THE PARENTING PARADOX

THE PARENTING PARADOX

Loving Our Children by Giving
Them Space to Grow

DR. JENNY BROWN

BLOOMSBURY ACADEMIC
NEW YORK • LONDON • OXFORD • NEW DELHI • SYDNEY

BLOOMSBURY ACADEMIC
Bloomsbury Publishing Inc, 1359 Broadway, 12th Floor, New York, NY 10018, USA
Bloomsbury Publishing Plc, 50 Bedford Square, London, WC1B 3DP, UK
Bloomsbury Publishing Ireland, 29 Earlsfort Terrace, Dublin 2, D02 AY28, Ireland

BLOOMSBURY, BLOOMSBURY ACADEMIC and the Diana logo are trademarks
of Bloomsbury Publishing Plc

First published in the United States of America 2026

Bloomsbury Publishing Inc does not have any control over, or responsibility for, any third-party websites referred to or in this book. All internet addresses given in this book were correct at the time of going to press. The author and publisher regret any inconvenience caused if addresses have changed or sites have ceased to exist, but can accept no responsibility for any such changes.

A catalog record for this book is available from the Library of Congress.

ISBN: HB: 979-8-7651-6196-8
ePDF: 979-8-7651-6198-2
eBook: 979-8-7651-6197-5

Typeset by Deanta Global Publishing Services, Chennai, India
Printed and bound in the United States of America

For product safety related questions contact productsafety@bloomsbury.com.

To find out more about our authors and books visit www.bloomsbury.com and sign up for our newsletters.

To David—

my co-parent and co-grandparent,

still learning as we go.

And to the many parents

who have taught me so much

about commitment, courage, and love—

through their willingness to grow themselves

in order to nurture strength, character,

and resilience in their children.

CONTENTS

FOREWORD

by Dr. Kathleen Smith

Parents know that our worry isn't working. Every parenting style and strategy of this era seems to invite more focus on our kids, who already feel immense pressure to regulate their emotions and achieve their dreams. As societal anxiety increases, so does the intensity of our attempts to love our children and meet their needs.

Wading into the field of parenting advice is not for the faint of heart. But Dr. Jenny Brown has taken up the challenge, offering a much-needed alternative to child-focused approaches. Her long career of clinical work, research, and leadership in the field of family systems is more than impressive, but what strikes me the most is her non-judgmental, generous, and curious spirit as she's worked with families with every imaginable challenge.

We tend to think of parental worry as a modern dilemma, but Dr. Brown outlines the long history of child focus in our society. For over a century now, parents have been primed to scan, label, and treat potential problems in our children. And in today's self-help saturated landscape, there is no shortage of advice to treat the worry that advice has created. Yet, Dr. Brown has chosen to do something rare in the parenting world—she engages the expertise of the families she encounters.

Bowen family systems theory, developed by the late Dr. Murray Bowen, provides an off-ramp for the parent worry cycle. Because when people get interested in their part in relationship patterns, they create breathing and growing space for those they love. Dr. Brown has taken the central concept of Bowen's theory, differentiation of self, and created a project for parents to take up on life's journey. The project of developing your best thinking, rather than your worry, for how you show up with your children.

Differentiation-based parenting is for anyone who wants to relate to their child from a more solid, principled position. It is for more than just the classic helicopter parent. It's for parents who struggle to control their anger when a child acts out, or those who can't stop giving in to a child's demands to keep them calm. For the stepparent who isn't sure where they fit into a new family structure, or the divorced parent who wants to be an example of maturity for their kids. This is also an important book for helping professionals who are recruited to "fix" the family problem when parents are overwhelmed.

When a parent makes themselves the project, and not the child, everyone is freed up to be a little more responsible for themselves. Dr. Brown also explores how differentiation-based parenting creates the space for grandparents and other family members, no longer overmanaged by an anxious mom or dad, to play significant roles in a kid's life. When a parent is managing their worry more thoughtfully, other communities and their cast of characters become the soil for a child to grow and tackle challenges.

Parents and helping professionals know that a worry-based approach to parenting is failing us. Dr. Brown is offering us an alternative, something meatier than the suggestion to calm down or simply sit on our hands while a child struggles. She's given us a framework for parents to get interested in ourselves, to be more thoughtful about what we do with our own anxiety and our own sensitivity to our children's distress.

As a parent, it is a relief to be told that I can play the long game. That there will be plenty of moments to pay attention and experiment with how I show up in my relationship with my child—not to change her, but to create the space for her to grow. As a therapist, it's a joy to be able to hand a parent this book and say, "There is no greater gift for a child than a parent who is growing themselves up."

Dr. Kathleen Smith, *PhD, LPC, is a therapist, author, and international speaker who teaches globally on systems thinking and emotional resilience. She is the author of* Everything Isn't Terrible *and* True to You, *and writes the newsletter* The Anxious Overachiever.

PREFACE

The idea for this book has been growing in me for decades, shaped by my personal experience as a parent and grandparent, and by my professional work in child and family mental health since the 1980s. I've had the privilege of walking alongside hundreds of parents—each devoted, thoughtful, and doing their best. Their challenges and insights have taught me more than any textbook ever could.

Today's parents are more informed and engaged than ever before. They build online communities, seek expert advice, and strive to raise emotionally healthy children. Yet, many still find themselves asking: *Why is my child struggling when I'm doing everything I can?*

In recent years, I've watched as concern over children's mental health has grown. I've also seen the increasing tendency to look outward—to experts, programs, and treatments—for answers. While professional help has its place, I've wondered whether this reliance has inadvertently diminished parents' confidence and clarity in navigating family challenges. This book emerged from that wondering.

Rather than offering another set of techniques to manage behavior, this book introduces a different lens. At its heart is a paradox: that loving well often means stepping back, not leaning in more tightly. Our most significant influence doesn't come from changing or fixing our children but from growing our capacity to be clear and loving leaders. These ideas are grounded in Dr. Murray Bowen's family systems theory and the perspective of *differentiation-based parenting*. I also explore the broader cultural and historical forces shaping modern parenting—the pressure to do more, control more, and never let go—and how these forces can leave parents unsure and children anxious.

Letting go doesn't mean withdrawing care or connection. It means making space by releasing anxious over-involvement in favor of calm, thoughtful presence. This path isn't about perfection—it's about self-awareness, clarity, and steady growth. It helps parents see where they end and their child begins, allowing love to flow from wisdom rather than worry.

If you've picked up this book, it's likely because you care deeply for your children and are open to reflection. That willingness is a powerful starting point. My hope is that these pages will affirm your commitment, bring fresh clarity to your role, and offer a path forward that is both encouraging and empowering.

JENNY BROWN
MAY 2025

ACKNOWLEDGMENTS

I'm so grateful to the many people who helped make this book possible.

To my agent, Jessica Felleman at the Jennifer Lyon Literary Agency, thanks for your steady belief in this book and your wise, cheerful guidance every step of the way. To my editor, Christen Karniski, and the Bloomsbury team, thank you for helping bring this book into the world. I'm grateful to all the parents I've worked alongside—you've taught me so much more than any textbook could. Thanks for the learning partnership with my colleagues in the Parent Hope team, the international Bowen family systems network, and the Family Systems Institute in Sydney. To my church community, Scots Church Sydney—you've helped keep my eyes lifted and my work grounded in a deeper perspective. To my friend Jill Grundy—I'm so grateful for your encouraging editing support. And to David, my biggest supporter—thank you for reviewing many chapters to help pull it all together. Finally, to my broader family—thank you for the legacy, lessons, patience, and love. This book is rooted in the journey we've inherited and shared.

INTRODUCTION

A NEW JOURNEY IN HOW
WE LOVE OUR CHILDREN

Truly loving our children means not loving or focusing on them too much. It requires knowing ourselves in our parenting relationships, recognizing our responsibility, and understanding when and how to step aside so they can grow.

Today's parents are more conscientious and committed than previous generations. Their devotion to their children from pregnancy to the school years and beyond is striking. I'm amazed at the attention both mothers and fathers give their children compared to my parenting in the 1980s and 1990s. The contrast is even more significant when I think of how I was parented in the 1960s and into the 1970s, when my four siblings and I were left to our own devices, and I don't mean the screen version, in terms of creating our playtimes and getting ourselves to and from school. I recall the mixture of joy and fear in my early parenting experiences in the 1980s as if it were yesterday. I was confused by the divergent advice that was doing the rounds, and with every new challenge, I tried to implement one version of advice I'd read, but was still left wondering if I might be damaging my child somehow.

The plethora of parenting approaches currently being sprouted has indeed multiplied since then. I greatly respect today's parents' efforts to apply the right parenting style, whether gentle parenting, emotion coaching, or some other approach, and build online communities to affirm their daily choices. Fathers are more involved than in earlier generations, and the seemingly unlimited array of stimulating activities for kids provides parents with more options than ever before. Amid such commitment, parents quietly ponder a profoundly challenging question: How is one or more of my children struggling when they have received so much devoted care? With studies showing that we're now seeing an epidemic of mental health issues for children, parents want to know how they can build protective factors for their kids' mental health. We read about the impact of the smartphone on mental health, but how do parents know where to begin in turning this around for children and adolescents, especially when it seems for so many that the digital horse has already bolted?

I have worked in child and family mental health since the 1980s and witnessed a concerning reduction in children's coping capacities. Additionally, I see from my consulting and research in the field how much parents want to find the best "expert" help for their children. Parents have embraced the value of early intervention. In turn, the demand for child mental health interventions is skyrocketing. I have wondered if the increase in relying on external treatment and experts in the child development field has reduced parents' confidence and increased their worry that they are not up for the task.

This book aims to make sense of the age of anxious, intensive parenting in a way that helps today's parents reclaim their clarity and confidence. It won't advocate for a sentimentalized return to previous eras. Parents of every generation have had their versions of self-doubt about their role, and today's societal landscape is dramatically different for families. Instead, it will help parents channel their conscientiousness effectively, allowing their child to develop age-appropriate independence and coping skills. It will help parents to become proficient observers of themselves in their relationships so they can make informed choices about what to adjust. Herein lies the heart of the parenting paradox: truly loving our children means not loving or focusing on them too much. It requires knowing ourselves in our parenting relationships, recognizing our responsibility, and understanding when and how to step aside so they can grow.

Central to understanding this paradox is shifting the focus from monitoring our children to focusing on what is within a parent's control to adjust. It's also about knowing when to hold back our natural urge to nurture—an instinct that, under stress, can easily become overblown. The result? Children who grow overly reliant on adults to soothe, affirm, and direct them. This kind of restraint can feel counterintuitive, even cold, to many parents. But what if we got curious about this discomfort? What if we stop making a project out of changing our children and redirect our attention to ourselves? This change of energy direction was a groundbreaking discovery made by psychiatrist Dr. Murray Bowen way back in the 1950s in researching whole families with a young person with severe mental illness. More of these discoveries are to be unpacked later. The following chapters show parents how to turn their focus of attention around, enabling them to build hope that their parent-led love cultivates resilient and responsible young people. Indeed, parents will discover a clear hope-building approach that leaves them feeling better about themselves and their parenting role.

All the hundreds of parents I've met over the past decades of family and child clinical practice have genuinely wanted the best for their children. They are often disillusioned and frustrated when a child struggles, but they never stop loving them. Parents want to find out how to bring their best to their children's well-being and are willing to consider their part in the development of problems if they believe they can make a positive difference. They get that intense "helicopter parenting" is unhelpful, but have not been given a clear alternative. Indeed, much of the advice they read is about giving their child enough attention to be secure. Parents hear in the media that they should stop being anxious, but such messages can add to parents' guilt and leave them feeling patronized. How can they turn off their protective, loving focus on their child? What if, in doing this, their child falters?

This book isn't about turning off love but redirecting the anxious energy that often accompanies it. The path isn't a quick fix or an endless search for the next external treatment offering, but rather a patient, big-picture effort, with parents buoyed by the signs of profound progress for their children along the way. It's a shift in perspective, a fresh lens, if you will.

We've Thrown So Much Love at Her!

Several years ago, while conducting research at a child and adolescent mental health treatment service, I met a mother named Rachel, whose story made a lasting impression. I have changed names and identifying details in this and all the case examples in the book. This family's situation is at the more severe end of the current child mental health spectrum.

Yet, some aspects of their experience seemed to resonate broadly with parents whose children had less confronting vulnerabilities. Rachel spoke of her terror when she entered her fourteen-year-old daughter's bedroom a year earlier and discovered that she had overdosed on her prescribed medication and paracetamol. Emergency services were activated, and Jessica was taken to the nearest children's hospital. After a time in an adolescent acute mental health ward, Jessica was moved to an intensive behavioral health treatment program to address her emotional health and disrupted schooling.

When I interviewed Rachel as part of my efforts to better understand parents' experiences of their child's mental health challenges, I was struck by this mother's process of coming to terms with Jessica's severe symptoms. Rachel conveyed her helplessness and understandable fear for their daughter's future mental health trajectory. What could explain Jessica's depression? She could not think of any traumas in her life. Had she missed something? How did her other two children seem to be doing well in life? At that moment, Rachel declared, "How could this happen to Jessica? We've thrown so much love at her!" These exact words have stayed with me. Rachel went on to reflect on all the positive supports in Jessica's life:

> I thought surely she'd be happy! Both her parents show her lots of love and attention. She's got my parents and in-laws, and we're really close. She's got lots of aunties, uncles, and cousins, and she's the only one with such terrible depression. It's a shock to everyone.

Can you relate to Rachel's question? Are you perplexed that children from loving, supportive families can struggle to cope? Rachel and her partner, Sam, are like many other conscientious parents. They have two other children on either side of Jessica, a daughter, Talia, aged seventeen, and a son, Miles, aged eleven, who are doing pretty well. They have a supportive extended family and are reasonably financially secure, with Sam in a small business and Rachel working part-time in an office admin role. Rachel has been committed to not letting work get in the way of being available to her children during their school years. Sam works hard Monday to Friday but is present at his children's school and sporting events in the evenings and weekends. Both sets of grandparents are present in their children's lives and have helped with childminding in the early years.

Family life had been relatively steady, with all children adjusting reasonably well to early transitions. That was until Jessica began to show symptoms of anxiety around age eleven. Previously, Rachel sensed that Jessica was a cautious child who depended on her support more than her siblings. By age thirteen, Jessica expressed reluctance to go to school, complaining of stomach pains. Rachel quickly found expert help for her middle daughter, enrolling her in a highly regarded university child anxiety treatment program. There were some initial improvements, but her symptoms reignited when Jessica moved to year seven at a new school. Midway through the school year, Rachel discovered that Jessica had self-harmed, and she and Sam were aghast. Rachel noticed her daughter covering her arms and was distraught to find signs of cutting. She sought out psychologists and psychiatrists, doing whatever she could to help thwart her daughter's diminishing mental health. There wasn't anything Rachel wouldn't do to find the best help for her daughter. Her question about how this could happen to such a well-loved daughter is entirely reasonable.

I've heard numerous versions of Rachel's query over my years of clinical practice and presenting to parents in schools and the community. Committed, loving parents struggle to understand why one or more of their children struggle to handle life's stressors. They are anxious about school and friendships, and separating from their parents remains difficult well into the school years. Others are not managing their frustrations and seem to be taking versions of toddler tantrums into later developmental stages. Parents know they're not perfect, but they keep loving their children, especially those who seem a bit different and more fragile. They are confused about how any of their children could show signs of emotional issues when they are investing so much support in them. That care and love may come through extra educational tutoring, more children's activities, advocating for their child's unique needs to teachers, or engaging experts to prevent worsening problem behaviors, emotions, or delays in achieving expected milestones. Many parents read and hear the latest parenting tips, especially the message of creating a loving and secure base for their children. They sift through the latest descriptions of current popular parenting styles. Armed with all this information, they then watch for any signs of insecurity and do what it takes to reassure their child. They're quick to let the child's emotions guide their responses and to coach their child to give words to the feelings triggered by the disappointment of not getting their way. Of course, there are nuances to parenting advice that easily get missed in the stress of family life. However, parents are increasingly trying to learn new strategies and are confused when these efforts don't bring the desired outcome of more secure and resilient children.

I, too, have asked my version of Rachel's question about how my child can be struggling when I've given so much support. One of the hazards of being in the helping profession is exposure to many interventions and an unrealistic expectation that this should shield us from the problems with which we help others. Professional helpers can be the most anxious of parents, as we're so committed to applying our knowledge to get it right. When one of my daughters confronted some emotional challenges in young adulthood, my husband and I found ourselves asking, "How could this happen with all the knowledge gained through my study and helping others?" I had to step back and reflect on my unrealistic standards, accept the messiness of life, and appreciate that setbacks are part of all life transitions. I also reminded myself of what I had learned—to work on myself now and not make a fixing project out of my child. She would find her way through this stage of her life, and I needed to be present, yet not anxious, in the ways I related to her.

More than ever, I see that this generation of parents desires clarity about their part in raising children who can withstand the pressures of growing up in our complex modern world. How can they prevent their children from being swept up in the current epidemic of mental health issues? They require answers to Rachel's question about how a child's coping can collapse when parents and other family members dearly love them. How can parents ensure that their earnestness in parenting is harnessed for their children's flourishing?

The Road Ahead—Parental Love That Finds Balance

If you're reading all this and thinking that the last thing you want is more parent blaming, I hear you! Judgment and criticism are the last things that parents deserve right now! I also do not want to add to the tribal defensiveness between particular parenting styles. It doesn't help parents to draw them into following any approach with religious devotion. What helps parents is when they learn what to observe in their parenting and make their own decisions about what is and isn't helping their child's growth of resilience. I assure you that this book seeks to convey empathy for current parenting challenges and to show how parents can have confidence that their investments in their children are delivering positive returns. Central to the book's message is recognizing how hard parenting has become, especially when a child isn't managing life stressors well. It also understands how confronting it is to question how much support a parent gives a child—surely, a child can never be loved too much!

In the following chapters, readers are invited to step back and consider the subtle ways parents can fall into overfocusing on children at any stage of development. What are the effects of too much support or correction in parenting? This is presented by explaining what the relevant research reveals about the impact of intensive parenting on children's well-being. I also address the issue raised by Jonathan Haidt in his groundbreaking book *The Anxious Generation*,[1] which speaks to over-involved parenting in the real world and under-involved parenting in the digital world. How has parenting become more intensive in real interactions with our children, yet disconnected in their online lives? The mainstream approaches to child mental health treatment are challenged, especially in how parents are often sidelined or given mixed messages. I aim to go much further than making sense of today's parenting culture. I am committed to helping parents discover an accessible pathway to gaining clarity and confidence. Access a different lens that helps, not hinders, your parenting journey.

The journey ahead unveils a parenting stance based on family systems theory: *differentiation-based parenting*. Dr. Murray Bowen's groundbreaking research,[2] shaping his family systems theory, is presented as a straightforward way to understand the drivers and impacts of intensive parenting. Bowen saw the paradox of family growth when a parent stopped their fixing efforts toward their child and made themselves the change project. This fresh perspective is paired with what the psychology research literature reveals about parenting factors that can compound children's mental health issues, laying the foundations for parents to make adjustments that increase their clarity and confidence. This understanding allows parents to build hope that their love balances the need for connection with the space to grow autonomy. They learn that changes they can make to their responses to their child can deliver far more positive results in their child's development of resilience and stability than the many child treatment approaches on offer. Indeed, parents will come to see that they are their children's most valuable resource for emotional and developmental well-being.

How the Parenting Paradox Became Part of My Research Journey

This question about parental investment in their children has become central to my professional journey. My early family therapy training confirmed the importance of seeing beyond each child to the family context, which promotes growth and reduces symptoms. I extended my study of family and society at Columbia University in the early 1990s, where I conducted fieldwork with the renowned family therapist and psychiatrist Dr. Salvador Miniuchin and his team at the Family Studies Institute in New York City.[3] This highlighted sustaining the parent hierarchy as vital for children's flourishing. Then, in further study at the Family Institute of Westchester, NY, I first encountered Dr. Murray Bowen's research and family systems theory. This theory made sense of the complexity of families with whom I'd previously worked, filling many gaps in understanding left by other approaches I'd been trained in.

Bowen's theory also turned on many light bulbs in making sense of my own family of origin. I've been committed ever since to continue to test and apply this family systems lens, which led me to establish the Family Systems Institute in Australia in 2004. A central premise is that when just one family member starts to change themselves in their relationships, the whole family benefits and grows. It's as if we are connected to a circuit like electrical wiring. Neuroscience research has increasingly demonstrated that our relationships profoundly shape the structure and function of our brains throughout life.[4] This can be incredibly freeing for parents and spouses who no longer get caught in endless efforts to change others, because when we change ourselves, this impacts those with whom we are connected. In 2012, I published my first book, *Growing Yourself Up*,[5] which outlined the magic that can occur through one person bringing their best to their significant relationships.

The most formative part of my professional journey has been teaching and supervising clinicians for over a decade at a particular treatment center in Western Sydney, Australia, which is affiliated with a large teaching children's hospital. I heard parents' desperation to help their struggling children and their frustrations in finding effective help. I began doctoral research to gain a deeper understanding of parent experiences and to identify what is most helpful in parents regaining their agency and hope. With this research backdrop, I developed the Parent Hope Project[6] to provide clinical interventions for children via their parents. I aim to have Bowen family systems' unique perspectives accessible to those working with children and families and, most importantly, available in easy-to-understand language to parents. This book is a culmination of my life's effort. It unfolds in three parts:

Part One first makes sense of this age of intensive parenting, looking historically at how parenting advice has led us to where we are today. It includes an exploration of the exceptions to intensive or highly protective parenting, such as with children's screen time. Dominant treatment approaches in child mental health are unpacked, with parents shown how to be a central resource to children's recovery from mental health vulnerabilities.

Part Two offers a unique framework for regaining balance so parents can provide love and support and allow their child to grow responsible autonomy in both the embodied and online worlds. It also provides ways for parents to get out of futile cycles of worry and conflict, and how to hold limits by drawing on a parent's "I" position. Three different families and parents illustrate the application of differentiation-based parenting throughout this part.

Part Three examines how parenting is a broader family and community affair, emphasizing that the parent–child relationship does not exist in isolation. This is vital for parents, who are becoming increasingly isolated from such support, which can add to feeling overwhelmed and stressed. It truly should take a village to raise a child. I reflect on the value of extended family, neighborhood connections, and faith communities in my parenting experience and childhood.

Each chapter uses real-life examples of families working through different scenarios and ends with a summary of reflections to assist parents in implementing the ideas presented, which are built on in the following chapter. My priority is to help parents understand that *how* we respond to parenting dilemmas matters more than the specific issues themselves. This is encouraging because it means that parents don't need to be experts on every topic—they just need effective ways to respond that guide children toward mature, thoughtful decisions rather than reactive or rebellious ones. While I touch on topics like young people's mental health and online lives, the core principles for responding are broadly applicable. What you'll read is less about the issues themselves and more about how to respond in ways that strengthen your relationship with your child. Whether the topic is alcohol, sleep, diet, gender and sexuality, exams, racism, religion, or any other complex topic, the emphasis is on how we engage, not how much we know. It's about understanding the power of a relational process with parents and children listening to each other. Our children grow in maturity and confidence, rather than reacting to parents' worry or control. The ideas I present have had both professional and personal resonance for me. Applying Bowen family systems theory to helping many people gain awareness of themselves in their relationships has paralleled my gradual growth in how I relate to others in my family—the hard work of learning not to get in the way of their growth while staying connected.

By the end of this book, I hope parents will feel confident that they can continue loving their children as they always have, while reducing the intensity of their parenting and becoming catalysts for their children's maturity. Most importantly, you'll discover how to grow yourself and find balance—to love and support your children without hindering the development of their problem-solving and distress management capacities. Parents can push back against the cultural norm of intense focus on children. You'll come to see how subtle shifts in how you respond to your child, at any age, can yield more lasting gains in resilience and emotional stability than many traditional, child-centered treatment approaches. This alternative, hope-filled path restores clarity and brings more profound purpose to the parenting journey. As you embark on this journey, *The Parenting Paradox* extends a liberating invitation—to love your children by making space for them to flourish, and for you to become the calm, loving leader you aspire to be.

PART ONE

AN AGE OF INTENSIVE PARENTING

1

TODAY'S OVERWHELMED PARENT

HOW WE GOT HERE

Programs meant to support your child might sometimes make you feel less confident in your most important role—as their steady guide and most significant resource.

I recently searched the internet to see what questions parents are asking online. These responses, which reflect every parent's rollercoaster of emotions, made me smile: "How do I get my kids to sleep?" "How do I get my kids to wake up?" "How do I get my kids to eat more?" "How do I get my kids to eat less?"

The following questions, however, replaced my smile with concern as I considered the challenges parents face in navigating uncertainty and responding to the overwhelming—and often contradictory—advice available. "How do I find the right school for my child?" "How do I deal with my child's screen obsession?" "Am I a good parent?" "Am I getting it right?" Can you identify the questions you most frequently ask as a parent? There's no shortage of opinions ready to answer your every concern—offering any number of parental directives, each claiming to be the right way forward.

I see today's parents walking a tightrope, conscientiously trying to meet their children's different needs. It's seriously perplexing for parents to sift through all the parenting advice to determine what's best for their children. It's even more complicated when parents see their children growing through different stages and figuring out how their needs change as they develop. I'm mindful that all of this external advice has parents increasingly monitoring their children to try to get things right. The amount of parenting advice on offer is overwhelming and makes it harder to address the surge of intensive parenting. The internet has allowed parenting blogs, vlogs, and forums to flourish. Social media platforms like Instagram, TikTok, YouTube, and Facebook have amplified the voices of parenting influencers and various experts. Among these digital voices, a new role has emerged in our cultural lexicon—the "mumfluencer," a social media–savvy parent who shares advice, products, and glimpses into family life with a broad audience. Now, artificial intelligence adds another layer to this ecosystem, offering a depersonalized platform for parenting suggestions. Every parent with internet access can share advice, adding to the unprecedented volume of information. Compounding this is the professionalization of parenting, expressed through the authoritatively labeled *evidence-based* approaches—studies on child psychology, development, brain function, sleep, and nutrition (and the list goes on)—now more accessible than ever. To top things off, parenting has become a money-making business field where advice gets monetized, blurring the line between guidance and marketing.

Parents Are More Stressed Than Ever

What an intensive climate today's parents are facing! Striking a balance between seeking guidance and trusting common sense has become a modern challenge. Indeed, all the signals point to a crisis of stress and overwhelm for many parents. In 2024, US Surgeon General Dr. Vivek Murthy issued an advisory highlighting parental stress as a serious public health issue.[1] The advisory noted that 41 percent of parents feel "so stressed they cannot function" most days, and nearly 50 percent said their stress completely overwhelms them. Similar reports are coming from other countries, such as the annual surveys by the United Nations Children's Fund (UNICEF) UK, revealing in 2023 and 2024 that many British parents are worried about their mental health, with almost half reporting being overwhelmed.[2] While multiple factors contribute to this, it's worth considering how this has emerged and any common themes that give clues to how to turn this around. A fresh look at how we arrived at this moment in parenting history can be foundational to giving parents a more confident path forward. Over the past century and more, every generation of parents has experienced the changing trends of professional parenting advice. Before we go there, let me share some of my parenting journey.

A Personal Story of Becoming a First-Time Parent

I first became a parent in the mid-1980s and remember with striking clarity—as if it were yesterday—the anxiety I felt when faced with the helpless, vulnerable baby for whom my husband and I were now responsible. This was heightened when the dreaded colic set in. I recall the helplessness of not being able to soothe my crying baby (or, more like, screeching). Everything in me turned to finding a *fix* for the unrelenting evening crying—and this was before I had access to the internet. Somehow, I still found various things to try to settle my daughter, such as chamomile tea in a bottle. Nothing worked, but somehow, the effort of trying did steady me a little. As my daughter's cries persisted, I became fearful of the damage this might be causing her. Would she be traumatized, and would her development of self-esteem be scarred in some way?

Where did these ideas that were fueling this fear come from? I recognize that some of this anxiety is an instinctive protective response; however, the extent of the fear went beyond my instincts. I can look back and see that it was part of the societal messaging of my parenting age—the 1980s. My influential go-to book was *How to Raise Your Child's Self-Esteem* by Dorothy Briggs.[3] It gained prominence in the 1980s, during the self-esteem movement, which saw an explosion of books and guides focused on building children's confidence and emotional health. The books I read and the conversations at my community playgroup connected my parenting to whether my child developed appropriately and grew this essential dose of *self-esteem*. Of course, there were other influences from my family of origin and the values embedded in my faith. Still, the societal trend of my day was a dominant drumbeat over my formative parenting years. Thankfully, alongside my husband, I managed to find my way through each stage's parenting dilemmas. Nevertheless, I can see how easy it would be to give way to fear-driven parenting and monitor my children for any possible signs of damaged self-esteem. In Chapter 2, I explore this fear-driven monitoring that all parents experience at times and to varying degrees, to see how any fixing effort can help steady a stressed parent. For now, I want to introduce the idea that outsourcing, professionalizing parenting wisdom, has been around for a long time and has laid much of the foundation for today's intensive parenting era.

The Societal, Historical Backdrop to Today's Parenting Climate

I wonder which decade of the twentieth century you would guess showed the most significant rise in parenting uncertainty and anxiety. I often ask this question when presenting to groups of parents. Many suggest the 1960s, with so much social change, while others go straight to the last decade of the century with the introduction of the internet. Unsurprisingly, everyone wants to go straight to our current century and the impact of the digital age and smartphones. The actual answer revealed is the 1920s—a surprise indeed. I am drawing from the fascinating historical research of Dr. Peter Stearns, a historian and scholar of cultural history. He has explored the history of American parenting through various works, including his book, *Anxious Parents: A History of Modern Childrearing in America*.[4] His research looked at markers of parenting anxiety from varied sources, including analyzing parenting literature, mass media, public health campaigns, personal accounts, and statistical data. While the last century saw substantial improvements in the lives of children with decreased mortality and protections from child labor, Professor Stearns revealed a paradox that as children's lives became objectively safer, parents' worries increased. He saw a steep rise in parent uncertainty in the 1920s. What do you think fueled this rise in parent anxiety over a century ago? The key factor was the first appearance of manuals on parenting.

In *Anxious Parents* and more recent papers, Stearns highlights the impact of the rise of expert-driven parenting advice. He writes that the "publications were designed to provide answers to parental concerns but also to offer standards that might lead parents to feel concerns where none had existed before."[5] I find it profoundly insightful to consider that many seeds of today's parenting worries are embedded in the issue of too much parenting advice! There have been some other books with a profoundly helpful historical analysis of the changing landscape of parenting—most notable for me is Haidt's recent analysis of the impact of the internet since the 1990s (alongside his valuable analysis from the 1980s to the 1990s of *Safetyism*[6]—avoidance of risk with increased fear of harm to children). I've also valued the book by Jennifer Senior, *All Joy and No Fun*,[7] which examines how the roles of parents, particularly mothers, have shifted over centuries. She highlights how parenting moved from focusing on survival and economic contribution to prioritizing children's emotional and cognitive development. Like Stearns, she shows the historical emergence of *intensive parenting*, especially in the mid-twentieth century, and how it became a societal norm in Western countries.

What I find especially revealing from Stearn's work is the longitudinal effects of professionalizing parenting. Different themes of advice and subsequent parental fears have represented each historical period. In the emerging Western world, the church and elders were the primary sources of parenting wisdom before industrialization. The focus was on moral development and submission to elders. Most families lived with grandparents and extended family. The term nuclear family only came into being in the early twentieth century. Children in the nineteenth century were significant contributors to the economics of the family. Late in the nineteenth century, the trends were changing. Parenting shifted from a focus on authority to nurturing children. This was accompanied by the rise of science and the beginnings of the field of psychology. The early twentieth century saw a dramatic expansion of expert influence over parenting and childhood. Pediatrics became recognized as a distinct specialty in medical licensing and certification in 1930. The first child guidance clinics were established in the United States in 1912. The child guidance movement expanded in the United States and the UK, driven by growing recognition of the importance of early intervention in childhood psychological and social problems. Child guidance clinics began to appear in the UK in the 1920s, influenced by Freudian psychoanalytic ideas and early child development theories. This growth of specialized child treatment centers that prevailed into the 1960s messaged parents about the value of early diagnosis and the treatment of emotional and behavioral issues. Child guidance centers have morphed into many new public and private services.

Over the last century, the growing professional field of child development added new levels of complexity to raising children that had not previously been seen. Parenting was becoming more child centered, and parents expressed increasing worries about their children's development. In each decade, worries shifted from concerns about children's posture and were replaced with hygiene concerns and even worries about correcting left-handedness. Hyperactivity was a prevalent area of concern and treatment from the 1960s and 1970s. Every era had diagnostic categories that became the focus for parental and professional concerns and treatment. I'm sure you can see the dominant ones in your current context. The arrival of cars exacerbated safety issues, and children's comic books fostered worries about exposing children to violent content. Increasingly, children were viewed as vulnerable. From the post–Second World War period, adults were implored not to overburden children and risk crushing their self-esteem. Professionals added to the dialogue that children were vulnerable and needed protection and external treatment when things went awry.

The Impact of Increased and Shifting Parenting Advice

With every new worry, a host of advice followed, and vice versa. With every wave of new advice, parents had more to be worried about. It's somewhat of a chicken-and-egg dynamic—advice creates worry, worry invites more advice. I think the 1946 enormously influential book, Dr. Benjamin Spock's *Baby and Child Care*,[8] is a good case in point for the impact of advice, even when the message tries to be reassuring. Spock's book was on my mother's shelf and that of numerous parents of the 1950s and 1960s. It encouraged parents to trust their instincts, which, on the surface, sounds like it is reversing the flow of parents' inadequacy—however, the endless list of things to watch out for neutralized the encouraging tone. Peter Stearns writes,

> Spockian recommendations about such simple acts as bathing a child, with a massive list of dos and don'ts about what to wear, how to regulate temperature, and so on, could fluster far more than reassure: parenting seemed very difficult.[9]

When looking at how messaging to parents has changed over time, it's pertinent to consider the rise of pharmaceuticals for children's mental health. In the 1980s, there was a sharp rise in attention deficit hyperactivity disorder (ADHD) diagnoses, which brought a wave of new medications and shifted how parents thought about managing their kids' behavior. With this, pharmaceutical companies actively marketed stimulants to parents and educators as solutions for improving academic performance and behavior. This was followed in the late 1980s with the introduction of antidepressants that were directly marketed to parents/consumers. In my own clinical experience, I've seen a gradual increase in parents' expectations of accessing medication to deal with their child's behavioral and mood concerns. This can leave parents invested in expert treatment but without a clear path for how they can make a difference in their children's growth of resourcefulness.

Over the past century, more external advice and marketing have been added to amplify parents' and caregivers' fears surrounding children's safety, education, and emotional well-being. This doesn't discount the influence of other social forces, including wars and dramatic economic and technological changes. Nor does it discount many positive shifts in caring for and raising children. Yet, it highlights the correlation between expert parenting advice and uncertain parenting. Can you see the ways that external advice can exacerbate parental anxiety by creating unrealistic standards and fueling a sense of inadequacy? It isn't that it causes parental anxiety per se, as parenting is naturally full of protective urges, but it certainly has played a significant part in amplifying parental overwhelm.

Recent Indicators of Intensive Parenting

Many papers in more recent times speak to the impact of parenting and childhood being medicalized and professionalized[10]—and with that, parents intensively outsourcing and giving it their all to ensure their children are happy and successful. Yet, as we've been exploring, this isn't a new development. Current literature speaks to the use of medical explanations for children's difficulties as a way of absolving parents of guilt. Mothers are more prone than ever to feeling guilty about parenting—are they neglecting their children when they return to work? (Questions that I don't see have not been asked equally of men.) Fathers have increasingly become more involved in parenting with each generation. However, with this comes a growth in their own doubts about parenting capability and a tendency to defer to mothers or outside *experts*, bringing its own set of parenting style tensions. Studies show that new fathers' brains adapt to caretaking similarly to mothers, but societal messages leave them feeling they're not up for the task.[11]

Our society is increasingly contributing to the intensity of parenting. Despite the time pressures many of today's working parents experience, research indicates that in most Western countries, parents spend more time with their children than in the 1960s, when most mothers were stay-at-home parents.[12] Back then, childcare often involved supervision rather than direct engagement. This shift reflects a stronger focus on children. The early twenty-first century saw a dramatic rise in programs and opportunities for children whose parents had the means to pay. Parents had more options for outsourcing to reduce their sense of not being up to the task of child-rearing and relieve worry about competition for success. Markers of poor mental health have skyrocketed in affluent suburban communities, where young people often have packed schedules, with high school students juggling multiple activities to boost their college applications.[13] Stearns's more recent work reveals that 73 percent of Americans rated happiness as the most important goal in raising children, and assessing the results of education far ahead of any other option. I wonder if you can see these trends of high investment in children in your communities. Consider how the goal of raising happy, successful children may feed the rigor and stress of today's parenting.

Interestingly, the significant increase in intensity that started with more affluent parents has spread to working-class families. A recent study found that both middle-class and working-class parents considered intensive parenting ideal. Middle-class respondents emphasized activities fostering cognitive and social development, while working-class participants prioritized more pragmatic approaches due to economic constraints. The concern to protect children from risk is shared across socioeconomic groups.[14]

Current anxiety revolves around the deleterious effects of the digital age and the smartphone. In his best-selling book *The Anxious Generation*,[15] Jonathan Haidt makes a compelling case for the harms of a phone-based childhood—social and sleep deprivation, attention fragmentation, and addiction. The facts are undeniable. However, viewing the bigger picture lens of over a century of increase in parents' anxiety reveals that the foundations of this generation's crisis in emotional health were well and truly established.

As I see it, the challenge is not adding more worry for today's parents. Any parenting out of fear leads to increased intensity, inadequacy, and ongoing reactivity in our children. It also contributes to parents' stress levels and a desperate need for respite. Haidt's observation that children are overparented in the embodied, real world and underparented in the digital world requires further understanding. I wonder if the smartphone has been a place of respite for kids and their parents. The relationship distance created by a digital world is an understandable place of respite in stressed families. I unpack this further in later chapters.

Less Is More in Parenting

Parents can be reassured that they don't have to constantly pour love and support into their children for them to thrive, and they genuinely don't need to listen to and read every new piece of ever-shifting advice. Advice to build parents' confidence should avoid intimidating or adding to their worries. Anyone speaking into the parenting space must go beyond revealing problems and their sources. Parents need to discover a pathway to recover confidence and to uncomplicate the journey of raising the next generation. I suggest that such a path is full of paradoxes or seeming contradictions.

1. Perhaps the overriding paradox is that less information is more helpful. It allows parents to focus on how they relate to their child rather than stressing about how much they need to know.

2. The second paradox is that a lower focus on children is required. This means parents pay attention to their stress and how it affects their relationship with each child. When parents turn their attention to managing their reactions to their children, they don't need to have all the latest information about their children's development.

3. Thirdly, the pathway to less overwhelm will paradoxically require substantially reduced outsourcing to expert advice and child-focused interventions so parents can recover trust in their version of *good enough* parenting.

A Mother Begins to Manage Her Fear of Damaging Her Child

Let me introduce you to a parent who managed to reverse her overwhelm under the weight of external advice. Marie (not her actual name) was referred to me by her psychiatrist. She had struggled with a severe episode of depressed mood after the birth of her second child. One of her chronic struggles was her guilt that her lack of presence after her child's birth was going to leave the child damaged. Her doctor thought an approach to build parent hope rather than guilt was needed. Marie told me about the vast collection of parenting books she'd purchased over the years, focusing on healing emotional wounds in children. Her daughter was now aged six and was attending a university anxiety treatment center for children. Marie was coaching her daughter to follow the treatment manuals and was desperate to see signs that she was growing in confidence and well-being.

The key message Marie heard in parenting books was the damage caused by early disruptions to parent–child attachment. She was terrified that her period of depression had left her daughter neglected and insecure. Each day, she monitored her child for signs of what she feared, and what do you think she found? Yes, she found evidence of what she was looking for and started a journey of external treatment. This predictable pattern of finding evidence for what we fear is a form of confirmation bias. What Marie wasn't seeing was how much her husband had stepped up in caring for their daughter as an infant and how her older son was thriving during the period when she was struggling. The bigger picture was of a family, including extended family, caring well enough for its members—no one was neglected or damaged.

In our conversations, Marie began to explore ways she could support her child's growth through how she related rather than outsourcing her parenting to the next trend she heard about online and to the clinicians at the behavioral health center. With each step, Marie regained some confidence and realized that her daughter had more capacity than she initially thought to make friends and enjoy school. It wasn't long before her daughter stopped her anxiety treatment and was fully participating in school. Yes, there were some hiccups of separation anxiety at the school gate, but Marie stopped labeling this as a sign of a damaged child.

I could see that Marie represented the many parents and caregivers today who are caught up in the sense of inadequacy in the face of messaging about children's complex needs and vulnerabilities. The parenting wave they're riding is mixed with fear about getting it wrong and harming their child. Even if there is some soundness to the advice, parents deferring to it add to a stressed and overwhelmed cohort of parents. What will it take to turn this around, given that the age of intensive, anxious parenting, fueled by external advice, has been incubating for decades?

Cultural Variations in Parenting

The trends explored have been drawn primarily from Western contexts. Are there signs of growing intensive parenting in different cultures? The literature on cross-cultural comparisons begins by acknowledging the common aspects of parenting that all humans share.[16] Universally, parenting and raising the next generation include caregiving, learning support, nurturing, supervision, and discipline. However, parenting practices look different across cultures. In Eastern cultures, parenting norms tend to emphasize authority, family honor, and collective social order. Indeed, the influence of the West has shifted many parenting practices and brought with it the stress of generational disagreements about what should be expected of children. Reviewing popular parenting books in Chinese cultures, there is a blend of integrating traditional respect for authority with a growing emphasis on nurturing creativity and individuality. Parents across cultures increasingly turn to and defer to *experts* for help. In China, the government provides regularly updated parenting guidelines for young children on responsive parenting, early learning, and healthy environments.[17] These texts draw on traditional cultural wisdom and modern research on child development.

When stress is added to any cultural parenting norms, these norms become tension issues for families. For example, more traditional expectations—such as emphasizing academic excellence, respect for parents and elders, and family harmony—contribute to elevated parenting stress around failures to meet expectations. For every culture, parenting stressors may take different forms. Still, it's worth considering that the common feature is increasing intensity across the globe, with children's mental health difficulties on the increase.[18] Recent research indicates that mental health problems are increasingly reported among children and adolescents in many Eastern societies. The perfect storm of traditional academic pressure and high cultural expectations for achievement, combined with the modern stressors of rapid urbanization, evolving family structures, and social media, can compound mental health challenges. And with this comes many overwhelmed and confused parents struggling to navigate this complexity.

Sifting Through the Advice—Where to Go from Here?

I hope that laying out some historical backdrops to this intensive, stressed parenting age will promote a climate of empathy for the challenges you and all parents confront. Additionally, this discussion sheds light on how programs meant to support your child might sometimes make you feel less confident in your most important role— as their steady guide and most significant resource. As I write this, I am mindful that my efforts to support parents might unintentionally add to the noise of all the advice surrounding them. Those of us in the helping professions easily contribute to the problem of turning parenting from an everyday experience into something overly academic and intimidating. My guiding question to test what I write for parents is "Does it help parents to think and act for themselves rather than follow others' directives?" The goal for parents is finding their sweet spot—not stepping back too far but staying present in a way that provides both loving support and space for children to grow independence. It's also about figuring out how to wisely use external resources without losing sight of your resourcefulness and values as a parent. The following chapters take you on a surprising journey to finding a wise balance. I hope you're beginning to appreciate that it must be your discovery journey, not something that outside experts prescribe.

For Reflection

Questions About the Impact of Parenting Advice

1. What have been the most influential parenting advice/ approaches for me?
2. How have they impacted my confidence and clarity as a parent?
3. What triggers my worries for my children?
4. How might my parents and grandparents have answered these questions?
5. How can I reduce my absorption of too much information?
6. How can I take fear out of my searching for expert advice?

2

WORRIED PARENTS

The first step in ending intensive parenting is raising awareness of worry patterns and their effects. This, in turn, opens up choices that parents can make to benefit their children and the family.

More than ever, parents are bombarded with advice about things to watch out for, which may be warning signs of problems or risks for their children—indicators of possible developmental delays, mental health vulnerabilities, or dangers in the outside world. We're told of the importance of staying attuned to our children. When you add this message to every parent's natural protective instinct, it's predictable that the levels of worry are amplified. Worrying seems part and parcel of responsible parenting—it often feels like being on high alert comes with the territory. If you've ever felt this way, you're not alone. A 2023 Pew Research Center survey found that 40 percent of US parents are extremely worried that their children might struggle with anxiety or depression at some point.[1] While rooted in love and responsibility, this heightened sense of vigilance for warning signs of problems in our children can leave parents feeling overwhelmed and uncertain about how to balance caution with confidence. But it starts with making sense of what generates our worry in the first place.

A Closer Look at Conscientious Worried Parenting

I recently heard a mother, I'll call her Michelle, reflect that "Ninety percent of my energy goes into worrying about and reasoning with my son and calming my husband. This leaves ten percent over for trying to calm myself and steady myself." Michelle has the extra pressure of working as a psychologist. She's especially alert to what research says is essential for her twelve-year-old son Jake's healthy development and the risks he may face as he enters his teen years. As she talks over the problems of too much screen time or issues around eating a healthy diet with Jake, she notices that he is rolling his eyes and switching off from her. This intensifies her efforts to get through to him. As she moves into lecture mode, Jake increasingly seems not to care. She becomes worried that she's losing touch with him. Lately, he's been making dismissive backhanded comments like "Whatever!" "Yeah, Yeah, Mom!" In response, his dad, Mick, gets angry that Jake is disrespectful. He moves in to chastise Jake, and they get caught in a verbal boxing match. Michelle then finds herself trying to calm her husband down and worries that he is too harsh on their son. She jumps in and says to Mick, "Don't use that tone of voice! It's unnecessary!"

All of this comes from the best of intentions for these parents. Michelle is well informed about what the experts in her field deem essential and is doing her best to create a healthy life for her eldest son. But can you see the effect of this kind of worried parenting? The more energy Michelle puts into shaping her son, the more he pushes back and detaches. Then, as her husband reacts, she finds herself trying to manage them both, leaving her with few resources to steady herself. Michelle and Mick have increasingly become focused on Jake, and it isn't delivering the happy family to which they're committed. They are inadvertently contributing to a growing worry-based family environment. As they try to shape their son, he becomes more sensitive to their corrections, and they become more irritable with each other in response to their perception of problem signs in their son and their different ways of handling things. They're left feeling more worried and more exhausted.

To stem this surging current of escalating worry, one of these parents will need to recognize their part in it and use that awareness to make changes. Michelle can replace her efforts to manage her son and husband with a focus on managing herself. She might express her worry more openly and calmly, saying what it's like to try to be the best parent she can be for her teenager. This would be a step toward *relating rather than reacting*. Mick could start noticing the impact of his worry-driven directives on his son and how sensitive he's becoming to his wife's responses. Any parent who pauses and becomes more aware of the effect of their worry on their parenting is taking a significant step toward a more open and growth-building family environment. In a later chapter, I write more about the worry cycle with more parent examples to bring it to life.

Dr. Murray Bowen's Insights into the Common Patterns of Parental Worry

Discovering the research of psychiatrist Dr. Murray Bowen has been transformative for me, both personally and professionally, in understanding the drivers and impacts of worried, intensive parenting. When I first started reading and hearing about Bowen family systems theory in a post-grad family therapy training institute in New York in the early 1990s, I could recognize and make sense of my family growing up and the many families represented by my clients. I had young school-age children at the time and was grateful for insights that helped me reduce my worried involvement with them. Murray Bowen, a pioneer of family systems theory, observed whole families in a research setting[2] and saw the pattern of parents focusing much of their energy on their struggling child.[3] He called this the *family projection process* to describe how parents' worries and sensitivities can be transferred to their children. Before you start hearing this as a message of *parent blaming*, let me reassure you that Bowen noted that every family has some degree of overfocusing on some of their children, and recognizing when we're doing this as parents allows us to tone down our worry levels. Can you see this in the previous example of mom Michelle and dad Mick, who were caught up in monitoring and trying to change their son? Jake was part of the dance, reacting to his parents' worried attention. This is also bigger than the family in the present, as the patterns get transmitted from one generation to the next.

It also helps alleviate parental guilt when we appreciate how society has contributed to parents' increased awareness of potential problems in their children. When society's messaging emphasizes the myriad potential problems children may face, it amplifies parents' natural urge to protect, adding stress and uncertainty and creating heightened intensity in parent–child relationships.

Three Steps of Worry About a Child — Scanning, Labeling, Treating

Bowen observed some predictable steps of a parent's worry focus. The first is when a parent perceives or assumes something is *wrong* with one of their children. Bowen called this step *scanning*. The second is the diagnosing or *labeling* step, which occurs when a parent observes behaviors or traits in the child that confirm their concern. The feelings of concern can exaggerate the view of behaviors that may be a regular part of development. This is like confirmation bias, where we look for evidence of our fear and pick up on any signs confirming our concern. The third step is *treating* or fixing the perceived issue. A parent's heightened attention to fixing the perceived issue can reinforce the child's part in the dance, where they can get stuck in problematic emotional or behavioral patterns.

As you think about this three-step worry process, scanning, labeling or confirming, and treating or fixing, I wonder if you can see this pattern in your current family and the family you grew up in. Bowen noted that a parent's worry focus was rarely spread evenly to each child. It's interesting to reflect on which of your children triggers more worry for you. How does this affect how you relate to them and how they relate to you? Did your parents worry more about you or one of your siblings, giving one child an extra focus of concern? I reflect on how my parents' worry shifted from one child to another. I had some medical conditions in the early years that led to extra checking from my mother. This certainly had ripple effects on my early resilience. However, as a new stage unfolded, a younger sibling became the focus of concern as they entered the rocky seas of adolescence. In reflecting on such family patterns, it's helpful to be aware that when worry takes hold of any relationship, it intensifies interactions and affects how people navigate daily life. Recognizing how worry patterns move through our families — past and present — can offer powerful insight into how anxiety shapes relationships, helping us respond with greater awareness and intention.

Consider how this three-step worry pattern can balloon enormously in the digital world. We search for evidence online of what we fear and then find diagnostic labels, advice, and offerings for treating and fixing our child. We can even become ensconced in online communities to affirm the labels and fix them in place for our child. This label is shaping the child, and we, as parents, are developing an identity as the carer of a child with this diagnosis. It isn't easy to step back and see this process in action, as so many reinforcing voices are online. In the moment, it can feel like we're doing the responsible thing—researching, connecting, getting answers—but without realizing it, we may be narrowing our child's path instead of widening it.

What the Research Says About Intensive Parenting

I know many parents are eager to jump straight to ideas to apply, but it's worth grounding our actions in solid research. Dr. Bowen's ideas, though decades old, are strongly supported by recent studies showing that parenting styles deeply influence children's emotional development. Yet, in today's landscape—dominated by medication and diagnoses— the role of the child's environment is often overlooked.

Psychological research links children's anxiety and emotional symptoms to key family factors: *parental overprotection*, *overcontrol*, and *overaccommodation*, alongside stress and conflict in the home.[4] These intensive styles gained attention in the late 1990s, revealing that when parents step in to reduce a child's distress, they may reinforce the child's avoidance of challenges.[5] When parents modify routines or avoid situations to prevent their child from feeling anxious, it can unintentionally shore up fear and avoidance. This limits children's opportunities to learn resilience and face their fears. It's like keeping them out of the deep end so they never feel scared—only to find they never learn to swim.

At Macquarie University, Ronald Rapee highlights how overprotection and control restrict children's autonomy and resourcefulness.[6] Similarly, Yale's Dr. Eli Lebowitz shows that parental accommodation—adjusting routines to ease a child's anxiety—offers short-term relief but reinforces long-term fear and avoidance.[7] Avoiding the *deep end* may reduce fear today, but it also keeps kids from learning to swim.

This evidence supports Bowen's view—an anxious focus on a child can hinder emotional and social growth. But this isn't about blaming parents. As discussed earlier, overprotective parenting stems from deep-rooted cultural shifts over the past century. A helpful first step is simply noticing how worry shapes our behavior. Awareness creates space for new choices that support our kids and the entire family. You're not alone. Many of us are swept up in these patterns. But with reflection, we can begin to see—and choose—differently. Parents need to tolerate their own discomfort as they watch their child experience necessary challenges and discomfort during growth. In other words, at each stage of their child's development, parents must manage their own anxiety in order to allow their child to face and cope with new situations.

The Impact of a Parent's Worry Across Childhood

Pause for a moment and think about the effect on a child of being monitored by parents. Have you ever had somebody worry about you and increase their focus on what you are doing—perhaps in the workplace or from your spouse? For example, has anyone started monitoring your eating with the view that you're gaining weight, or watching how you're using your time at work to lift your output? It doesn't bring out the best in us. We react with either irritation or anxious wariness. It's not much different for the child who gets a hefty dose of worry and supervision from others. Children more caught in the parents' *projection process* may become insecure, anxious, or overly sensitive to their parents' emotions. Over time, they may absorb the labels that come with their parents' worry, shaping their identity and making it harder for them to develop emotional independence. Unless a parent can recognize and change their part in this, it can become an endless carousel ride where the child's reactions reinforce the parent's anxieties.

Other children in the family who experience less worry will have a less anxious path in their lives, leading to distinct emotional dynamics among siblings. Over time, this can quietly shape sibling roles and relationships—where one child becomes the *fragile one* and another the *resilient one*, without anyone meaning to assign these parts. I return to this fascinating exploration of sibling differences in a later chapter.

When I've presented these ideas about over-worrying to parents and professionals in child and family health, I've found that the metaphor of *breathing space* is a helpful illustration. This is how I wrote about it in a journal article about the problematic impact of an intense *child focus*:

> It presents significant developmental challenges to the young person as they come to function in reaction to others. This leaves them with little emotional breathing space to grow in thinking, feeling, and acting for themselves.[8]

Of course, the crowding of the emotional breathing space goes both ways. In the early stages of this three-step worry pattern, the parent reduces their tension by their fixing efforts. However, as their child grows in reactivity, it also presents a crowding effect for the parent. Parents start to find that they shift back and forth between trying to help their child and needing space to recover from the parenting stress. Both parent and child experience impediments to their well-being. What begins as a well-intentioned effort to soothe a struggling child can gradually evolve into a cycle of emotional exhaustion. We saw this in the earlier example of Michelle and Mick with their son Jake. As Michelle becomes increasingly preoccupied with managing her son's development and her husband's reactions, her emotional space shrinks, making it harder for her to stay grounded amid the escalating tension.

Recognizing that love for each child must also include the breathing space they need to grow in how they relate—rather than react—to others is a crucial insight. Naturally, parents will be uncomfortable as they recognize how they can participate in the worry dance. But remember that growth is only possible when we tolerate some discomfort. This discomfort isn't a sign of failure—it's often a signal that something important is shifting. With awareness and compassion, even small changes can open up new possibilities for connection and calm within the family.

When Parents' Worry Gets in the Way of Support

Steven is a dad who relishes his role in supporting his four adolescent children. He's an energetic guy with lots of friends. Being liked by others is high on his list of priorities—something he brought from his growing-up experiences, where he knew how special he was to his mother and how much he secured himself with being the loyal friend who'd go to the ends of the earth for his *buddies*. As a dad of teenagers, it was no surprise that he found himself deeply invested in their social lives—especially when it came to his youngest daughter, Ellen, for whom he had always felt a particular protectiveness. After Ellen was born, the family faced a series of added challenges, as his wife, Trudy, experienced a prolonged period of low mood and emotional struggle. Steven stepped in to be more involved in Ellen's early care than he had with their other kids. Ellen had always seemed more fragile to Steven, and he quickly jumped in and bolstered her confidence. His worry for Ellen got ramped up when she had an injury that kept her out of her basketball team for the coming season. Steven feared this setback would socially isolate his daughter and get in the way of connecting with peers at junior high. He became increasingly concerned about whether she was making friends and being included. He would pick her up from school while she was in an orthopedic boot, and the first thing he would ask her about was . . . Can you guess? Who did you hang out with? Ellen would respond with a shrug, and Steven would ask more questions about what she did during her break. Who would she like to invite over? Has she tried chatting to the girls from their neighborhood—asking more questions and giving suggestions. The more he worried and tried to help, the more withdrawn and disengaged Ellen seemed. This added to his worry that she would be the shy, left-out kid at school. The more he acted from his worry, the more real his worry seemed.

Steven could pause and observe how he was playing out his worry with Ellen. He could see it wasn't helping. In particular, he realized he wasn't the kind of support for his daughter he wanted to be—a parent who his daughter felt able to come to for a chat, a good listener who could offer ideas without getting in the way of his children finding their way through social and schooling dilemmas. Steven was redirecting his energy from monitoring Ellen to clarifying what kind of parent he wanted to be. He knew he needed to stop worrying about how she related to others. As a first step, he experimented by picking her up from school and not asking about friends. Instead, he asked about what music she was listening to and what she suggested they listen to on the drive home.

What do you guess were the outcomes of this switch? To his surprise, Steven found that when he stopped focusing on who Ellen connected with at school, she started to share more about her day. Steven refrained from letting his worry hijack this more open conversation, practicing tolerating more silence. He shared a bit about something interesting he experienced that day, ensuring that it wasn't a hidden directive about how to make friends. When Ellen mentioned any of her peers, Steven made every effort to be curious and not anxiously interrogative. The relationship between dad and daughter was becoming a positive support rather than an intense project driven by a father's worry. Steven shifted from keeping a worried eye on his daughter to being genuinely interested in her. This shift brought more calm and connection to their interactions. Consequently, some breathing space opened up, enabling Ellen to relate rather than react.

When Parents Don't Worry Enough— Children's Digital Worlds

You may well be asking the question, are there parents who should worry more? Parents who are so detached from their children that there is an absence of age-appropriate scaffolding? Chapter 3 explores the variations in parenting responses to feeling stressed in these intensive times. There is a version of intense parenting that plays out as helplessness. The intensity of helplessness can be as hindering to a child's development as excessive attention.

It's worth noting that while parents have increased their worry and focus on their children in the real or embodied world of relationships, they have been under-worried in their children's digital world. Jonathan Haidt has highlighted this, laying out the evidence of "overprotecting our children in the real world and underprotecting them online."[9] How can we make sense of this contrast? I suggest that the degree of pressure that parents feel in the modern world primes them for any respite on offer. The more they worry and invest in their children, the more they are stressed. Sustained stress seeks any available relief, and what can be more attractive than a child not requiring anything from a parent? The tablet and smartphone screen delivers parents the break they crave. In my era of parenting, this was confined to the TV and later to the invention of portable DVD players. I recall how glad I was for a break when my children sat quietly in front of the TV.

Parents are increasingly worried about their children's safety, success, and happiness in the real world. At the same time, driven by a legitimate need for a break from parenting and life stress, they may be under-worrying about the impact of excessive screen time on their children. This paradox—protective in one realm, permissive in another—points less to neglect and more to exhaustion. This has become such a significant challenge for today's parents that it deserves a whole chapter. We return to parenting in the digital world later.

Curiosity—a Bridge for Redirecting a Parent's Worry

In the previous examples of parents Michelle and Mick, their worry focused on their son Jake and his *attitude.* Steven's worry drove him to ensure that Ellen wasn't left out by her peers. It seemed counterintuitive to reduce the loving concern with which they were surrounding their child. From my experience, telling a parent to worry less doesn't provide a clear alternative. So, a parent tries to stop worrying so much. What do they do in its place? One place to start is bringing curiosity into the place where worry once reigned. As in the example of Steven and his daughter Ellen, he shifted his focus from what he was worried about and got curious about his daughter's music tastes. As Ellen began to open up more, when there was less pressure for her to reassure her dad, she allowed her father the opportunity to get to know her better. And, in turn, for her to get to know her dad. This doesn't all happen in one week, of course. However, a less worried and more interested parent lays a foundation for a parent–child bond that helps children develop their capacities and gradually launch.

Loving Parents—Observe More, Worry Less

This chapter outlined the detrimental effects of monitoring our children to prevent our worries from coming to fruition. Such worried, intensive parenting has become the norm and is often viewed as an ideal form of conscientious care. It's tricky to see the problems that flow from worried parenting when it has become part of the air that parents breathe. The trend is that parents and others who are charged with helping raise the next generation are led by children's struggles and perceived vulnerabilities. Adults are watching out for things to be fixed or corrected in children, which adds to the crowding of a child's developmental breathing space. With awareness of the impact of this worry-driven focus on children, we can begin to reverse the direction of our change efforts and focus on ourselves as loving leaders. It's not an easy shift in this day and age, but one that gives a resilience-building channel for our parental love.

For Reflection

Consider Your Own Experiences of Being Over-Monitored

1. What have been the effects of someone making a project out of trying to change you?—When another suggests what they think you need to change, they watch you to see if you're following their advice.

2. Have you experienced such monitoring from a parent, a boss, a friend, or a spouse?

3. Have they tried changing areas of your life that concern them, such as your diet, habits, career, work process, or perhaps

your friend choices? Maybe you've experienced another concern from them about how you're parenting!

4. Can you see the intensity and reactivity this triggers? How, while it may be intended for good, has it disrupted your own sense of competence?

5. How does this shed light on the impact of overfocusing on a child?

THE MANY FACES OF INTENSE PARENTING

Because parenting starts with such a dependent infant, it's very easy to overdo our nurture beyond the child's actual needs.

I think everyone these days has heard about concerns regarding "helicopter parenting," in which parents constantly hover over their children. Julie Lythcott-Haims, a former dean of Stanford University, is one of the writers speaking to the effects of the over-involved parent in her book *How to Raise an Adult: Break Free of the Overparenting Trap*.[1] On the university campus, she has witnessed firsthand how overparented students lack life skills, confidence, and the ability to navigate challenges independently. In the early 2000s, awareness of helicopter parenting increased as colleges and university faculty began noticing over-involved parents who would call professors or even attend job interviews with their young adult children. The main argument of writers in this space is that overprotective parenting creates fragile, anxious children who struggle with the predictable stressors of life. This fits with the discussion in Chapter 2 about the impacts of worry, driving parents to make a project out of their children.

I see two things that are missing from much of the current discussion. The first is providing a path for parents to develop a balance beyond merely describing the problem and its effects. The second is an appreciation of how all parents are prone to versions of intensive parenting—and they don't always look like classic helicopter parents. When parents begin to recognize their own version and tendencies toward intensive parenting with honesty and self-compassion, they can take comfort in knowing they're not alone—and that they can make logical adjustments for their children's growth and well-being.

Overdoing or Overfeeling for Our Children

A mother, I'll call Rebecca, who worked with me using my semi-manualized program (The Parent Hope Project[2]) to help parents recover hope in their capacities, said that she never thought of herself as an intense parent until she started tracing her patterns of relating to her struggling teenagers. She didn't make her teens' lunches or drive them to school anymore. As a teacher, she was clear that it was not her role to do her kids' homework for them. This is one of the recognized features of helicopter parenting, with research highlighting that a growing proportion of parents, in their desire to support their children's academic success, become excessively involved in homework tasks.[3] Rebecca, however, saw that she regularly interpreted her children's feelings in her mind and acted on these perceptions to try to calm her children and prevent additional upsets. This was a different version of intensive parenting, with a parent doing the feeling work for their child. Rather than *overdoing* for her children, she was *overfeeling* for them. Her radar was highly alert for any sign of her children being unhappy. When she sensed a child was in a low mood, she would be cautious not to add any stress. She spoke softly and suggested things like walking to the park to lift their spirits. She avoided any conversation that might be upsetting. Rebecca came to recognize that this was getting in the way of her adolescents speaking and acting on behalf of their own emotional experiences. It helped to make sense of how two of her children, whom she worried about the most, were increasingly withdrawing. This does not mean that Rebecca's parenting was causing this, but it was playing a part. Rebecca's awareness of this gave her something clear to work on adjusting that could contribute to her children's growth in their capacities to manage their feelings.

The Balancing Challenge—We're All Prone to Versions of Intensive Parenting

In these anxious times, and with every parent's good and natural protective instinct, it is unrealistic to expect that we can always get the balance right. We will hover into overdoing it in myriad ways in our parenting, especially when our stress ramps up. Rebecca came to see that she was overdoing interpreting the feelings of her most sensitive children. The more her teenagers' moods went down, the more alert she became to monitoring their emotions and responding to her hunches. As a worried mom, Rebecca tried to do the feeling for her children rather than being responsible for her own thinking and feelings. In this nuanced way, she was losing the balance of being connected and not doing too much for the child.

Again, I turn to wisdom from Bowen family systems theory[4] to make sense of the balancing challenge. Bowen describes two essential counterbalancing life forces: the togetherness, connection force, and the separateness, autonomy force. We need both to function as humans and as social mammals. We need to be attached to and appreciated by others, have sufficient space to be individuals, and live out our responsibilities. In any of our relationships, we function best when there's a pretty even balance between being connected and being separate (except for being in an intensive care situation when dependence on others is necessarily high). This is the concept of differentiation of self. It is vital to make clear that separateness is not about selfish individualism, which is autonomy without valuing and honoring others in connecting well. Conversely, connecting is not about being so invested in others that we cannot function without others needing and validating us. In raising children, finding the balance between attachment and not stifling is the essence of *differentiation-based parenting*. It's a challenging balance that looks a little different at each stage of children's development as they grow in their capacities to be separate. Even in infancy, however, there are many ways a baby is learning to function as an individual little person while also attached. Intensity in parenting occurs when either side of these life forces gets out of balance. Consider how this plays out in parenting and shapes various excess styles.

Overdoing Connection

Because parenting starts with such a dependent infant, it is very easy to overdo our nurture beyond the child's actual needs. Caring for a tiny, vulnerable infant also releases lots of feel-good hormones as a way of securing the parent–child attachment (mostly oxytocin: a hormone produced in the hypothalamus and released by the pituitary gland that promotes bonding[5]). One often-overlooked trap is that a parent can become too attached to this feel-good experience and unknowingly keep facilitating their child's dependence beyond what is helpful. It can provide a parent with a sense of security and identity, and who doesn't need a bit more of this in such a chaotic world? One insightful mother shared with me that she came to see that after an intense conflict with her teenage daughter, she would relish the impact of repairing the rift. The intense togetherness and feelings of reattachment had become essential to her feeling good about herself.

When connection overrides separateness in parenting, it can manifest in different parenting styles. Each is an expression of intensity in that the loss of balance shapes it. The overfocus on connecting with the child impinges on developing their autonomy and prevents the parent from focusing on their separate part in the relationship. In Bowen's theory, this is called fusion (in another family therapy approach, it is called enmeshment[6]), where boundaries between parent and child get blurry. Each reacts so much to the other that they lose the ability to reflect on themselves. Hence, when a parent can reverse this by increasing their self-reflection instead of frequently ruminating about their child, it generates a growth-promoting balance. Here are some examples of over-connecting parenting styles:

1. The Over-Nurturing Parent

Meena is an example of a doting mother who cannot imagine she could shower too much love on her children. In particular, her baby daughter Asher seemed to be the cutest girl on the planet, and she adored fixing her hair and trying new outfits. She would stroke Asher's head to soothe her to sleep and tell her repeatedly how beautiful and precious she was. Meena was also devoted to her older son, Ravi, but sensed that he was more confident and didn't need quite the same validation as Asher. Ramit, as the father, supported his wife's commitment to nurturing both children and contributed to treating Asher as their princess.

There is no doubt that these children felt loved. The problem, however, was that Asher was becoming dependent on her mother's soothing even as she approached school age. At age five, she could not fall asleep without her mother's stroking, and separating to go to school proved impossible unless Meena stayed in the classroom for the first part of the day. Both parents were being called to take Asher home early because of her distress. As new problems arose, the only response both parents could find was to increase the soothing and validation of their daughter. Throwing more love on Asher seemed the only solution to what appeared to be her lack of confidence. The connection investment was increasingly getting out of balance with separateness and space for Asher to begin learning to manage life changes.

2. The Over-Accommodating Parent

Joe is an example of a dad who goes too far in the connection side of his parenting relationship with his son, Blake. In the early years, his wife Shelley was more involved with their kids, but as Blake started to reach his preteens, Joe worried that he would lose his friendship with his son. Blake was showing signs of being detached from the family and preferring to be on his Gameboy rather than spend time with the family. Joe had a tense and distant relationship with his father and was anxious not to repeat this father–son pattern. As a result, he started to praise his son more at every opportunity and to make allowances for his son's poor treatment of other family members. When the family went out for his older sister's birthday, Blake said he didn't want to go. Joe started bribing him with the promise of more gaming apps. When they got to the restaurant that was his sister's favorite, Blake refused to eat anything on the menu, and Joe promised to get him takeaway food on their way home. Shelley would give Joe a critical stare, but all Joe could think about was not losing his son's affection.

When both parents talked, they discussed concerns about their once sweet boy becoming so entitled. Both began to search the internet for what might be wrong with him and considered finding professional help. What they were overlooking was the effect of how one parent's fear of loss molded a style of accommodating too much. Neither parent was confident they could turn this around and hoped a diagnosis and treatment might be the answer. There are many versions of accommodating a child's behavior—going along with a child's anxieties or demands. All of us get caught in this at times when wanting peace overrides holding out for what we believe is right.

3. The Co-Achieving Parent

As a star student growing up, Helena knew she had made her parents proud. As an adult, she relished achieving and knowing that others admired her. She took this pattern into her parenting—to be a successful mom, as evidenced by her successful kids. I imagine you can predict how this unfolded. When each of her children showed signs of talent and intelligence, Helena would throw all her support their way. This meant lots of time together, coaching her children and praising their success. Certificates and trophies covered the living room wall. As Helena surveyed these markers of her children's talents, she felt proud of her children and equally proud of herself. Gradually, she became more involved in all her children's competitions and concerts as if they were her achievements. There was little separateness between mother and children regarding markers of talent. Alex, the father, saw his wife's happiness, absorbed in the children's achievements, and went along with it. When his wife was happy, he felt she expected less from him. The children's grandparents were also involved in the project of their grandchildren's achievements. A generational pattern of co-achieving parenting was in place.

4. The Overdirecting Parent

As with many dads, Brad was sensitive to feeling left out when his first child was born. His wife, Sasha, happily cared for the children, and he wondered if he could find a meaningful role as a father. He began to feel left out in his marriage and as a parent, and started trying harder to be recognized. Brad quickly stepped in to tell them how to do things as he focused on finding a role with his two children. This started with more positive directives, such as showing them how to complete a Lego project and tie their shoes. Over time, the pattern moved to explain how they should behave, giving multiple reasons why they should heed his advice. Can you see how the stress of adjusting to parenting amplified Brad's loss of balance? He was becoming an overcontrolling parent who was so alert to when his children needed correction that he lost sight of considering the effects of his parenting and whether this fitted the kind of dad he wanted to be. This parenting style may look like it is overdoing separateness because of the negativity developing in the father–child relationship. However, the energy was not going into being separate as a dad but toward a connection filled with giving directives. Overparenting can be both positive and negative and is often a mixture of both, where a heated argument with overdirecting is followed by over-nurturing in repairing the damage. Both sides of the coin are filled with an intensity that can equally crowd a child's breathing space.

Overdoing Separateness

Both over-connecting and over-separating are driven by intensity in reaction to the child. Many parents find that as they watch their children develop, they experience a sense of being overwhelmed and anxious that they are not up to the task. When I think of it, I remember occasions like this and see that all parents have times when they use distance to manage the sense of impossible demands of parenting. It is often not recognized that distancing parents are doing this as an expression of intensity in their relationship with their children, not from a place of absence of care about them. Here are some examples of distancing parents where stress is managed through excessive separateness.

1. The Outsourcing Parent

Dean and Clare are busy people. They work long hours to pay their hefty mortgage and to give their children a good life. Their version of intense child focus is envisaging the opportunities they are working to create for their three kids. While they focus on giving their children lots of stimulation and the best education, they do this through their separateness rather than over-connecting. They don't realize that they are out of balance because of all the things they can see they provide for their kids, such as sports, art classes, afterschool clubs, and when there is any sign of a child not coping, they send them to a local child therapist. Even the annual family vacation is filled with outsourcing as they go to a location with varied activities for all ages.

Many busy parents resort to outsourcing many services and activities for their children. A degree of external resourcing can be well balanced with relaxed quality time; however, when done anxiously to fill gaps in parent availability, it becomes part of today's intensive trend, leaving children with little free, unstructured time.

2. The Give Me a Break! Parent—Including Allowing Lengthy, Unsupervised Phone Time

Jasmine and Terence faced the complexity of managing their blended family, which included children from previous marriages. They worked in the hospitality industry, which involved shift work, and had children ranging in age from five to seventeen, adding to the complexity and stress of their family life. They are devoted parents and stepparents when they get the time. They watch their kids' sports and stay aware of their school progress. At the same time, like so many of today's families, digital devices have provided a welcome respite for them as adults who relish the distraction of their phones and the way they keep their children occupied. This is an unbalanced loss of connection and awareness of what goes on in children's digital world. The relief of the space that devices provide is complex to relinquish. Deep down, Terence and Jasmine are uncomfortable with the impact of their children's device time, but they are too exhausted to step up and represent their values.

What parent doesn't need a break from the full-on nature of caring for children? I remember the smothering sensation of life with a toddler, not being free to have my bathroom space to myself. Parenting can be exhausting, amplified by the loss over past decades of nearby connection with extended family, support from family and support provided in faith and social communities. We all need respite to re-engage in our relationships, but if we take it too far, the imbalance leads to checking out of parenting responsibilities.

3. The Shut-Down Parent

Most cases of overdoing separation with children result from the overload of life and family demands. Distancing is the fastest way to relieve stress and discomfort when intensity is high. The more extreme version of this imbalance occurs when parents experience helplessness about raising their children. Shona had come to parenting with a fantasy that she and her child would have the perfect relationship. Her childhood had been severely disrupted, moving home and location numerous times and having to adjust to changes in carers from her broader family and kinship network.

When Shona first held her baby girl at not quite twenty years of age, she saw this as a positive turning point. Her baby would be loved and secure in a way she never experienced. There was so much intense need for this positive relationship to come to fruition that Shona felt panicked when her baby would not settle. She received many support services that gave her lots of information and provided parent groups to teach her how to attach as a teenage mom. Shona gave her all to achieve an idealized mother–child bond, but as she entered the toddler phase and confronted her child's defiant pushbacks, she went into shut-down mode. This did not fit her fantasy about being the perfect parent, and Shona was left with a sense of helplessness. Not seeing the intensity behind this, family support workers began to label her parenting as neglectful. Shona was shutting down to cope with the overwhelming feeling of her positive dreams of parenting not being delivered.

The Value of Recognizing the Imbalance

As you reflect on these different parent examples, you may see elements of yourself in them. We all vary in the degree to which we overdo (or underdo) it, but we all fall into times when we lose the balance between connection and separateness as parents. Reflecting on my parenting journey, I was prone to being a co-achieving parent. It's good to be interested supporters of our children's talents. However, there were times when I became overinvested in my daughters' areas of potential success, imagining where it might take them and feeling a level of personal satisfaction when they were in the spotlight. It helps to notice when we are ruminating about one or more of our children—about their strengths or vulnerabilities. The danger of any version of intensive parenting is that we blur the boundaries of what belongs to them and what is ours.

To be clear, as a parent, you are not the only one participating in intensive patterns. The child responds to a parent's focus and reacts in ways that perpetuate the cycle. The other parents and family members all play their part. But change always starts with us. Toning down our positive or negative responses to our children will reduce the stressful intensity around our children and have a positive ripple effect on the whole family. You're not alone in this—every parent finds themselves caught in these patterns at times, and our children play their part in perpetuating them. Recognizing them is already a decisive first step.

Getting the balance right requires first seeing the versions of intensive parenting that we fall into. Remember that all parenting will contain some elements of these different intense styles. We play them out usually without awareness. The path to balance starts with stepping back, shifting our lens to ourselves, and considering our patterns. In the regular stress points of responding to our children, do we intensify our connection at the expense of allowing space for our child to grow, or are we more likely to distance ourselves and lose consistency in staying connected? Rebalancing doesn't happen through reversing from a negative to a positive, intense child focus. Instead, it occurs when a parent can remain separate and aware so that they can connect in ways that support their child while also creating space. In this balance—between presence and perspective—we give our children what they need most: the room to grow into themselves, knowing we are calmly and consistently there.

For Reflection

On Patterns of Intensity

1. Which of these parenting patterns am I most likely to exhibit, especially when life is stressful?

    Overdoing connection?

    - The over-nurturing parent
    - The co-achieving parent
    - The overdirecting parent

    Overdoing separateness?

    - The outsourcing parent
    - The give me a break! parent
    - The shut-down parent

2. Which of my children is most likely to trigger an imbalance in how I connect and stay separate?

3. Which of these styles is my parenting partner prone to? How might they be reacting to my style?

4. What were my parents'/caregivers' main styles? Did their style change from early childhood to facing the challenges of raising an adolescent?

4

PARENTS ON THE SIDELINES

RETHINKING MESSAGES ABOUT CHILDREN'S MENTAL HEALTH

The parent–child relationship is pivotal to children's well-being, so leaving parents on the sidelines doesn't make sense. At the same time, parents need to experience compassion and respect, not blame or criticism.

All parents are concerned about the news reporting crisis levels in children and young people's mental health. Parents are impacted by alarming headlines such as this one from the *New York Times*: "'It's Life or Death': The Mental Health Crisis Among U.S. Teens," with the tagline: "Depression, self-harm, and suicide are rising among American adolescents."[1] There is clear evidence that children's mental health has seen a significant decline in recent years, with various factors contributing to this concerning trend. The impact of the smartphone, growing social and academic pressure, and the effects of the pandemic lockdowns are all getting attention as contributing factors. Perhaps what's being overlooked is that mainstream treatment approaches are failing to reverse the decline in children's functioning. Parents want clear information about child treatment options and guidance in understanding what is available. They also often face numerous roadblocks when trying to find services for a vulnerable child. Perhaps most concerning is that parents are rarely invited to take a central role in a child or teen's mental health practice. If you're a parent who has tried to navigate the maze of mental health services for your child—facing long waitlists, confusing options, or feeling sidelined in the process—you are not alone, and this chapter is especially for you.

First, a brief overview of the growing evidence pointing to a crisis in children's mental health. This is not to alarm or add to the anxieties of parents and caregivers, but to underscore how essential it is to rethink conventional approaches to supporting struggling children and young people. In the United States, recent data reveal that over one in five teenagers aged twelve to seventeen have experienced symptoms of anxiety. At the same time, over a two-week period, nearly 17 percent have struggled with depression.[2] In the UK, during the 2023–24 period, the National Health Service (NHS) recorded a staggering 204,526 referrals of children seeking mental health support for anxiety. It's sobering to see this dramatic rise from just 3,879 referrals in 2016–17, highlighting a rapidly worsening crisis.[3] Meanwhile, in my home country, Australia, concerning trends reveal that children's mental health challenges are emerging at an alarmingly young age. Recent research indicates that mental health decline now begins as early as eight years old, with over one-third of children as young as four and five already showing low levels of well-being.[4] These findings paint a distressing picture of a generation grappling with emotional struggles even before reaching elementary school. With such statistics, it isn't difficult to make a case for a reimagining of mental health care—one that prioritizes prevention, parent involvement, and a society-wide commitment to nurturing the environments of its youngest members. Parents can play a central role in such reimagining.

A Parent's Bewilderment About Their Struggling Child in a Loving Family

In this book's introduction, I presented Rachel and Sam Ritchie and their fourteen-year-old daughter Jessica (not their real names), who had been increasingly depressed and having suicidal thoughts, culminating in serious self-harm. I met the Ritchies as a researcher at the partial hospital intensive treatment center where Jessica had been admitted. Rachel and Sam were hands-on, responsible parents who were living a nightmare, facing their middle daughter's severe symptoms. They expressed understandable bewilderment about how their daughter could struggle when she came from such a supportive family. Rachel and Sam are illustrative of many parents trying to find answers to why one or more of their children could be struggling so much. They would do anything to find the right help for their daughter and were willing to persist in exploring all available treatment options. We'll return to the example of the Ritchie family later in this chapter. They are not alone in their experience of the confusing and tumultuous journey of trying to navigate today's mental health service options.

Navigating the Overwhelming Process of Finding Mental Health Support for Your Child

When I began researching parents' experiences with their child's mental health treatment, one theme stood out immediately—the arduous and often heartbreaking journey of seeking help. Parents spoke about navigating a complex, frustrating, and sometimes discouraging system. Their stories revealed that the search for support for their seriously emotionally struggling adolescent was just as critical to understanding their experience as their stories of their interface with their child's treatment service. Exploring the emotional, logistical, and systemic challenges they faced in getting help for their child, commencing a program was essential to grasp the depth of their journey. Rachel Ritchie expressed the common sentiments of parents I interviewed:

> When we started here, we were exhausted. I mean, it's three years of constant turmoil, like it just never ends. We're tired, and I mean not just the sleeping tired, we were running out of options, running out of ideas, running out of connections, getting her to the right people; you know, we were just running out of choices.

Here are more examples of similar parent accounts describing the struggles to find effective mental health services for their adolescent who had ongoing complex mental health symptoms such as self-harm, psychosis, and high-risk behaviors.[5] Listen to the repeated expressions of frustration, confusion, hitting roadblocks, and going around in circles.

> You're going here, there, and everywhere, and you're sort of going in circles and not finding the right people that you need.
>
> I was looking up on the internet, "googling," and there was nothing really there. I rang anyone possible, anyone I could find, and the children's hospital, just trying to find any contact to get someone suitable.
>
> They had a long waiting list, so I was stuck as a mother; I've gone from here to there. But there's nothing out there. I was at the stage where I didn't know where to turn.

When parents seek support services for their children at any stage, the landscape can be confusing. Who is the relevant professional? Do I access public or private services? What approach is best? Can I afford it? What is my role?

Parents' Involvement in Their Child's Treatment—Do They Have a Role?

Rachel Ritchie and the other parents I interviewed were attending a service that embedded meaningful parent involvement as an expected part of the young person's admission. This service started in the 1970s with a psychiatrist trained in family therapy, who wanted this treatment center to honor the importance of family for every adolescent.[6] This is not always the case when a child receives treatment. For most parents, the next challenge is knowing what involvement is expected of them once they find a service to see their child. Across most Western countries, there are clear legal and policy directives that parents must be involved in mental health treatment planning for children under sixteen or eighteen years of age.[7] Sometimes, the age recommended for parental involvement is up to twenty-five years.[8] The reality, however, is that there is often a disparity between policies about the importance of parent involvement and the reality of service delivery. A review of published papers on parent engagement with their child's mental health service reveals that many services have token parent involvement with passive attendance at some meetings, rather than the policy guidelines of parents being genuinely engaged in contributing to treatment planning, goal setting, and decision-making.[9]

Many parents find themselves on the sidelines once their child is seeing a mental health professional. At one level, they experience great relief to have found support for their child. On the other hand, they often feel that they are shut out of information about their child's therapy and are sensitive to feeling judged by their child's clinicians. The parents in my research spoke to this often shared experience of feeling that their voice was not valued before coming to this new program:

> The counselor didn't meet with me. She just went straight into her, which I thought was bizarre because maybe she wanted to talk to me about why I wanted her here.
>
> They ask me to leave while they do a survey, and then they called me out, and I'm pretty excluded from anything from there on.
>
> One of the issues is that the child's point of view is always correct, while our point of view is less so. To me, it needs to be getting information from the child and also having information from the parent.
>
> Well, I've been kept at arm's length. I don't know a great deal.

Parents reported that medical decisions were often made without sufficient consultation:

> She tells me that my daughter is now going to be on antidepressants because she didn't do well in this survey. I don't get why I have to be just told that. I should have been part of the decision.
>
> There was no communication between me and the psychiatrist, and it didn't seem to be getting any clarity about how to deal with the anxiety. So, she was just medicated.

Another common experience for parents was feeling judged or blamed:

> However, I object to my wife and me being labeled. It's mentioned that we're not good parents in one way, shape, or form. I mean, we do try our best.

Well, my first meeting with the psychologist, the way he spoke, he sounded condescending to me, as if it was all my fault. It happened sort of indirectly, by tone rather than actual words.

It is incredibly challenging for parents to determine what role is helpful and available in their child's behavioral and emotional health treatment. Knowing that policy is on your side can help parents to advocate for meaningful involvement in their children's treatment. Based on solid research that the parent–child relationship is pivotal to children's well-being, leaving parents on the sidelines doesn't make sense. At the same time, parents need to experience compassion and respect, not blame, when involved in any child treatment service.

Chapter 3 presented the family systems perspective that if parents can reduce the intensity of their worry in their interactions with a child, the child can recover breathing space to lift their coping capacities. This perspective lays out a pathway for effective parent involvement in their child's treatment—and for prevention and amplifying children's mental health symptoms. The parent can collaborate with a clinician to understand and adjust their worry reactions to their child. Parents can be empowered as they discover their importance in turning around their child's trajectory from becoming an ongoing patient to a child who recovers their responsible independence. Such a pathway, however, isn't easy to find in the current child mental health treatment landscape. The dominant approaches convey different messages to parents about their role in their child's recovery.

Shortcomings in Current Treatment Paradigms

Every approach to helping a child whose ability to cope with life is disrupted by anxiety, low mood, or high agitation is ultimately aiming for recovery. Plenty of research shows that treatments like cognitive behavioral therapy, emotion coaching, behavior modification, and medication can be effective. But even with promising research behind them, many families and clinicians find that symptoms often come back—and that the positive effects of treatment may fade after just a few months. A standout study (The Child/Adolescent Anxiety Multimodal Extended Long-Term Study)[10] evaluated the long-term efficacy of interventions for anxiety disorders in youth. The results are nothing to celebrate. Year after year, follow-up assessments showed that only about 22 percent of kids stayed well. Around 30 percent remained unwell, and nearly half had ups and downs—getting better, then worse again.

Even though governments are putting more money into child mental health services, it's becoming clear that more funding alone isn't enough to truly change what's happening. Change at a societal level, limiting children's access to smartphones and social media, will hopefully start making an impact. Parents, however, have such a short time frame to raise their kids. They need real hope and practical options that can make a difference sooner rather than later. That's why it's essential to take a closer look at the approaches we're already using to support children's mental health, think honestly about their limitations, and explore positive, more effective paths forward.

The Medical Model Looks for a Cause and a Fix—Where's the Support for the Family Environment?

While there are strong biological expressions of mental health symptoms such as anxiety, depression, and attention issues, a medical model will fall short if it primarily attends to the brain and doesn't appropriately address the environment in which the symptoms have arisen. The field of child psychiatry endorses the vital interplay of nature and nurture, advocating for a holistic approach that considers the complex interplay between genetics, biology, and the environment as essential for effective prevention and treatment. It also recognizes the importance of supporting the family as the most influential aspect of a child's environment. Nevertheless, the dominant treatment remains the individual child with token family involvement. A significant focus is on coming up with a primary diagnosis and medication. Any diagnostic label gives the impression that there is a cause and a fix. At least two-thirds of children between the ages of five and seventeen in treatment for mental health conditions were prescribed medication. The majority combined this with individual counseling.[11] Understandably, parents invest their hopes in finding a straightforward one-directional solution. If only it were that simple! But children's mental health doesn't follow a simple cause-and-effect path—it's shaped by a web of influences, from relationships and environment to biology and stress.

Treating the Individual—Where Is the Family?

Despite the recognition of the impact of the relationship environment on children's well-being, the vast majority of treatment offered to emotionally struggling children is focused on the child as an individual. I hear from many parents who are frustrated that their child's therapist doesn't provide them with information from the clinical sessions that could help them to support their child's recovery. While policy is clear about the importance of family and parent involvement and addresses the school context, this does not adequately translate into what is offered. In a survey conducted by the American Psychiatric Association, 90 percent of clinicians reported that involving parents in child mental health treatment is effective; however, only 25 percent felt adequately trained to engage parents in therapeutic processes.[12] This disparity suggests that there is a substantial gap in the training and ongoing professional development of mental health professionals who feel more comfortable relating to the individual child than helping engage the family. I've heard this repeatedly over the years in my supervision of clinicians and have written that

> Clinicians in child and young people's mental health services are aware that family dynamics play an important part in the "stuckness" of symptoms. Still, they struggle to find a way to translate their treatment approach into a family or parenting intervention.[13]

I believe it's useful for parents to be aware of this area of uncertainty for many professionals and to specifically request a worker who is trained in and comfortable with involving parents. Asking for this isn't overstepping or being difficult—it's aligned with current best practices and many child mental health policies that recognize the family as a key part of the treatment team.

Not Everything Is Trauma—the Risk of Over-Labeling Childhood Challenges

Are you noticing the increase in labeling challenges in life as *trauma*? Not that long ago, a traumatic event was defined as a catastrophic stressor outside the range of usual human experience, such as war, torture, or natural disasters.[14] More recently, any adverse experience causing distress may be labeled as trauma. Today, trauma can be seen to stem from events that contradict our worldview—in other words, people expressing different opinions could be labeled as unsafe and traumatizing. This expanded use of the word trauma fits with the growing social trend of *safetyism* put forward by Greg Lukianoff and Jonathan Haidt in their 2018 book, *The Coddling of the American Mind*,[15] where all threats, both real and imagined, are to be avoided. The risk of calling too many things trauma in child mental health is that it can foster increased avoidance, anxiety, and fragility in our children.

Trauma-informed practices have gained significant momentum in recent years in child mental health services. In many ways, this is helpful as it appropriately acknowledges environmental influences. No one can argue with the detrimental impact of major life disruptions on a person. The problem is when such cause-and-effect thinking blocks out all the other influences on a child's coping in life. I have spoken to many parents who are in search of an undiscovered trauma as a way of making sense of their child's struggles. When clinicians, parents, and teachers go in search of a traumatic event in a child's life, they will always be able to find something that has presented a substantial stress for a child. But the picture is always more complex than that one thing. It risks detracting from seeing the child's markers of resilience. Too much explanation and treatment based on trauma also misses accounting for the many variations in people's capacity to bounce back after adversity, with different relationship protective factors. Rather than searching for a traumatic cause, we can helpfully ask: "What's helped my child cope—and how can we build on that?"

Attachment Theory—the Traps of a Focus on Attuning to Our Children

As a parent, have you ever felt that no matter how closely you tune in, it still doesn't feel like enough? That pressure might not be your fault—it could be built into the very models we're being asked to follow. John Bowlby's attachment theory,[16] generated by observing the impact of children being separated from caregivers during the Second World War, has become the central relationship-based model for understanding and treating children's emotional symptoms. Some people have described the field of child mental health as *swimming in a sea of attachment theory*—which reflects just how much this way of thinking has come to shape how we think about and support children who are struggling.[17] While attachment theory has offered valuable insights, relying too heavily on it can sometimes limit our perspective and stop us from seeing the bigger picture of what children and families are really dealing with.

Attachment theory has been widely researched and expanded on over the decades and is indeed the go-to model for addressing the family environment in child mental health. At risk of simplifying this theory, the focus is on the importance of secure attachment for a child to thrive. Conversely, some form of faulty attachment with caregivers is viewed as a core part of the problem when a child struggles. Hence, when parents are involved in any treatment or preventive courses, the effort is to help them correct their attachment style and strengthen the security of the parent–child bond. They are taught how to co-regulate their child's emotions—to come alongside their child and speak to what a child is feeling. Additionally, parents are encouraged to become better attuned to their child's needs. It just sounds right. No one could argue with the benefits of children experiencing security in their relationships. What may be missed in this approach is that when stressed parents (which most of us are) are given messages to attune more to their children, they increase their focus on and monitoring of their child.

While recent versions of attachment theory include the need to grant children space to explore and become more autonomous, the message for parents is that you need to be able to read your child's needs and use parenting techniques that ensure you provide that enshrined secure base. Where does this focus parents' energy? Not to grow their self-awareness of how they respond differently with each of their children, but to improve the mind, mood, and behavior of the child they worry about most. Consider the effect of the primary focus going toward the child to help them feel more secure. It raises the possibility that this favored approach may inadvertently add to parent–child intensity, leading to the squelching of children's growth of their capacities.

A Family Systems Understanding of Mental Health Symptoms in Children

What if helping your child didn't start with focusing on them, or looking for a cause of their symptoms, but with understanding yourself and how you respond to the emotional currents in your family? Chapter 3 introduced Murray Bowen's family systems theory. In this theory, reducing intensity and fusion in family relationships is the path to forging a secure relationship for a child. Can you recognize how this is different from the above perspectives? Rather than parents becoming more focused on their child, the emphasis is on parents focusing first and foremost on ways they may be adding to becoming overly responsible and reactive to their child and parenting partner. It can seem counterintuitive, but the goal is not to fix or attune to the child but to be a separate and connected carer with the child.

This is *differentiation-based parenting*, distinct from *attachment-based parenting*. From this lens, parents come to see how everyone in the family is affecting each other, hence all are part of co-regulating the emotional experience of the other. This includes how each child in a family affects the parents differently. Parents also attend to how they react to the parenting partner and how this impacts the child's life. Every child is part of such a triangle with their parents, shaping how they learn to relate. The good news with this perspective on how each family member affects each other is that when a parent adjusts their expression of emotions and their consequent actions, they can cultivate a more growth-promoting environment, over time, for all.

I like the garden metaphor for seeing the family as an emotional system—it's an organic way to think about how families function and change. "The family emotional system: seedbed of symptoms or garden of recovery" is a phrase that captures this dual potential, tied to the work of Dr. Daniel V. Papero from the Bowen Center for the Study of the Family.[18] I heard this explored in depth during his keynote at the Twenty-First Annual Conference of the Family Systems Institute,[19] which took place in Sydney, Australia, in 2024. In his talk, Dr. Papero described how the emotional system within a family can be the soil where symptoms take root—but also where recovery and growth can flourish, depending on how much intensity the system generates.[20] Overwatering—what Bowen theory would call overfunctioning—leads to emotional saturation, where anxiety grows instead of a resilient individual. But when families cultivate space, allowing each member the room to develop their own functioning, that's when real recovery becomes possible. It's not about controlling growth, but about creating the conditions where growth can happen.

Returning to the Question—How Can My Child Be Struggling When We've Shown Her So Much Love?

Rachel Ritchie asked the question so many confused and fearful parents ask when they have a child with such deep fragility needing help from mental health services. With her daughter Jessica having harmed herself with an overdose, she looked back on their family life and couldn't make any sense of this harrowing situation:

> How could this happen to Jessica? We've thrown so much love at her! Both her parents show her lots of love and attention . . . and she's the only one with such terrible depression. It's a shock to everyone.

Rachel and her husband, Sam, were influenced by all the messaging about children's mental health. They thought that this only happens to children who are neglected or abused in some way. They looked for medical causes. Is this in the family genetics? Has Jessica experienced a trauma that she hasn't disclosed? How is it that after some initial improvements in her individual treatment with a psychologist she liked, her mood became darker?

Rachel and Sam had the opportunity to be part of parent sessions while Jessica was in her treatment center. They were helped to map out the timeline of their family and to see the way Jessica had been parented with more anxiety than the other children. Here's how they began to put the puzzle pieces together.

Rachel reflected on her parenting and recognized she had always sensed that Jessica, her middle child, needed more support than her siblings. As a toddler, Jessica caught every virus going around, and Rachel became increasingly protective of her often-unwell daughter. Although Jessica managed early transitions like school and sleepovers, she remained more emotionally dependent on Rachel, who described herself as Jessica's *security blanket*. Rachel took pride in this nurturing role—it affirmed her identity as a good mother.

Sam, meanwhile, recalled feeling sidelined after their children were born. Rachel's focus shifted to parenting, which brought more peace to their marriage. He didn't complain about the loss of closeness, relieved that her criticism of him as a husband had eased. He went along with Rachel's parenting efforts, especially when Jessica's anxiety surfaced.

Parent sessions helped Rachel and Sam recognize that Jessica had a different relationship dynamic than her siblings. She had become the focus of heightened worry and protection—primarily from Rachel, with Sam joining in to help her feel secure. Jessica naturally responded to this anxious attention with greater neediness, creating a reinforcing cycle of reassurance and dependency. Even the extended family joined in efforts to boost her confidence, yet by adolescence, Jessica still struggled to cope beyond the safety of home.

Through these sessions, Rachel and Sam began to see how their attempts to fix Jessica were backfiring. Instead of fueling worry, they shifted toward a calmer interest in her ideas and strengths. They didn't blame themselves. Instead, they appreciated how this was activated by her frequent illnesses. It was also clear that genetically, she had a more inhibited temperament, like her dad.

Parent sessions became a turning point. Rachel and Sam learned to adjust their approach and support Jessica's growing resilience. While Jessica also received other forms of treatment, her parents became less focused on fixing her and more confident in their role as her steady, supportive foundation—benefiting not just Jessica, but the entire family.

Putting Aside Expectations of a Quick Fix

One of the other mismatches of the medical model in mental health is the expectation that there is a quick fix for a complex, multifaceted set of symptoms. I do acknowledge that there is a place for symptom relief if it also helps a child grow their resourcefulness, not dependence. More sustainable change, however, takes time—and it often starts with parents being willing to shift how they see and respond to their child's challenges. Rachel and Sam Ritchie appreciated that changes to their previous intensive parenting and improvements in Jessica's coping would not be immediate. They reflected that the road to Jessica's loss of inner strength was many years in the making. It wasn't like catching a virus a week back that could be treated with immediate symptom relief. As parents, they could see glimmers of improvement that helped them tolerate the long road to their daughter's recovery of her life resources, which was the best route to take. This removed an urgency to fix, which helped create a calmer tone for the relationship. They were confident that they now knew how to work on their part in promoting Jessica's growth in independence and resourcefulness. The push toward fixing a diagnosis was replaced by a steady path of promoting balanced relating that enables all family members to become their best.

Sifting Out What's Helpful in Children's Mental Health

It's a massive challenge for parents to determine the best approach to helping a child who is struggling on multiple levels engage with the tasks of growing up. They see their child struggle to engage with school and peers, struggle to restrain anger when instant gratification is withheld, struggle to mobilize to take small risks, and struggle to access their resources to calm their upsets. The helping options on offer are deeply confusing for parents. Is this a medical problem that needs a diagnosis, or is it a trauma that has occurred in the past? Is it enough for our child to be seen individually, or is parental involvement necessary? Will we be blamed in some way if we are involved? Do we need to learn more about our child's needs and attune to them better? Or are there small but impactful steps we can take to reduce the worry around our child and give them space to get back on track?

While every treatment approach may have helpful elements, it's useful to consider what messages fall short and sometimes make recovery more difficult for our children. I am convinced that the broader perspective of family systems deserves to be an offering for parents and mental health professionals. This confused system that struggles to implement policy for non-blaming, family-based involvement is ripe for transformation. What if, instead of assuming the child must change first, we saw the family as a living system, where small shifts in one part can lead to powerful, lasting changes throughout? Imagine the impact of mental health support services that empowered parents and ceased putting the burden of change on the child, with their diminished coping and maturity resources. Imagine more support services for the family and community that promote the resourcefulness of our young, rather than giving labels that can fuel dependency. Can you begin to see a fresh and hopeful way forward where parents play a central role?

For Reflection

Questions to Consider About Mental Health Treatment for Your Children

1. Will this approach involve me so that I can grow in confidence as a support for my child?

2. Will I be helped to see a big-picture lens rather than a narrow cause-and-effect view of my child's struggle?

3. Will I be treated with compassion and respect?

4. Will treatment increase a fixing focus on my child that might add to them staying in a patient role?

5. Will the service add to my overfocusing on my child or help me recover my path as a parent?

6. Will the service help me discover what's in my control and adjust to assist my child in having more space to grow?

7. Am I willing to take a longer road to my child's recovery of well-being instead of investing in finding a quick fix for their current symptoms?

FROM CONFUSION TO CLARITY

THE PREVENTIVE ROLE OF PARENTS IN CHILDREN'S MENTAL HEALTH

A key to health-promoting parenting is allowing space for your children's transitions and adjustments to a new stage of maturity— space for them to struggle a little and experience their newfound coping skills.

Chapter 4 examined the limitations of current approaches to understanding and treating children's mental health. Building on these ideas, I want to empower parents with a perspective that strengthens their confidence in supporting their children through life's inevitable challenges. I often hear parents asking how they can protect their children from becoming part of today's youth mental health crisis. Is the answer early intervention, seeking professional help at the first sign of trouble, or gaining a deeper understanding of mental health diagnoses and their implications? While these may play a role, the most potent influence lies closer to home. The family environment shapes a child's emotional resilience more than any external factor. Parents can grow their capacity to foster a foundation that enables children to navigate seasons of emotional vulnerability. This doesn't need to be perfect at all. Instead, it calls for a little less intensity in how we respond to our children's inevitable upsets. And for us to tolerate that family life can sometimes be messy, and that doesn't call for panic. We can be going through a storm, and while waiting to come out the other side, our best efforts are managing the storm inside of us.

Firstly, I want to clarify the idea of prevention. As you saw in Chapter 4, a prevention mindset can lead to excessive monitoring of children, looking for early signs of mental health problems. In this way, it can become part of what worsens kids' emotional health. So, as we consider how parents can play a role in building a health-promoting family environment, remember that this is not about having a checklist of warning signs, adding to an intense focus on our children.

Social Prescriptions Rather Than Medical

Before focusing on a central preventive effort that parents can make in their relationship with their kids, I want to clarify that this sits alongside many other family and social initiatives. There is a small but growing movement in the mental health field to apply social prescriptions rather than rely on pharmacological prescriptions. One example is a report in the UK that conveys how connecting young individuals to community activities and services can improve their health and well-being.[1] This is certainly an encouraging trend, where social engagement opportunities, meaningful activities, diet, and exercise receive the attention they deserve. Alongside this is the vital call for a whole society response to the detrimental impact of the smartphone and social media on children. This results in legislation and school policy reform that provide necessary backup for parents as a preventive measure for the coming generation.

At a family level, many adjustments can be made that will improve mental health outcomes for our children. You can probably list many of these—family dinners, connection to the extended family and community, one-on-one relaxed time with children, joining children in their favorite online games and shows, walking to places rather than driving, and jointly planning a holiday. I invite you to expand this list. Such intentional activities will counteract the intensity of worry with our children, where too much of our connection is around our concerns. We don't want our worries to prevent us from seeing our children's capacities.

As I speak with educators and school well-being staff, I hear about the many efforts schools make to incorporate mental health literacy into their curriculum as a preventive measure for children. I question the effectiveness of this approach, as it may mirror the constant monitoring of children for clinical issues, potentially leading to the discovery of problems simply because they are being actively sought. Some recent studies show evidence that such programs can exacerbate children's mental health issues.[2] Do you recall how this is the same pattern that often occurs in our families, where parents scan for what they fear and amplify the problem? The most valuable preventive measures focus not on symptoms but on children's resourcefulness. A fabulous example is the Let Grow organization,[3] which creates school and parent partnerships to support children's independence. We explore more of these social supports for parents and children in later chapters, but for now, let's focus on a core prevention aspect of parenting—how to reduce intense reactions to children's distress or defiance.

Facing Our Children's Distress and Defiance—Allowing Space for Them to Struggle

Two of the most common and confronting aspects of parenting are dealing with our child's distress and defiance. Can you recall your earliest memories of dealing with these emotional breakouts for each of your kids? I recall the first times my sweet infants metamorphosed into tantrummy toddlers whose favorite word was "No!" What can prepare a parent for this great challenge to their reasonable requests? Equally, I tremble when I remember the shock of my young child melting down with the most dramatic display of upset and tears as I was leaving them at nursery school. I now get to witness similar predictable displays of upset from my grandchildren and hear from my grown children their appreciation for what I've been through in raising them. These dramatic emotional displays are expected as children leave infancy behind and gradually become more competent in containing their upsets at not having a parent on tap or not getting their way.

The key to health-promoting parenting is not to interfere with your children's transitions and adjustments to a new stage of maturity. It means allowing *space* for your children to struggle a little and experience their newfound coping skills. This is challenging for any parent. A child's distress naturally stirs deep emotional reactions within us. I hear parents express how one of their children's crying and clinging trigger a surge of protection and a desire to buffer them from the world. And other parents recall their fuming offense to a child speaking back to them and not following a request. These are primary triggers that all parents can recognize.

How Children's Mental Health Symptoms Show Up—Internalized or Externalized

Pause and think about your experiences with your child's early tears or anger. Consider the difference between a child fearful of the world and one who reacts aggressively to limits. Both present unique challenges that shape family dynamics and parental responses. A clue to understanding prolonged helplessness or opposition is how parents responded over time—and how children, in turn, reacted to those responses. Of course, it's never just two types of distress. In all my clinical work, I've never met a child who didn't show some helplessness, withdrawal, or pushback. These reactions often draw intense responses that can unintentionally reinforce the child's emotional state. We'll look at real-life examples soon, but first, let's consider how mental health symptoms are categorized as internalized or externalized.

Internalized symptoms are inward: emotional distress, withdrawal, or poor self-regulation. They often show up as anxiety, fear, sadness, low energy, or social avoidance—sometimes with physical symptoms like headaches or stomach aches. Eating disorders fall into this category, and at the more severe end, thoughts of not wanting to live.

Externalized symptoms are outward: poor impulse control, aggression, or defiance. These may be expressions of anxiety, with the child using dominance as a way to regulate. More severe behaviors include violence, bullying, lying, or property destruction, usually toward authority figures. While a neurological basis is often assumed, caregiver responses also play a key role in escalation or de-escalation.

Some children show both types of symptoms and may be labeled with a personality disorder—marked by both withdrawal and high-risk behavior. With ongoing intensity, reality distortions like psychosis can appear. I've yet to see a case without some level of anxiety. It seems to underlie both withdrawal and aggression. Over time, I've come to see anxiety as a meta-symptom—at the core of both neediness and opposition. Anxiety is the most common mental health diagnosis for children and teens, and it is often coupled with other issues such as internalized depression and externalized hyperactivity.

We've already looked at some of the staggering statistics, but they are worth revisiting. The rise of anxiety among our young is quite staggering. In a US report in 2023, just over 16 percent of adolescents were diagnosed with an anxiety disorder, with girls especially affected (over 20 percent for girls). Shockingly, the data shows a 61 percent increase from 2016.[4] Anxiety can be truly debilitating when it sets in for any of us as day-to-day life gets sabotaged by excessive fear that plays out in our minds and bodies. But remember that a calmer and less intense relationship environment, that doesn't fuel worry and tension, is the best seedbed for an anxious child to start to flourish.

Working Out the Place of Diagnoses

The different expressions of internalized and externalized symptoms earn specific diagnostic labels from the DSM, or the *Diagnostic and Statistical Manual of Mental Disorders*.[5] I understand that many parents invest a good deal of effort in finding a diagnosis, hoping it will be matched with straightforward treatment. Diagnoses describe how a child's sustained symptoms present themselves. They may lead to treatments that help children face their fears or correct negative thinking. They may provide behavioral management protocols and often involve prescribed medication. These *fix-the-child* treatments miss a key point—sure, symptom relief can help, but it doesn't give adequate attention to the environment that seeded the child's limited tolerance for distress.

All the above symptoms are highly distressing for the child and the parent. A child's engagement with education, extracurricular activities, and peers is compromised to varying degrees. It can quickly become a revolving door of efforts to fix it, with some initial improvements followed by a regression when the next challenge presents itself. Parents and professionals want a map to exit such a roundabout. Rarely, however, is this exit a shortcut. Instead, the best route is a slower road where parents start relating to their struggling child differently. They begin relating to their capacities for learning how to deal with upsets and limits, distinct from relating to their child's symptoms and problems. Let's unpack this with some examples.

What About Neurodiversity?

A note on where diagnoses can have their place. I hear some parents say that when they realized that their child had a particular neurodivergent diagnosis, they stopped trying to rewire their child's brain and started to accept them as they were. This sounds like a positive outcome as it reduces the parents' efforts to fix and frees up space for the child to develop to their best and unique capacities. The neurodiversity movement emphasizes that diagnoses such as autism and attention deficit hyperactivity disorder (ADHD) are natural variations of the human brain rather than deficits or disorders that need to be *fixed*. More and more diagnoses seem to be added to this list, which appears to be reflecting society's ongoing investment in the medical model. While a reduction in a fixing effort takes pressure off children, I also caution that giving a child a fixed label might lead parents and others to treat them as less capable than they might otherwise be. Whatever a child's unique temperament and neurological wiring, we do well to treat them as an interesting young person to get to know rather than a label that emphasizes limitations.

A Personal Story of Being the Symptomatic Child

Much of my writing comes from decades of experience in the child and family mental health field. But I also write from a personal place—

as someone who, at eleven years old, found themself in treatment for psychosomatic symptoms. I had symptoms that appeared as biological but were, at heart, psychological. My headaches and dizzy spells emerged following a few years of adverse events in my family, including the sudden death of my grandmother, my grandfather's severe stroke, bringing him into our household for care, and culminating in a fire that gutted our house. I had an infectious illness for a time that kept me isolated for many weeks. After returning to school, I began to exhibit symptoms that resembled something concerning happening in my brain, including headaches and fainting spells.

My mother had invested a hefty dose of worry and care when I was genuinely medically ill. She had a brother who died of an infectious illness aged four, and understandably was highly protective and monitored any signs of ill health in her children. I can look back as an adult and see how her extra attentive response to my health contributed to my withdrawal from life into my symptoms. Of course, the terrifying experience of our house fire and the other griefs in the family added to my vulnerability. What is important to note, however, is that I am one of five siblings and was the only family member to develop symptoms at this time. It is clear to me that the extra protective investment from my mother, combined with my time as a sick child needing quarantine, influenced my slipping into a withdrawn and anxious state. As my family got back on track after this tumultuous period, I lifted out of my symptoms and happily re-engaged with school and life. While I can't be sure, my reflections all these decades later are that the individual psychiatric treatment I received did little to contribute to my recovery. The return of some family stability was the most significant factor in getting back on track.

My mother's response to my illness was a factor in my getting stuck in symptoms. My father would have supported my mom's worry. I am not blaming my parents for this in any way, as they were doing what came naturally at a challenging time for all of us. My mother's experience of her older brother's childhood virus and death in her family of origin also fed her intensity in parenting a child with an illness. Looking at parenting stress responses to one or more of their children provides valuable clues to ways parents and others can assist a *mentally unwell* child recover their functioning.

As a side note, I find it fascinating that my symptoms would be labeled differently today. The current label for psychosomatic illness in the DSM-5-TR (2022) is functional neurological symptom disorder (FNSD). This term replaces conversion disorder[6] and refers to apparent neurological symptoms that have no medical explanation and are believed to have a psychological origin. Does this give you a perspective on the changing nature of diagnostic labels? It isn't very clear for us in the field, and is surely confusing for parents.

How Our Family of Origin Experiences Can Drive Over-Caring Responses

Understandably, my mother brought a heightened sensitivity to children's illnesses to her parenting. This meant that any significant health issue in her children was met with a good deal of support. Parent support is terrific, but the problem is when it continues beyond the child's need for it. This can keep a child in a less capable state than their stage of development. For me, as an eleven year old, it made the safety of being cared for as a needy patient hard to leave behind, not that I was consciously plotting this. For my parents, the added stress of dealing with the loss of our home and possessions alongside caring for a disabled, elderly granddad would have amplified my mother's sensitivity. That is what stress does. It turns up our intensity dial, which will get mixed up in our parenting responses.

A Dad Reacts to How He Was Parented

Alan wanted to be a very different parent from his father. He recalled that his dad worked long hours and that he often harshly corrected their behavior when he interacted with his two sons. When Alan was raising his kids, he was determined to be different. He gave his children lots of affection and time to support their activities. When his youngest son,

Aaron, started to oppose his parents' instructions, he was susceptible to not being harsh. He met his son's tantrums with lots of effort to make him happy, trying to distract him with special treats. When his son wouldn't eat the food cooked for the family, Alan would find alternatives for him. As Aaron grew, he became increasingly oppositional and would be incredibly disrespectful to his dad. Alan felt discouraged as he experienced a harshness from his son that he had felt from his father. Without awareness, he had gone so far in the other direction that Aaron had not had sufficient practice at tolerating not getting his own way. It was important for Alan not to become self-critical but to see that he could adjust his parenting not to accommodate his son's demands. He appreciated that his over-accommodation came from a well-meaning place and that, gradually, he could reclaim balanced parenting where connection and limits went hand in hand.

I've met other parents who have such a strong sense of their role as an authority that they fall into overdoing correction and control. This is just as unhelpful as Alan's over-accommodating. It's useful for all of us to consider the reactions we bring from our own experiences of being parented to understand how one or more of our kids can push our stress buttons. With awareness, we can make choices to respond more helpfully for the sake of our children's healthful development.

Parents Dealing with a Child's Upset Without Relying on the Latest Techniques

When a child is upset, a parent's body reacts automatically—stress rises, heart rate increases, breathing quickens. The brain releases cortisol, activating the fight-or-flight system. Mirror neurons make us feel our child's emotions as if they're our own. Bonding hormones like oxytocin drive us to protect. In the face of this intense surge, it's tempting to jump straight into soothing or fixing—offering comfort, or using bribes or threats to stop the child's distress. However, a parent's awareness of their own emotional state is just as important as their awareness of the child's upset. Our job is to respond, not over-respond. That urge to shut down distress may need to soften so we can adjust to our child's new stage of development.

Throughout history, parenting approaches have shifted between extremes. Some eras emphasize soothing and involvement, while others lean toward detachment and ignoring. But rather than grabbing at techniques, it's more helpful to focus on regulating our stress and relating calmly to an upset child. A pause to reflect often does more than a technique. Questions like: What's my child stepping into developmentally? What do they need to learn for responsible independence? What helps or hinders that? These shape thoughtful responses. Children benefit from gradually learning to manage in the world without constant holding. They also grow from hearing No. A highly stressed parent may struggle with limits, while a steady one can hold them confidently. That reflective pause gives both parent and child resilience—and helps prevent caregiver burnout.

Parents Staying Steady as Their Children Learn to Handle Separation and Limits

Do you recall Rachel Ritchie's reflections on her parenting history with her middle daughter, Jessica? She could see that she was much more protective of Jessica than her other children, allowing her maternal comfort to be a security blanket well into her school years. This worked during the elementary school years because Jessica had just one class teacher at school to be her mother's replacement. However, transitioning to the high school context tipped Jessica's upset over the edge of her resources. Her dependency on her mother and other nurturing teachers had provided stability in the early years, but it could not sustain her in the more complex environment of adolescence. Rachel and Sam did their very best to parent Jessica and followed many messages about meeting their daughter's security needs. Without realizing it, they had parented in a way that kept Jessica at a level of dependence in line with a much younger child. This was maintained over the years because Jessica presented to her parents as more needy. Her temperament was likely to be naturally reserved and shy, but the extra protectiveness prevented the emergence of sufficient maturity for early adolescent challenges. This helps to make sense of the development and worsening of her depression.

For other families, their struggling child has always been experienced as demanding rather than needy. Parents have floundered in their efforts to set limits and often keep the peace by giving in to a child's defiant behaviors. A child who doesn't get to experience parents holding a calm and consistent line on appropriate conduct when young (according to their parents' values) will predictably struggle to contain agitated responses. As I write this, I think of all the loving parents I have met who have struggled with an oppositional child. It is always more complex than what can be captured in a few sentences. Often, biological factors are at play, and the pattern of tension between parents has them adopting opposite parenting methods to manage the child. One becomes extra harsh, while the other goes in the opposite direction, adopting extra nurturing methods. The key idea here is that an environment that is either intensely positive or correcting will lack the nutrients for a child to grow, whatever potential they have for steadying themselves in their relationship environments. I trust you are taking in that over-positive nurturing is as unhelpful as over-negative correcting, as both sides of the coin crowd the child's growth of their responsible independence.

Parents Reducing Their Need to Be Needed

In reflecting on ways that parents can reduce over-caring for their children, we would do well to consider the subtle ways we can gain rewards from our children's dependence on us. I recall a mother having a light bulb moment as she read an example from another parent who gained a strong sense of comfort from making up with her child after a fight. She said to me:

> I see that's just like me! I realize I soothe my stress through emotional closeness with my teenage son, especially after intense arguments. I need to find healthier ways to connect with him that aren't driven by deep emotional involvement to help me feel better about myself.

One of the challenges of giving our children space to grow is that being needed by them gives us parents emotional and psychological rewards. We experience the feel-good bonding hormone oxytocin and can unknowingly start reinforcing moments of experiencing our child's need for us. As parents, we can find a sense of steadiness in caretaking. When a child shows neediness, we may feel stronger in our role as comforter—but this can unintentionally keep them more dependent than their age requires. Ask yourself: *Do I feel good when my child needs me?* Could I be holding on to their dependence more than necessary? Some may see this as guilt-inducing, but that's not the aim. If you can tolerate the discomfort of honest reflection, you're already on the path to growing confidence in your parenting. And with that confidence comes real hope—hope that you can support your child's growing resilience and maturity.

Hope for Parents and Vulnerable Children

Parents can always find ways to reduce the intensity of their responses to a child with whom they are concerned. Murray Bowen described this way of viewing mental health as a family system that unevenly distributes their worry in ways that affect one member's growth more than others. When a family member gives up the development of a separate, resourceful self in the back-and-forth of relationships, they are most prone to struggle with symptoms. The good news is that the family can adjust to enable all members to reinstate their growth of a resourceful and responsible self. Part Two outlines this pathway, presenting it as *differentiation-based parenting*. Balanced parenting helps a child maintain a strong sense of self while staying emotionally connected to others. In child mental health, this means that when parents provide support while allowing their child to navigate separations and limits, they help build resilience. This approach can prevent a child's struggles from escalating into more severe coping difficulties. I've heard from those who worked closely with Dr. Bowen that he often liked to say, "That which was created in a relationship can be fixed in a relationship."[7] Can you see the hope generated from such an idea? Our family relationships can be a fertile garden for children to regain their best functioning and well-being. And it is never too late for parents to contribute to this. Part Two helps you see more clearly how to apply this, whatever stage of parenting you are in.

For Reflection

Parenting as Prevention

1. How have I experienced my children's distress and defiance?

2. Have my reactions ever been exaggerated with one or more children?

3. How might my family of origin experiences have contributed to worry or over-caretaking in my parenting?

4. Am I overcorrecting or overprotecting in ways that limit my child's coping and self-regulation?

5. Do I sometimes need my child to need me beyond what fits their age?

6. What helps me reflect on my parenting with honesty and openness?

7. What's one insight I can take away about parents' preventive role in children's mental health?

PART TWO

A UNIQUE APPROACH TO REGAINING BALANCE

INTRODUCING DIFFERENTIATION-BASED PARENTING

6

THE PARENT IS THE PROJECT, NOT THE CHILD

This approach is marked by a surprising pivot that shifts the focus from the child to the parent. This shift means parents can reverse the current anxious focus on children, and in turn, children can grow in age-appropriate levels of coping and responsibility.

Bravo for sticking with me through Part One. I imagine many parents are eager to dive into practical strategies, but I hope you've found the groundwork we've laid worthwhile and enriching. We've taken a step back to reflect on how society is fueling the intensity of parenting, often crowding a child's breathing space and getting in the way of their full development. We also explored the current landscape of child mental health approaches and considered how a parent-led approach can offer something powerful and preventive. If you've made it this far, I trust you've already begun to see how some simple shifts in perspective can start to relieve the pressure. With that foundation in place, we're ready to dive into what you've been waiting for— principles for application to help parents reclaim balance and lead with confidence.

Drawing from Bowen's family systems theory, *differentiation-based parenting* combines loving connection and space for autonomy. I figured that a Bowen family systems perspective on parenting deserved its own title. I could see that the core goal of lifting out of intense parenting is facilitating what Bowen called differentiation of self. The parenting paradox is woven through this concept, marked by a surprising pivot that shifts the focus from the child to the parent. This shift means that parents can turn the tide of the current anxious focus on children. In turn, children can grow in age-appropriate levels of coping and responsibility, and isn't that what we all want for our children? When one parent changes, the emotional space between people changes, leading to changes in the child. In my first writing about differentiation-based parenting, I conveyed, "It is not specifically a parenting style but a longer-term parenting project. . . . The core aim is fostering connection without over-fusing with our children."[1]

In this chapter, we meet three sets of parents who take courageous and positive steps to regain balance in their parenting—connecting without crowding. Throughout Part Two, we journey alongside these parents and their children (not using real names or identifying details), considering what applies to our unique family contexts and parenting challenges.

A Mindset Shift—Reduce Attention on Our Children, Increase Attention on Ourselves

Any change of direction starts with a mindset shift. Techniques and strategies without a clear understanding of the thinking behind them won't bring sustainable change. The mindset shift for parents is about a change of focus and attention. The focus of our energy is best invested in ourselves as parents and what we can change, rather than trying to fix or change our child. It might sound somewhat radical that we reduce our attention on our children and increase our attention on ourselves as parents. Not attending to self-interest but to our growth in awareness. In this way, the parent and what we can adjust become the project, not the child.

I wonder if you're asking yourself if such a shift is possible. It feels like so much of our parenting instincts are deeply attuned to protecting and watching over our children. All the messages about attuning and attaching to children add to parents, making children the main project. The key is to manage those good and natural instincts and not let them get the better of you. When instincts start running the show, the balance gets lost, and the investment in our children prevents us from developing ourselves as parents. Parents who can cultivate self-awareness are best positioned to provide a growth-enhancing environment for their children.

Introducing Parents Who Shifted from Child Focus to Parent Development

Jason and Amy are committed parents. They've been married for fifteen years and have three children. Sophie is thirteen, Henry is eleven, and Charlie is eight. Amy has always taken the lead in parenting, taking time out from her career for a year after the birth of each child. She has read many parenting books and attends parenting talks at school or in the community. Jason is supportive and often joins her at these events. He listens to Amy's parenting ideas and tries to be on the same page. Over the past few years, they have increasingly struggled to manage Henry's strong will as he becomes defiant when either parent tries to direct him. Jason finds that he frequently loses his cool with Henry, but keeps trying to show his son that he must respect his parents. Henry has always been a strong personality and does not cope well if he doesn't get his way. This contrasts with Sophie, who is quieter in nature and generally compliant. Henry's tantrums as a toddler were regular and often extended into marathon episodes. Amy saw this as expected for his age and applied many techniques she had read about to help him express his big feelings. Charlie showed some similar traits to Henry but was less disruptive.

At age eleven, Henry's episodes of shouting and protesting continue. He is increasingly absorbed with the video games Jason and Amy originally purchased for him as an educational stimulus. Amy has spoken with Henry's teachers over the years about ways to help him stay focused in class and, more recently, about his reluctance to attend school. As with any family, there are many other details to the changes in life over their parenting years and the various health challenges that children have gone through. Henry is the child who always seemed to catch whatever virus was going around and would often be at the doctor's to address fevers and earaches. Amy always felt that Henry needed extra support from her and Jason. She wonders what kind of support Henry needs to manage these critical preteen years.

Brianna and Carter are raising two children, seventeen-year-old Jada and fifteen-year-old Xavier. Carter partnered with Brianna two years after her separation from the kids' father, with whom they have minimal contact. Jada was four, Xavier was two, and Carter willingly stepped into an active parenting role alongside Brianna. He always felt somewhat outside Brianna's close relationship with her daughter Jada, but accepted that this was a mother-and-daughter thing. Both children showed talent in sports and music, and their parents devoted significant time and resources to supporting their children's activities and tuition.

At age fourteen, Jada was identified as a gifted dancer and accepted into a local special program that served as a feeder for the country's top contemporary dance companies. One year after starting the program, Jada asked to drop out. Brianna noticed that she had lost weight and was increasingly avoiding socializing. As loving parents, Carter and Brianna researched treatment offerings for their daughter and stepdaughter. They both took time off work to be with her and involved their grandparents in rallying to help Jada get back on track and fulfill her dream of being a professional dancer.

Natalia and Adrian are deeply enamored with their only child, Elena, who is four years old. Natalia was in her mid-thirties when she married Adrian, who had previously been married and had two children aged nineteen and twenty-one from that relationship. It was always a fear for Natalia that her biological clock would sabotage her desire to be a parent, so when Elena was born after IVF treatment, she was over the moon. Adrian relished the chance to be a better dad than he thought he had been with his other children. He and Natalia had satisfying careers but knew that Elena would always come first. Knowing that work often got demanding, they enrolled her in enriching activities such as music and kids' gymnastics. They appreciated that there were some downsides to being an only child, so they prioritized Elena's socializing with her cousins. At home, they were delighted with Elena's imaginative play and wondered about the satisfying, creative life that would unfold for her. However, with the joy of Elena in their life, they were aware that she was becoming increasingly entitled. She was expecting her parents to give her the food she wanted and many other requests for TV, the iPad, not having a bath, delayed bedtime, and so on. Adrian relied on promising treats to get the desired behavior from Elena, and Natalia became anxious at any sign that her daughter was unhappy. If she was firm with Elena, she repaired the negative vibe with extra cuddles and affirmations.

Each of these parents is tackling different challenges with children at various stages of life. Their family stories and backgrounds also vary. However, one central element is shared—to varying degrees, they've become so focused on their child that they've lost their compass as parents. Their parenting is shaped by their concern for their child, rather than by clear principles. They all sincerely want their child to be happy, but their investment in this goal doesn't yield the desired result of a resilient, flourishing child. Each was so focused on helping their child that they had not had the space to reflect on the effect of their parenting responses. The amount of energy going into their children overshadows the energy required to develop as parents. While you may not see the same degree of intensity in your parenting, we all get caught up in too much reactivity with our children at various times. Learning to recognize it is the first step to rebalancing our parenting.

The Interaction Map—Observing and Discovering a Parenting Pattern

We can all acknowledge that with the many pressures of modern life, creating space to pause and reflect often goes begging. Yet, no change is possible without it. The first critical step is to take some time to reflect on our parenting patterns, not just our worries or dreams for our children, but more importantly, our responses to them. What is the effect of our reactions on our children? Are we adding to our children's reactivity or anxiety? Is our response trying to change our child and make them who we wish they could be? Or are we seeing that we can only change ourselves and what is in our control? I often use the word reactivity, so a definition is required. Reactivity is when a child or adult responds impulsively with strong emotions—a knee-jerk rather than a thought-through response. We don't want our reactivity to cast a shadow over our children's development.

Murray Bowen saw that the most valuable questions for gaining awareness of ourselves in relationships start with who, what, where, and when. They help us zoom out and see the family as a system.

Bowen observed that asking questions that begin with "Why?" is less helpful because it limits our perspective to finding a single cause for an individual's symptom rather than recognizing how everyone contributes to the family dynamic. He writes:

> Systems theory . . . focuses on what happened, how it happened, and when and where it happened. . . . It carefully avoids [our] automatic preoccupation with why it happened.[2]

When we focus too much on the details of every story in family life, we become overwhelmed by the issues themselves and lose sight of our own responses. I've heard many parents go into great detail about an argument or the child's symptoms, which helps with venting but not with new awareness. To help them gain a fresh perspective on what they can do differently, I ask them to describe in detail what happened. This shifts the focus from offering opinions to uncovering insightful "aha" moments.

We need to see the regular back-and-forth responses with our child and parenting partner to determine which of our responses are helpful or unhelpful. Yes, this is often confronting and uncomfortable. Yet, isn't our discomfort worth it if it results in a growth-enhancing environment in our families? Let's look at the interaction patterns that each of the example parents could observe.

The Pattern of Interaction with a Reactive Preteen

Amy and Jason recognized how much focus they gave Henry compared to their other children. Henry's temperament and frequent sicknesses had added fuel to this, especially for Amy, the more hands-on parent. Their next step is unpacking the pattern they get caught up in with their middle son.

Amy and Jason described a recent challenging interaction with Henry. As you read the details, try to identify the emerging back-and-forth pattern.

Amy asks Henry to finish up his game and get ready for dinner. Henry ignores her. She responds calmly and firmly, saying, "Henry, you must not ignore me. I know finishing the game you enjoy is hard, but it's time to wrap it up now." Henry responds with an angry "Leave me alone!" Jason hears this and steps in, saying with annoyance, "You are not to speak to your mother that way. I'm going to take your gaming privileges away as of now!" Henry is enraged and yells at his father: "You're so mean! I just need more time to finish this game." Jason now thinks he would never have spoken to his father this way. He also wants to show Amy that he's supporting her. He counterreacts, raising his voice with Henry and moving toward the device to take it away. A struggle follows, and Amy steps in, telling Jason, "It's OK, I'll handle it." Jason steps back, feeling frustrated. Amy sits beside Henry and rubs his back, saying, "I'm sorry you feel we don't care about your games. You have lots of strong feelings right now, don't you?" Henry is sheepish and quietly snuggles into his mother, thanking her for letting him keep playing. And declaring, "I don't need any dinner anyway." Amy feels somewhat helpless. She doesn't want more conflict, so she leaves and returns with a plate of food for Henry to eat while he finishes gaming. She uses the technique of setting an alarm, saying the game must stop when the buzzer sounds in fifteen minutes. Henry complies.

It's a challenging pattern for Amy and Jason to reconsider. They both acknowledge that it is a common scenario. They do their best to apply parenting strategies but are left feeling helpless. While their intentions come from a loving place, the impacts of some of their responses deserve reconsideration. Previously, all their problem-solving focused on Henry's behaviors, understanding his needs better, and trying different techniques. All the attention toward Henry hindered them from reflecting on themselves and what they could do differently. How much of their energy was spent trying to change Henry? What could each start adjusting about each of their responses? Amy reflected that her effort to be calm was helpful. She also values her ability to affectionately connect with Henry after a conflict. However, she also saw that her taking over from Jason put him in a one-down place and elevated Henry's sense of being her special one. She wondered if Henry's defiance was reinforced by his sense of winning and being nurtured by his mother, with his dad being sent out of the room. Jason felt justified in being firm with Henry, saying, "It's my job to show him that I'm in charge." At the same time, he could step back enough to see that his coming onto the scene in a combative way was fueling conflict and setting it up for Henry to feel like the "kingpin."

Both started to think about how they could stop doing what was unhelpful. They couldn't yet see an evident approach to improve their way of relating to Henry, but appreciated that it would bring gradual progress if they stopped doing things that dialed up the intensity. This is the kind of progress that builds on itself. Amy and Jason could start to be better observers of themselves when things get heated with Henry. They started to observe how the incident unfolded:

1. How did the incident start?
2. How did I respond? What was my tone? What was I thinking?
3. How did my child respond? How did the other parent react?
4. What happened next—and next—and next—until it ran out of steam?

They could recognize their interaction map in a way that helped them see more of themselves rather than the challenges their child presents. Amy found it more accessible than Jason to become more of an observer, but she refrained from trying to do the work for him. Just as Henry needed space from being reacted to, each parent needed space to progress at their own pace. They have started turning the tide away from making Henry the project to making the parents the project.

As you read this interaction, I wonder if it opens up insights into what is and isn't helpful in each parent's responses. Rather than focusing on Henry (which is so easy to do, given his challenging behaviors), what's it like to shift the focus to what the parents are doing, feeling, and thinking? Can you glimpse the value of examining how family members affect each other, and that when one parent changes their part, it can contribute to better outcomes for others?

Amy and Jason are becoming curious about their parenting responses, asking themselves:

1. Are they focusing too much on changing Henry rather than adjusting their own responses?

2. How can they better reflect on their own parenting goals instead of solely analyzing Henry's behaviors?

3. How much of their energy is spent trying to control Henry's actions rather than adapting their own responses? How can they adjust their responses to create a less intense dynamic?

Amy is asking herself:

1. How does my effort to reconnect affectionately help in the short term? Are there any unintended negative consequences?

2. Is my tendency to take over from Jason making Henry feel like my special one and placing Jason in a one-down position?

3. Could Henry's defiance be reinforced by feeling like he's "won" when I remove Jason from the situation?

And Jason is reflecting:

1. Does my effort to be firm truly establish steady leadership, or does it escalate conflict?

2. How might my combative entrance into the situation set up Henry as the "kingpin" who can defy me?

The Pattern of Interaction with a Withdrawing Adolescent

Let's look at the patterns with our second example family. Brianna and Carter are desperately worried for seventeen-year-old Jada. They're throwing all their energy into her recovery of confidence. The problem is that the more they support her, the more closed off she becomes from life. They begin to reflect on whether they have overinvested in their daughter's success, and that Jada has not had sufficient inner commitment and coping capacities to manage the pressures of the intense and competitive special program. In her family, Jada experienced herself as highly talented and constantly applauded by her family. However, she was no longer the shining star in the gifted dancers' program, topped up with her mother's affirmations.

In describing a recent interaction with Jada, Brianna recounted how she knocked on her daughter's door, suggesting she might come for a walk. Jada was on her bed and responded by pulling her blanket over her head. Brianna came and sat beside her, reminding her of the psychologist's advice to exercise daily. Jada murmured back to her mother that nothing was working, and she didn't want to go back to counseling. Brianna felt panicked and thought that she must find a way to keep her daughter in treatment. She responded, "I will take a day off work to take you to sessions, and we can go to your favorite café afterward." Jada responded with a mumble and a reluctant "OK." Brianna left her room and vented her worries to Carter. He saw she was stressed and anxious and said, "You tell me what you want me to do, and I'll help out." He admitted feeling concerned that all the focus on treatment seemed to be making things worse, but he didn't want his wife to be upset with him, so he stayed silent.

As Brianna reflected on this interaction, she wondered if she was pushing Brianna too much. Clearly, the more she tried to lift her daughter's spirits, the gloomier Jada became. It's challenging for her to consider connecting in a less worried way, as the stakes seem too high. Jada had been assessed as depressed and with indicators of a developing eating disorder. What a challenge this presents for any parent! If I back off and stop pushing, will things get worse? Yet, shifting the focus to the parent is not to be confused with backing off and not being available. Instead, as Brianna began to consider, it can mean being present in a less intrusive way and tolerating a child passing through a challenging phase of life without trying to rescue them. In pausing and reflecting, Brianna began to think about ways to connect to Jada's capacity to find her way through this difficult time and start to think and speak for herself. Carter began to recognize how much he walked on eggshells around his wife regarding parenting, which coming into the family as a stepdad had played into. As he examined his ways of interacting, it opened up the option of sharing his thoughts and observations with his wife, so that he could be a more valuable resource in their current situation. He would need to take a supportive, rather than a critical, posture when sharing his perspective. Carter will also need to be prepared to withstand pushback from Brianna, who has become accustomed to his always going along with her. Brianna knew deep down that she wanted Carter to speak for himself in their relationship, even if it was hard for her to hear.

Brianna and Carter are stepping back and considering the effect of their responses:

1. Have we overinvested in Jada's success rather than allowing her to develop resilience and coping skills?

2. How can I connect with Jada in a less worried and more constructive way?

3. What does being present in a supportive but non-intrusive way look like?

Additionally, Brianna is asking:

1. How can I tolerate Jada's struggles without needing to rescue her?

2. If I stop pushing, will things worsen, or could it help Jada build her inner strength?

3. How can I make space for Jada to start thinking and speaking for herself rather than relying on my affirmations?

4. Am I open to shifting my stance to allow Jada to navigate this challenging phase more independently?

As parenting partners, both Brianna and Carter are asking:

1. How can I share my perspective in a supportive rather than a critical way?

2. Am I open to hearing my spouse's thoughts even if they challenge my current parenting approach?

The Pattern of Interaction with an Entitled Four Year Old

And now to our third example family. Bedtimes had become increasingly exasperating for Adrian and Natalia as Elena mastered her art of delay tactics. They recount a recent typical interaction. Natalia had created a list of bedtime tasks for Elena, promising star stickers if she followed the sequence. Natalia notices Elena getting out more toys while she is reminded about getting ready for bed. She tells Elena there are special rainbow stars for following the routine tonight.

Elena looks up, interested in seeing the new stickers. She asks for one to put on her Bunny. Natalia says she can't have one until she starts to get ready. It's time to clean her teeth. Elena goes to the bathroom, and Natalia helps her put toothpaste on her brush. Elena asks for her sticker, and when Natalia explains that stickers are unavailable until she's in bed, Elena starts crying.

Adrian steps in and asks what has made his princess so sad. Elena complains, "Mom promised me a sticker for my Bunny." Adrian looks across at Natalia, who shrugs her shoulders to convey that she's feeling lost. Adrian tells Elena that not only will she get stars on her chart and her Bunny when she is all ready for bed, but he will also buy her another Bunny tomorrow.

Adrian takes over, helping Elena get ready for bed, reading her a story, and delivering the promised star for Bunny. It's already thirty minutes after their desired bedtime. Elena pleads with her dad to read some extra books. He initially says no, but then gives in. Natalia is relieved to have made it through the bedtime negotiations and to have some precious, albeit reduced, downtime to relax.

Adrian and Natalia have begun to get curious about their parenting responses:

1. How do our reactions contribute to Elena's bedtime resistance rather than resolve it?

2. Am I reinforcing Elena's delay tactics by giving in to her demands?

3. Are my rewards (stickers, toys, extra stories) helping or creating more opportunities for negotiation?

4. Am I consistently holding bedtime expectations, or do I send mixed messages?

5. Am I settling for temporary relief (giving in) instead of a long-term solution?

6. How can I allow Elena to develop self-regulation rather than relying on external rewards?

The most helpful part of tracing this interaction is that Adrian and Natalia can see how they contribute to Elena becoming demanding. This differs from seeing it as a personality trait that will never change. While Elena's temperament may be feisty, that doesn't lead to excessive entitlement unless her demands are met with rewards.

Just like Amy and Jason, and Brianna and Carter, Adrian and Natalia are confronted with seeing things they are doing that are becoming a problem for Elena's development. This is tough to swallow. It's easy to take this personally and wallow in guilt, but each of these parents knows that they love their children and want to do what it takes to give each child a better environment. They're adjusting their mindset from trying to make their child happy to making their maturity as parents their goal. Holding a fresh mindset and seeing a path forward lifts guilt and replaces it with hope.

Notice the Pattern of Over- and Underfunctioning

One of the most valuable aspects of Bowen's theory is the description of typical patterns in our relationships.[3] One recognizable pattern in parent–child and marriage relationships is the circuit of overfunctioning and underfunctioning. When a parent starts doing for a child what the child can learn to do for themselves, they're overfunctioning. It's not just when we do things for our child, but also when we think and feel for our child that we take over their learning to develop independent thoughts and feelings. Over time, the child adapts into the cycle and increasingly invites parents to take over their tasks and coping.

Can you see this pattern in the family examples? Amy is taking charge of everything—researching, contacting teachers, managing Henry's behavior—while Jason stays passive. As Amy ramps up, Henry becomes more defiant and dependent, expecting her to manage his problems.

Brianna is unintentionally overfunctioning in response to Jada's emotional struggles, checking in constantly and trying to fix things. Jada withdraws further, which further invites Brianna to manage her well-being.

Natalia continuously soothes and adjusts to Elena's emotions. Adrian joins her, backing down from limits. Elena becomes demanding and emotionally unregulated, expecting others to fix things for her.

Notice the Pattern of Triangles

These over-and-under patterns sit within another pattern: the triangle. Relationship triangles exist in all families. The tension and insecurity that inevitably arise between two people are managed by including a third person who becomes part of the pattern for tension relief. A three-person relationship plays its part in keeping the over-and-under pattern functioning.

As parenting worries grow, Amy and Jason increasingly focus on Henry, who becomes more oppositional and dependent. This forms a triangle where Henry is the focus, without each discussing their thoughts and feelings within the marriage. Additionally, Jason is more passive, which increases Amy's overfunctioning and Henry's underfunctioning.

Similarly, Brianna and Carter work together on the problem-solving project for Jada. Carter avoids speaking his mind to his wife to keep the peace. Instead of connecting directly with Jada, Carter supports Brianna's role, reinforcing her overfunctioning and contributing to Jada's emotional underfunctioning with her mother.

Natalia and Adrian's shared focus on Elena forms a triangle that positions her as the emotional center of the family. While the couple avoids tensions by focusing on their daughter's happiness, Elena increasingly relies on her parents for rescue and emotional regulation.

The triangle helps manage adult issues and tension in all three families by focusing on the child. This calms the grown-ups, but it so easily positions a child in an underfunctioning position and limits growth for everyone involved. Understanding these common patterns helps us better observe ourselves in our parenting and other relationships.

The Shift in Focus from Child to Parent

This chapter introduces three family stories where parents give their all but end up disillusioned. They're each doing some helpful things in their parenting, but can also see that some of their habitual responses are not constructive. Each reveals what happens when too much focus is placed on a child at the expense of the parent's own growth. I invite you to reflect on the patterns you recognize in your parenting. Yes, it may feel uncomfortable, but ask yourself if that discomfort is worth the long-term benefits for your family. Just like with our children, we can't rush growth.

We'll explore how parents can reduce stress, observe their patterns, and confidently support their children's development. Observing becomes powerful when we trace interactions and see our part. Instead of trying to change our children, we shift the focus to our own responses. Simply becoming curious observers of ourselves can reduce reactivity in the family. The act of stepping back to observe interaction is part of differentiating ourselves. We get more separated from our children's emotions when we get curious about what we felt, thought, and did. This aspect of differentiation occurs within us, yet its impact extends beyond us, creating more space and balance in our relationships.

The following chapters explore the patterns we fall into with kids and partners and how to recover clarity and calm. We consider what it looks like to offer love that fosters responsible autonomy, how to build self-regulation, escape cycles of conflict, and lead as a parent who speaks for oneself. This includes working out parenting principles that guide us. You'll see how each of our three families puts these ideas into action, gaining confidence and bringing their best to their children.

For Reflection

Do I Allow for Pausing and Observing Space?

1. Am I regularly stepping back and reflecting on myself as I relate to my children and parenting partner?

2. What's the focus of my reflection? Is it adding to worry about my child? Or am I thinking about my patterns of responding to my children?

3. What's the effect of my responses on my children? Am I adding to my children's reactivity or anxiety? Or am I reflecting on what's in my control?

4. Can I see what's helping and what isn't helping in my relationship with each child? Am I contributing to an independence-building relationship?

Noticing Overfunctioning and Triangles

1. How might I be doing for my child what they could be learning to do for themselves—emotionally or practically? How might this unintentionally encourage their underfunctioning?

2. When tension arises in my marriage or parenting, do I shift my focus to our child? Could this be a way of avoiding personal adult conversations—and if so, what impact might that have on our child's functioning?

7

THE CONTAGION OF CALM

The presence of just one less anxious adult can reduce the intensity level of the whole family system.

When parents start focusing on themselves and what's within their control, one of the first things they notice is that they can tone down the strength of their reactions. This is no small thing. In fact, it may be the most powerful thing a parent can do to improve the environment in which children are being raised. When a parent moves from exuding stress and worry directed toward their child to conveying calmer communication, it has an immediate ripple effect. Equally, an enraged parent who takes time to turn their heated tone down builds a foundation for a reactive child to become more thoughtful. The effort to be a little calmer is contagious—a positive form of influence. Just like when I'm flying and we hit turbulence, the flight attendant remains calm—their composed presence steadies the cabin, and I find myself calming down too, as if their ease quietly permits me to relax.

Today's popular parenting approaches pay close attention to ways parents can calm their children down and co-regulate their emotions. I propose an alternative perspective for parents to consider—shifting the emphasis from calming a child to calming ourselves is more productive. The emphasis is on mobilizing our capacity to self-regulate, and in turn, our children can grow their self-regulation capacities. Self-regulation is the ability to control your thoughts, emotions, and behaviors to achieve goals or respond appropriately to situations. As parents, when we practice self-regulation, we create a climate that allows our children to calm themselves and respond more responsibly. Let's explore how parents can best support this essential part of a child's emotional growth and resilience.

Journeying with Our Example Families

We return to the three families introduced in Chapter 6. Each is part of a stress-filled pattern of parenting with the child they are most worried about—a child or teen who is, in some way, struggling to manage their emotions and behaviors.

A Defiant Eleven Year Old

Jason and Amy have started to notice just how on edge they feel around their eleven-year-old son, Henry. It's like they're walking on eggshells, bracing for the next flare-up. Both parents are hypersensitive to any sign of pushback from him, like tiny signals of defiance, which are now alarm bells. Amy, especially, has been growing increasingly worried about Henry's recent school avoidance. She watches him closely, constantly scanning for signs of anxiety—slumped shoulders, that distracted look in his eyes, the way he disappears into his games. One evening, things boil over. Jason walks into the living room and tells Henry to focus on his homework. Without missing a beat, Henry snaps, "Leave me alone. My homework's stupid!" Jason's stomach tightens. His voice rises instantly. "You are going to fall behind at school, son. Now stop messing around and get out your work right now, or there'll be trouble!" Henry doesn't back down. He yells, "You can't make me! I don't care about my school stuff, and my friends don't do their homework!"

Jason feels the anger flood in—hot, fast, overwhelming. He blurts out a threat to remove his access to the gaming console. Beneath the anger, though, is a deep sense of panic: Why is my kid talking to me like this? Why doesn't he respect me?

From the kitchen, Amy hears the yelling, and her heart sinks. She drops what she's doing and rushes in, trying to calm the situation. She crouches next to Henry, rubbing his back, trying to get him to breathe. Her tone is soft, soothing. She's desperate to de-escalate, to get him regulated. But in Jason's eyes, it looks like she's taking sides. He throws up his hands and storms off. "Henry is wrapping you around his little finger!" he mutters on the way out.

Henry is now fully worked up and turns to Amy, "Dad is SO mean! Why is he always yelling?" Amy reassures Henry that dad loves him and only wants what's best. She also assures him that she'll do his work with him at breakfast time.

It's a familiar scene in their household. Jason feels like his authority is constantly under siege, and Amy—though outwardly calm—is quietly spinning with anxiety, always trying to pre-empt another meltdown. Henry, meanwhile, seems to know just how to press buttons. Whether consciously or not, Henry once again finds himself in the middle of his parents' frustrations with each other. He senses that he has mom on his side and dad on the outside.

Think about where either parent might start to bring some more calm to this dynamic. It's interesting for Jason and Amy to see how uptight they get with Henry compared to their eldest daughter, Sophie, and youngest, Charlie. Jason considers that, at times, he also gets riled up with Charlie when he doesn't follow his instructions, but Henry pushes his flare-up button the most.

A Withdrawn Teen Struggling to Eat

Brianna is consumed with fixing things for her seventeen-year-old daughter, Jada. Her mind is constantly spinning—appointments, meal plans, therapy notes—anything that might help lift her daughter's low mood and support her increasingly fragile relationship with food. She's doing everything she can think of, but it never quite feels like enough. This morning is no different. It's 7:00 a.m., and Brianna is anxious that Jada isn't up and ready for breakfast. She goes to her bedroom door and gently cajoles. "Come on, Jada, love. Time to get up." Her voice is soft and hopeful. She's laid out a plate of fresh fruit downstairs, just like the nutritionist suggested. She opens the door and reminds Jada about what her therapist said—about courage and facing fears one small step at a time. But as is becoming the trend, Jada doesn't move. She lies curled up in bed, eyes half open, a heavy silence between them. "Come on, Jada," Brianna urges again, her voice tightening. "You can do this. You just have to try." She's still trying to sound encouraging, but the worry is starting to leak through. Jada groans, turning away, murmuring, "It's not that easy, Mom. You just don't get it."

Something shifts in Brianna. Her heart races. Her frustration breaks through. "Jada, you need to cooperate with all this help, or you'll never be happy!" The words land hard in the quiet room. Jada pulls the covers over her head, disappearing. Brianna stands there for a second, her own breath shallow, then turns and walks out. In the kitchen, Carter is making coffee, and she immediately unloads—her voice shaking with fear and exasperation. "I'm trying so hard, and it's like nothing gets through to her."

Carter sighs. He feels it too—the ache of watching his stepdaughter struggle and the helplessness of not knowing what will make a difference. Both parents are scared. Beneath Brianna's relentless drive to fix is a deep, raw panic—What if she doesn't get better? What if I can't reach her? And Carter, helplessly, is holding his fear that he might not be the empowering stepdad he thought he could be. Is there a way that Brianna and Carter can bring a helpful calm to this challenging situation? They can see they are much calmer and less intense when parenting their younger son, Xavier. What will it take to tone down their reactions to Jada?

A Tantrumming Four Year Old

Natalia and Adrian are exhausted. Every evening feels like a battle for control with their spirited four-year-old daughter, Elena, and last night was no different. It starts calmly enough. Natalia crouches next to Elena, who's curled up watching Disney, and says in her gentlest voice (although inside, she fears the defiant response), "Sweetheart, it's time to turn off the TV and get ready for your bath." Elena doesn't budge. Without even turning her head, she belts out a firm "NO! I don't need a bath!" Natalia stiffens slightly but stays composed. "If you don't get ready now, there won't be any TV tomorrow," she warns, trying to hold the line. That's when Elena lets loose a full-body protest—crying, shouting, flailing— precisely the kind of meltdown only a four year old can pull off with such commitment. Adrian storms in from the hallway, already on edge from the day. "Stop that stupid crying, Elena!" he snaps. And just like that, things go from hard to harder. Elena's sobs escalate into full-blown shrieking.

Natalia scrambles to find a new angle. "Okay, okay—how about your new bath toys? I'll get them ready for you!" she says brightly, trying to turn the ship around. Adrian, now desperate too, jumps in with a sweetened offer: "And if you have your bath, you can listen to extra audio stories in bed. Deal?" His voice is tight, almost pleading. Elena pauses. The mention of new toys catches her attention. Slowly, she gets up and walks toward the bathroom, still sniffling but clearly intrigued. Natalia and Adrian glance at each other—part relief, part defeat. It's another night when bedtime has dragged well past an hour, full of bargaining, bribing, and emotional whiplash. They started the evening feeling stressed and finished it feeling exhausted and depleted. Adrian thinks about his regrets of not being very present in the lives of his older children from his first marriage. He is committed to doing it differently with Elena, yet his stress levels are so high in her presence that he resorts to the fastest, quickest fix he can access when interacting with her.

Each of our parents is overwhelmed by the cycle they seem to repeat with one of their children. The pathway to change is not a magic parenting technique, but each parent's ability to reflect on what triggers their version of intense reactions, and how those moments shape the emotional climate at home. By dialing down their own emotional intensity, they can begin to shift the family dynamic, bringing a sense of steadiness that's not only calming but contagious.

Contagious Calm

We can all recognize the positive ripple effect of one person's genuine, calm expression. You know the impact of watching a flight attendant when your plane is experiencing turbulence. They demonstrate a steady task focus while checking everyone's seat belts, then take their seat and retain a pleasant facial expression. It has a settling impact. We can tell it isn't a fake calm but a clarity that comes from experience and awareness of their role.

Research has many fascinating examples of the positive contagion of a person's effective stress management or negative stress management. One influential study on this subject, with the apt title "The Ripple Effect: Emotional Contagion and Its Influence on Group Behavior",[1] explored how emotions transfer between individuals and affect group behavior.

In this study, members functioned better when groups were exposed to calm and positive emotions. They demonstrated greater cooperation and resolved conflicts more effectively. On the other hand, when reactive negativity was introduced, disagreements increased, teamwork suffered, and members perceived their performance as weaker. It's not surprising, really. Our human brains are wired to mirror the facial cues and emotions of others—especially those important to us in our families. This is particularly impactful in the parent–child relationship. When parents calm down, their children's nervous system receives safety cues, and their stress hormones (cortisol and adrenaline) begin to decrease. This helps create a space for the child to use the part of their brain (prefrontal cortex) that controls reasoning, self-regulation, and impulse control. A highly reactive caregiver interacting with a distressed child leads to interactions fueled by our brain's fear and impulse system (amygdala).

Is It a Parent's Job to Co-Regulate a Child's Emotions?

Parents often believe it's their job to calm their children, rather than calming themselves. Many attachment-based approaches emphasize co-regulation—helping children manage emotions until they can do it independently. While this has truth, especially since emotional regulation develops gradually, the focus can sometimes go too far. A calm, nurturing parent is indeed vital. But when parents take on too much of the child's emotional work—interpreting every behavior and trying to soothe constantly—they may overfocus on the child and interrupt the child's growth process.

Another pitfall of the emphasis on parent co-regulation of the young child is that it can lead to a belief that young children lack the internal capacities to self-regulate and need adults to do it for them. Evidence is available to show that children can grow away from their parents quite rapidly, becoming less helpless and dependent in the first few months of life.[2] Here are some of the self-regulation resources that infants possess in small but essential measures well before they are verbal: controlling their breathing and heart rate, sucking to calm down, adjusting their sleep and wake times, looking away, and shifting attention when something is too much for them, as well as holding a soft object to feel better. Even impulse control starts to develop as the brain learns how to focus.[3]

In family systems thinking, all family members are co-regulating each other. Every family member affects the emotions and behaviors of the others, for better or for worse. Every person, including the young child, has biological resources to manage their discomfort. The child affects the parents just as the parents affect the child. We adults, however, have the maturity to take the lead in managing our emotions. The parent recognizes that their effort to self-regulate is the first step in a child's learning to draw on their capacities to self-regulate. In this way, the focus is firstly on the parent and secondly on being aware of the child's behavior and emotions. When the parent intentionally attends to improving their reactivity, they are differentiating from the child. This is the magic path to reduce intensive parenting and replace it with steady, balanced parenting.

Self-Regulation—a Road to Building Resilience

While co-regulation is always happening in relationships, self-regulation allows us to be separate and connected. Co-regulation is when two people shape each other's emotions, while self-regulation prioritizes handling one's own reactions. Each family member develops the ability to tone down their feelings and engage their thinking in ways that match their stage of development. Over time, we become less reliant on others to calm us down and more responsible for managing our emotional responses. As we reduce our sensitivity to the emotional states of those around us, we become better able to stay grounded, even when a child or another family member is struggling. This is how we build resilience in our relationships.

There is substantial evidence for the link between children's self-regulation and well-being. A review of research between 2010 and 2020 on student mental health outcomes shows that self-regulation strategies employed in the learning process are significantly associated with various dimensions of student well-being. Conversely, self-regulatory deficits were linked to decreased well-being.[4] I have valued the long research career of Professor Laurence Steinberg and his contribution to understanding the ingredients of well-functioning adolescents.[5] Steinberg has extensively researched adolescent development, emphasizing the significance of self-regulation in children's well-being. His analysis clarifies that self-regulation—managing emotions, thoughts, and behaviors—is crucial for achieving long-term goals and overall mental health. Notably, he highlights the role of parent–adolescent relationships in a child developing self-regulation. Essentially, self-regulation is central to building resilience—the capacity to bounce back when things don't go as we planned and hoped.

A Word About Anxiety—Short Term and Chronic

The opposite of calm is anxiety or tension. Although often viewed as an individual diagnosis, anxiety is a universal human experience—and because we're so attuned to one another, it lives in our relationship systems, not just within us. Bowen distinguished between short-term and chronic anxiety. Acute anxiety is a natural response to real threats and fades once the stressor passes. But chronic anxiety lingers. When we stay on high alert after challenges, it shapes how we see everything—especially relationships.

Over time, chronic anxiety can become part of a family's culture. Even minor issues trigger outsized reactions, creating a constant sense of threat. Our ability to self-regulate improves when we ask: Is this a real, immediate danger—or are we stuck in a long-term pattern of expecting the worst? I describe it as the difference between a "what now" challenge (acute in the moment) and a "what if" rumination (chronic and long term). Is it real or is it imagined? Dr. Kathleen Smith has written a fabulous book drawing on Bowen theory, titled *Everything Isn't Terrible: Conquer Your Insecurities, Interrupt Your Anxiety, and Finally Calm Down*.[6] It's a much-needed guide in this anxious age to recognizing and dealing with persistent anxiety. Dr. Smith writes about working on our differentiation to gain perspective on our fears:

People who have a higher level of differentiation still feel anxiety. They're just able to override it by slowing down its escalation. They're better able to tell what's a real threat and what's an imaginary one, and they can switch off the autopilot and grab the controls.[7]

Building our self-regulation muscles goes hand in hand with growing our maturity or differentiation. As parents, we need to replace being caught up with stepping back, panic with curiosity, and oversensitivity with separateness.

Differentiation-Based Parenting and Parent Self-Regulation

A parenting approach that begins with our own self-regulation offers a clear path to fostering this essential coping skill in our children. Focusing on differentiation of self means building the ability to balance emotion and reason—staying connected to ourselves while engaging with others.

This balance helps us recognize emotions without being overwhelmed, allowing for thoughtful choices. We learn to distinguish short-term anxiety from chronic what-if worry. Parenting naturally brings anxiety, often triggered outside our awareness. Our brains instinctively seek relief from tension.

The more aware we become of our anxiety triggers and automatic responses, the more we can influence the family's emotional tone. Differentiation is a slow, steady process—but one that brings early and lasting rewards. It calls for intentional effort in the following areas:

1. Parent's distress tolerance.
2. Parent calming their stress responses.
3. Parent's problem-solving effort.
4. Parent's awareness of how self affects others.

The best news is that rather than trying to verbally teach children self-regulation skills, if the parent is making progress on these, their children will naturally make their own progress. Think about the value of children learning to use these same resources:

1. Child's distress tolerance.
2. Child calming their stress responses.
3. Child's problem-solving effort.
4. Child's awareness of how self affects others.

The presence of just one less anxious adult can reduce the intensity level of the whole system. In turn, those around them can access their best resources to manage strong emotions, mobilize their best thinking, and be mindful of others.

Our Parent Examples—Beginning to Take the Lead on Their Self-Regulation

Each parent in our example families can reflect on how they can tone down the stress infusing their parenting. They are each caught in a repeated stressful cycle, with much love underneath. When a parent considers their self-regulation, it isn't about achieving a quick or perfect outcome, but it is a vital starting point. Things can feel messy for a while, but a parent can experience the reward of representing calmer leadership.

Jason and Amy are beginning to see the cycle they're in with their middle child, Henry. It's a cycle, laced with panic and frustration. But what might shift if, in that heated moment, either Jason or Amy paused and tuned into managing their panic instead of reacting to Henry's behavior? What if Jason, instead of snapping, could recognize the stress and fear rising behind his anger, and take a breath? He can see that the fear of failing as a dad with a child who doesn't show respect gets him unhelpfully heated in his responses to Henry and, at times, to his younger son, Charlie. He can discover that pausing and breathing is a valuable contribution as a parent. Perhaps he can show Henry what self-regulation looks like by speaking to his commitment to not be an angry dad and taking time out to tone down his unhelpful rage.

What if Amy could acknowledge her own anxiety before rushing to soothe Henry and approach the moment with a more grounded presence? Can Amy see how stressed she is when Jason and Henry clash and how it contributes to the father–son tension? Could she give Jason more space to determine how to respond to Henry? She can provide Jason with feedback on what she observes of the effects of his anger on her and Henry, but choose a calm space to have this conversation and remove any critical tone.

As Brianna struggles to respond to Jada's resistance, she can begin to see the dance of which she is part. The emotional climate is thick with worry, urgency, and heartbreak. But what if, just for a moment, Brianna could pause and notice what was happening inside her—the fear, the pressure, the anxious urgency to get her daughter fixed? She doesn't need to have any complex inner insight; she just needs to see what might shift if she could adjust herself instead of pushing so hard against Jada's resistance. And seeing that the more she anxiously pushes, the more Jada withdraws.

It's so challenging for Brianna and Carter to steady themselves with Jada, given how much they have invested in her giftedness and how fearful they are of seeing her opportunities for success slipping away. Then, to add to their anxiety, they are confronting their daughter's decline in mental health. Any parent would be struggling to stay calm in this situation. However, Brianna is beginning to see that it will be difficult for her daughter to lift her coping capacities without her getting steadier and less intense.

And for Natalia and Adrian, underneath the surface, both are anxious and desperate to find something that works for Elena. Can they each begin to see they're caught in a loop—trying to be firm, then pivoting to comfort and reward when things fall apart? It's a stress-filled dance of mixed messages, one they didn't deliberately choreograph but find themselves repeating night after night. The first effort is not solving bathtime but toning down their stress-driven responses. What if, instead of escalating or over-accommodating, they could center themselves first, grounding their response rather than reacting from panic? The first step to solving their parenting dilemmas with their precious daughter is to get sufficiently calm to do thoughtful problem-solving and work out which of their responses is helpful to adjust.

Being Real—Parents Don't Always Need to Keep It Together

As parents begin to reflect on toning down their stressed or fearful responses, it's essential to understand that this *doesn't* mean shutting down or pretending not to feel anything. Kids need parents to be real with them—authentic and present. That can include using a firm, serious, nurturing, or concerned tone when it fits. The key is keeping that emotional response proportionate to the moment rather than letting it flood the room or being overly focused on changing the child's mood and behavior. Sometimes, the most powerful thing a parent can do is notice their rising heat, whether it's frustration, worry, or overwhelm, and name it out loud in a grounded way. They might say, "I can feel myself getting too worked up right now. That's not how I want to handle this, so I will take a moment to calm down." This kind of moment sends a clear, impactful message to a child: emotions are real, and they don't have to take over. Even grown-ups can get overwhelmed, and they can also choose how to respond.

So be reassured, it's not always about being perfectly calm. It's about representing what it looks like to be emotionally aware and willing to take responsibility for how we show up. And that example? It's so much more effective than any perfectly worded lecture or parenting strategy. Parents who can better manage their stress responses are valuable resources for a child's growth in managing their worries and frustrations. This can happen in small steps. Even a slightly calmer parent can change the tone of family life from overheated to growth producing. When parents take responsibility for their own reactions, they convey to their children, "I care about how I impact you. I'm working on my part, too." This mature effort is the kind of contagion we want to infuse into our relationships.

For Reflection

Reflecting on Your Self-Regulation

1. What can I observe in myself that tells me my tension/worry levels are increasing?

2. Can I notice this happening with the children I'm most concerned about?

3. What do I notice in my body? My breathing, heart rate, stomach, and muscle tension?

4. What do I notice about my thinking patterns when tensions mount? (Negative thinking, blaming of self or others, anxious fixing of others, fear of the future.)

5. When does fear take over my parenting responses?

6. What is one area of my stress reaction that I can begin to adjust in my parenting?

Recognizing "What If" or "What Now" Anxiety

1. As a parent, how often do I respond to my child's behavior or challenges with a *what now* mindset (acute anxiety) versus a *what if* mindset (chronic anxiety), and how might shifting from reactivity to curiosity change my response?

Building Your Resilience Resources

How can I build on the following?

1. Using relaxation techniques? Ways to reduce my body's signs of tension.

2. Using my logic? Is this degree of worry proportional to what is going on now?

3. Using my principles? What principles for the kind of person/parent I wish to be can keep me in balance right now? (For example, I am committed to not attacking others, behaving with integrity, and being honest and direct . . .)

8

THE WORRY AND CONFLICT CYCLES

HOW TO GET OFF THE MERRY-GO-ROUND

Changing a worry cycle is not an immediate, quick fix but a parent-led process. The child is so accustomed to the old cycle that they'll continue to push back in familiar ways until they realize the parent will not participate.

We've already seen how many parent–child difficulties are embedded in repeating cycles. A parent's worry about their child can trigger reactivity in the child, reinforcing the parent's concern. Over time, this pattern can become a self-perpetuating cycle, keeping a child stuck in heightened sensitivity to their parent. As you read this, I hope you're reflecting, in helpful ways, on the cycles you find yourself in with your children when stress mounts—and let's be honest, stress is a constant drumbeat for today's parents. I imagine you're looking for fresh ideas to help you as a parent, and maybe hoping for strategies that are easy to apply. I'm convinced that the most powerful strategy for creating lasting change—and helping our kids flourish—is to become curious about the patterns of which we're all part.

This chapter presents the most common cycles parents find themselves in. The worry cycle can be found in any parenting of a child who appears to struggle in some way. When the emotions in this pattern turn negative, it triggers a conflict cycle in which the parent's response to the child's defiance unintentionally reinforces the child's sense of dominance. As with any cycle, it's hard to see any beginning and end, and how to get off the roundabout. When a parent finds a way to lift out of a worry cycle, they create space for children to learn to manage their intense emotions and to develop age-appropriate, responsible independence. In a conflict cycle, a parent can refrain from fueling negative escalations and turn the tide of a child developing a posture of opposition and defiance.

When I introduce the idea of the worry cycle to parents, I often hear them say, "That's exactly what's happening with us!" There's usually a moment of instant recognition and relief. It serves as a reminder that they're not alone—this isn't just their personal struggle, but a familiar pattern shared by countless families.

Take a look at Figure 8.1. See if you can recognize elements of it in your parenting. Or maybe reflect on how your parents responded to you or your siblings. You may be surprised by what starts to make sense.

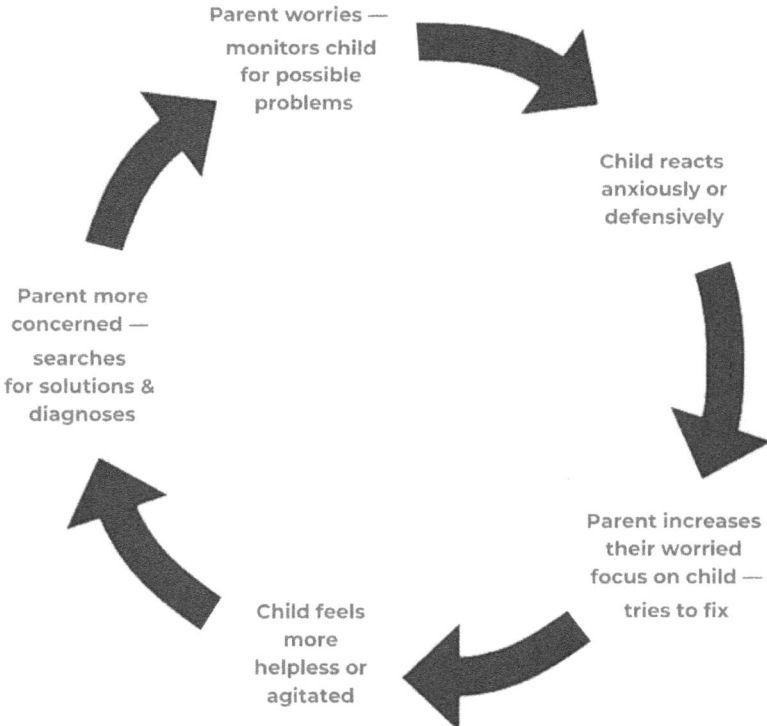

Figure 8.1 The worry cycle. *Created by Jenny Brown.*

Let's examine how our three sets of parents identified their version of the worry cycle and began to break free from it. Amy and Nathan, the parents of energetic and often oppositional eleven-year-old Henry, provide a clear example.

The Worry Cycle in Action for Parents and Their Eleven-Year-Old Son

As Amy began to direct her focus away from Henry and toward herself as a parent, she readily recognized she was in a worry cycle. She realized that her concern about Henry's ability to stay focused—and the possibility that he might have attention deficit hyperactivity disorder (ADHD)—led her to monitor him for any signs of these issues. Her constant watchfulness was contributing to Henry's reactivity. Here's how Amy could break down her pattern:

1. Amy's worry meant that she watched Henry more than the other children. She was alert to any signs of a deeper problem.

2. The more she watched him, the more agitated he became.

3. Amy began interpreting his responses as confirmation of a real problem and increased her efforts to help. She regularly jumped in to tell Henry how to stay more focused on a task.

4. In response, Henry seemed to struggle more and increasingly appeared helpless with schoolwork and managing routine chores at home.

5. Amy dove deeper into researching attention issues. She sourced a specialist to assess Henry and put him on an appointment waiting list.

A version of these five steps repeated itself day after day. Reflecting on the worry cycle, Amy realized her attempts to fix things for Henry added to his helplessness and sparked his outbursts. It felt liberating for her to think that things might settle if she backed off from her constant watch and corrections of Henry. Yes, he may still exhibit his high-energy temperament, but this might not mean he has a condition that requires a specialized fix. She realized she could apply this to her younger son,

Charlie, where she was in a similar but less intense worry cycle. Perhaps that was the same cycle her own parents had been in with her older brother during their growing-up years.

When Worrying About a Child Fuels Dependency

Amy's well-intentioned monitoring and helping efforts can inadvertently reward children who experience the specialness of a mother's attention. While balanced attention from a parent supports a child's growth, too much attention has the opposite effect, leading to a child reverting to an earlier stage of development and increased neediness. Kids in Henry's pattern easily come to rely on external rescue and soothing rather than building strong internal regulation pathways. This helps parents understand how the child invites the worry dance to continue.

Of course, Amy genuinely wanted to help Henry focus on tasks. However, the help inadvertently adds to helplessness. We've previously explored evidence for this pattern. Still, it's beneficial to appreciate the research that backs up the problem of too much attention, particularly because the literature is so strongly biased toward the importance of a child's need for attention and early intervention for neurological issues. A good example is a study that found that parental over-engagement, characterized by excessive assistance, was associated with poorer self-regulation in kindergartners. The researchers observed that when parents frequently intervened in tasks that children could manage independently, it limited their opportunities to develop their regulatory skills.[1] Amy was such a committed parent that she pushed past her guilt triggers when she saw what needed adjusting in her parenting and replaced them with feelings of confidence and hope that she could turn things around. This doesn't discount the possibility that Henry has some genetic learning challenges, but he will be best able to reach his potential in a non-worrying environment.

When a Worry Cycle Shifts into a Conflict Cycle

Henry's dad, Jason, identified a different version of his wife's cycle. He wasn't as concerned about a diagnosis. Instead, his worry centered on having disobedient sons. He noticed he was on high alert for signs of defiance, especially from Henry, and responded with frequent corrections. Jason's cycle can be summarized in these five steps:

1. Jason is alert to disobedience and is quick to challenge Henry at the first signs of non-compliance, telling him to follow instructions immediately.

2. Henry retorts angrily—"I don't want to!"

3. Jason's blood starts to boil, and he shouts at Henry—"You obey me now! Do as you're told!"

4. Henry's defiance goes to the next level, calling his dad a loser.

5. Jason is really stirred up now and feels ineffective as a dad.

Jason hadn't realized how often he got pulled into a worry cycle that had the tone of an escalating conflict cycle. He knew it was important to set limits and hold boundaries, but wasn't yet sure how to do that without escalating things further. Figure 8.2 illustrates this typical parenting pattern.

A Parent Recognizes When They're Fueling the Conflict

It wasn't easy for Jason to see his part in this pattern. His reaction to his son's disrespect kept him focused on how Henry needed to change, rather than looking at what he could start to change. The intense emotions that are part of any conflict made it especially hard for him to refocus on himself. Jason gradually pieced together the dance he was stuck in with Henry. This was helped by Amy refraining from getting in the middle and telling Jason to change. (More on this pattern in a marriage in later chapters.) As a parent, Jason believed it was appropriate for him to set limits and hold his ground on disobedient behaviors, but didn't yet know how to do this without adding to the escalation. Jason was helped by understanding how the cycle had become physiologically reinforcing for Henry.

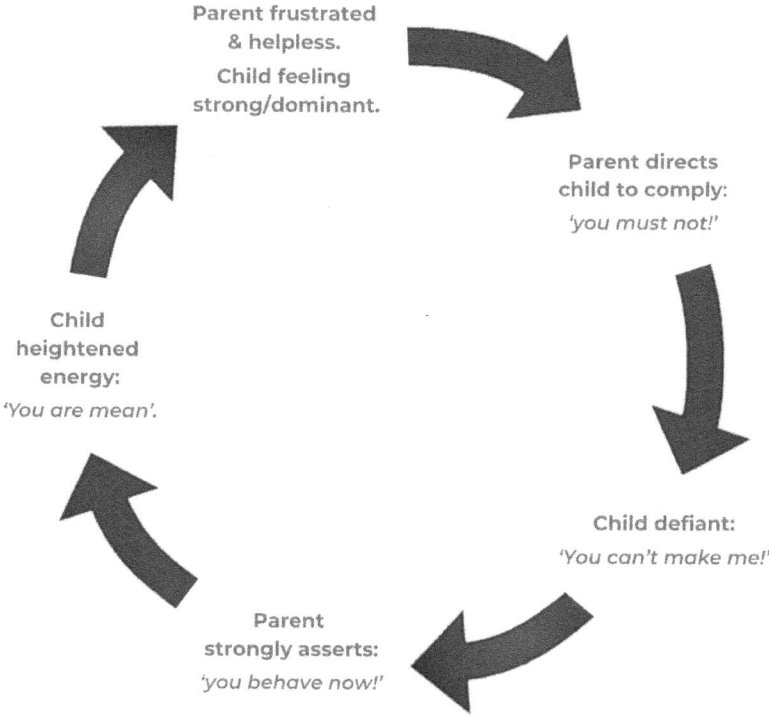

Figure 8.2 The conflict cycle. *Created by Jenny Brown.*

When Your Child's Defiance Feels Rewarding—to Their Brain

When parents (or any carer/teacher) give a child a platform for defiance, the child's brain responds with an injection of hormonal rewards, providing a temporary sense of euphoria and power.[2] Of course, this can be the same for an adult in a conflict cycle, but children and adolescents have reduced maturity to curtail their responses. When children and adolescents are in a defiant conflict state, their brains respond in complex, intense ways—it's not just about being rebellious. Preteen and adolescent brains are wired for risk and reward due to heightened dopamine and adrenal activity, meaning their defiance can feel rewarding or empowering. Younger children can experience a version of the same event. This was important for Jason to appreciate. A big part of the cycle is that Jason, asserting his authority to gain compliance, creates an opening that Henry is free to resist.

It's vital to recognize that Henry is getting a rewarding experience when he feels he can successfully oppose his dad. In the moment, it's reinforcing for Henry, but after the escalation, it leaves a child with many muddled emotions and thoughts that don't assist character development. One of the things that fuels this is that Jason is asserting his authority by trying to get Henry's compliance, which Henry is free to withstand.

Chapter 9 looks further into how Jason finds a way to hold his parental leadership without becoming entangled in a futile conflict cycle. He learns to set limits based on what's within his control, rather than trying to force change in his son. We'll explore this paradox more deeply, but Jason begins to make meaningful shifts even now. Simply recognizing his role in the cycle and choosing not to engage in verbal sparring have led to real change; escalations have dropped substantially. And what a difference this makes to the family environment!

Figure 8.3 shows how a parent can begin to adjust their role and step off the worry-and-conflict merry-go-round.

Can you see from Figure 8.3 that this isn't an immediate quick fix, but a process of change led by the parent? The child is so accustomed to the old cycle that they'll continue to push back in familiar ways until they experience that the parent will not participate. Here's how it looked for Jason and Henry:

1. Jason checks in on Henry, asking if he can remember what is expected in getting ready for bed.

2. Henry mumbles and nods but continues playing with his device.

3. Jason pauses to calm his anger. He says sternly, but not aggressively, that he wouldn't repeat his request, but would give Henry space to make a good decision.

4. Henry's so used to defiant escalations that he tells his father to go away.

5. Jason refrains from taking up the conflict invitation, making it clear he's not going to fight about this. He goes to the kitchen to help Amy clean up. Meanwhile, Henry continues to ignore the request, but as he sees his parents move toward the bedtime routine with his two siblings, he picks himself up and grumpily starts getting ready for bed.

For Jason, this was the beginning of a calmer parenting style that didn't mean giving up leadership. There would be slip-ups—however, Jason was tasting the new possibilities of getting off the futile roundabout he'd been on.

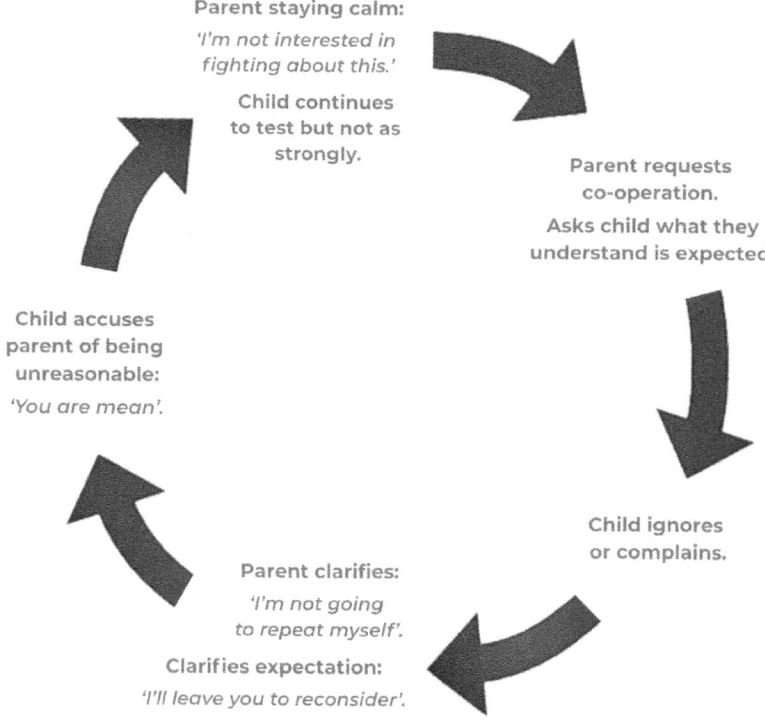

Figure 8.3 Getting out of the conflict cycle. *Created by Jenny Brown.*

Can Parents Be Expected Not to Worry When a Child Is Highly Symptomatic?

Every parent has different contexts for their worry cycles. This is illustrated as we turn to the other families we're following. For Brianna and Carter, viewing their daughter Jada's increasing depression and food restrictions, it seems illogical to parent without an injection of worried focus. Brianna and Carter are distraught that their gifted daughter has disengaged from her dance academy. Would this mean that all her chances for success in life could be squandered? Dance was what had seemed to give her joy and confidence. The urgency to intervene was understandably high—there was so much to lose. This level of worry for Brianna and Carter was heightened because of the apparently sudden onset of Jada's symptoms of depression and a possible eating disorder that had taken them by surprise. What had previously been focused on Jada's achievement switched to a worried focus on her treatment—was she complying with her therapist and nutritionist? Brianna was playing out the worry cycle in the following steps:

1. She constantly watched her daughter to measure her mood and check her eating.

2. Jada increased her withdrawal from her family.

3. Brianna increased her helping strategies by suggesting that Jada get back to dancing and reminding her of the nutritionist's advice.

4. Jada responded with annoyance and increased shutting her mother out.

5. Brianna increased her focus on getting more professionals and family members involved in fixing the situation.

When symptoms become more severe, it's an agonizing challenge for parents to break the worry cycle. Brianna certainly didn't want to treat Jada as a young child and made an effort to give her the space Jada was asking for, but her mind was increasingly consumed with concern about her daughter's mental health. This concern was dominating her relationship with Jada. It also dominated Brianna and Carter's conversations as a couple. They also included their son, fifteen-year-old Xavier, in their efforts to help Jada, asking him to get her out of the house and join him with his friends. The whole family, including grandparents, was part of the worry focused on Jada. Yet, the more effort that went into getting Jada back on track as a dancer and ensuring her treatment was followed, the more she withdrew and became secretive.

When Brianna and Carter saw their unproductive spiral, they knew it wasn't helping Jada recover her competencies to manage her life. It took courage to pull out of their worry cycle. They didn't stop Jada's treatment, as she was positive about her psychologist, and her symptoms were genuinely concerning. Brianna shifted to being curious and supportive of her daughter's journey. She said she knew it was Jada's journey through this trying time. As her mother, she was there to walk alongside her and get to know her daughter as a unique and engaging human being. She said she was worried about her daughter out of love, but didn't want her worry to crowd out their connection. Brianna began to put her words into action and connect with Jada around shared interests rather than focusing on fixing her.

Even when a child is exhibiting severe symptoms, it's possible for parents to exit the overprotective cycle, to lower the intensity, and to contribute to an environment that supports a turnaround for a struggling teen. It will require patience for Brianna and Carter as the symptoms their daughter was experiencing will take time to abate. It was important for Brianna to accept that the seeds of her daughter's collapse had been a few years in the making, as the intensity around her success had increased. Hence, it was realistic to expect that the road to Jada recovering her self-direction may take some time. The data on teenage recovery from depression, which co-occurs with other symptoms such as eating disorders and substance misuse, shows a multifaceted process.[3] A young person's recovery of life coping—encompassing physical, psychological, and behavioral aspects—often spans several years. Patience for the long game will be required. Brianna learned that she could replace her sense of urgent panic with patience and hope in seeing how she could profoundly contribute to her daughter's growth by getting off the worry-go-round.

The "Giving In" Cycle

Natalia and Adrian's parenting of four-year-old Elena reveals yet another version of a worry cycle. Natalia is driven by her concern for getting her parenting right, having waited so long for a child. Adrian's previous parenting regrets fuel his worries. There's an underlying imperative to have a close relationship with their daughter. Hence, any sign of her annoyance with them is met with a response aimed at smoothing things out and finding a happy space. This kind of worry sensitivity fuels Elena's sense of entitlement and elevated importance. Here are the steps in their cycle.

1. Natalia and Adrian are highly sensitive to Elena's negative reactions toward them as parents, and they quickly try to repair any tension by offering positive incentives.

2. In response, Elena increases her demands.

3. This is responded to with more efforts to have a cooperative child who's also happy with her parents.

4. This increases Elena's expectations of being served by her parents, and she protests when she doesn't like their responses.

5. Natalia and Adrian have even more worries that their daughter isn't approving of them.

Can you see the confirmation of the worry about not having a daughter who approves of and loves her parents? Such a worry focus ends up as a "giving in" cycle that fuels a child's sense of entitlement.

When Natalia and Adrian could see their dance pattern diagrammed as a cycle, their insight lights turned on. They had to get off this roundabout and halt their worry from fueling their accommodation of their young daughter's every wish. There was going to be plenty of pushback from Elena, who was so used to her parents giving way, but both parents had the clarity to hold their ground and deal with short-term disruption for the long-term gains for their daughter.

What Is Natural Versus Overprotective Worry?

All parents sometimes experience worry—it's a natural part of wanting our children to grow up safe and happy. Because humans have such a long period of dependency, this protective instinct often continues well into adolescence and young adulthood. When a child shows signs of struggle, wanting to step in is only natural. The challenge is distinguishing healthy, age-appropriate protectiveness from overprotectiveness, especially in a culture where parents are deeply invested in their children's success, happiness, and safety. A Pew Research study in the United States revealed that 94 percent of parents say it's "extremely" or "very important" for their children to grow up happy, and 88 percent prioritized success, primarily through education and career achievement.[4] A more recent Pew Research study found that 70 percent of parents say they worry "a lot" about their children being harmed physically or emotionally.[5] Another telling report found that 84 percent of parents of children under age thirteen say they frequently think about how to protect their child from physical harm.[6] Toning down overprotection isn't easy when it's wired into the role of parenting. The key is to get curious about our patterns with each child and ask whether our caring instincts have been caught in an unhelpful reaction cycle. Change takes time, but it begins with a patient, intentional effort.

I've been the beneficiary of a parent shifting their worry focus. As a symptomatic eleven-year-old child who was the focus of my mother's concerns, I relished her attention. I became easily jealous if one of my siblings was unwell, which diverted her focus of worry to them. For a time, it was relationally rewarding to be the sick patient and sustain my mother's fixing efforts. I look back and see that what changed for me was that my mother started to relate to me as an interesting human rather than a sick child. We developed a relationship based on sharing conversation and connecting over favorite foods and TV shows. My mother started to find me interesting rather than concerning, which contributed to my lifting up, and independent engagement with school and my peers. Sadly, my mother isn't around for me to hear her reflections on this season of our life as a family, but the lens of family systems theory helps me make sense of this childhood experience.

Stepping Off the Worry-Go-Round

As you near the end of this chapter, you may be seeking additional techniques for parenting a struggling or misbehaving child. I hope you can see that simply recognizing the cycle you're part of—and how it keeps things stuck—offers an alternative to the futile *worry-go-round* with a child. For any parent who finds themselves going around in circles in their parenting, take this as a signal to step off the roundabout. While your intentions are loving, you don't want to stay stuck in a repeated, unconstructive back-and-forth. Even if you don't know what to do in place, it's a significant first step to stop fueling the cycle of worry and dependence or stubbornness and defiance.

I like the metaphor of a playground merry-go-round as it vividly captures how everyone keeps pushing to maintain the spin. Yet, I wonder if another metaphor—a tennis or table tennis game—might better illustrate the impact when one person chooses to stop playing. Over the net, the child keeps serving the ball, trying to pull the parent back into the game, but the parent resists. The parents don't vanish— they invite a different kind of engagement. No more ping pong—instead, they go swimming or running together. Or with younger children, play on the swing or slide together. Still connected, but now creating space for the child's healthy growth toward autonomy.

For Reflection

Common Questions That Parents Ask About Worry Cycles

1. How can I avoid withdrawing too much once I step out of the cycle?

    Detaching can be as unhelpful as over-involving. The goal is to stay connected without merging with the child. The most helpful step back is one that lets us observe our part in the cycle.

2. When is worry appropriate?

    Telling a parent not to worry goes against nature. What matters is managing it. Can we keep worry from becoming part of a growth-blocking cycle? Can we accept that kids need life challenges to grow? Can we fact-check our fears and ensure curiosity, not anxiety, leads our parenting?

3.   When is external help genuinely helpful for a child?

External support can sometimes be valuable, as long as it doesn't lock a child into a position of dependency or tie their identity to a diagnostic label. Forcing a child into treatment is counterproductive. When parents address their own patterns, it often brings more lasting benefits.

4.   Isn't some children's behavior simply naughty, rather than part of a parenting pattern?

Both children's and parents' problematic actions can be selfish, well-intentioned, or driven by anxiety. Whatever the drivers of uncooperative behavior, they are always part of a system, meaning that the relationship is always playing its part. If a child is clearly misbehaving, a parent can respond in ways that don't fuel a reward-inducing defiance cycle. Parents can manage themselves in ways that allow children to learn the difference between responsible and selfish behavior.

5.   How can I handle the pushback from my child when I change the way I respond?

We can expect pushback whenever we change our part in a worry, conflict, or "giving-in" dance. This doesn't mean our shift isn't working—it requires persisting with a more constructive response to a child until a new, positive flow appears.

6.   What if my parenting partner isn't getting out of their cycle?

The most helpful first step is to focus on changing how we respond, instead of trying to change our partner. If we come across as critical or try to push them to change, they're likely to get defensive and push back. Instead, we can share what we're noticing and how we feel about it without insisting they see it the same way. This can soften reactivity in the parent–partner–child triangle. (More in Chapter 13.)

9

PARENTS STEPPING UP

HOLDING LIMITS AND DISCOVERING YOUR "I" POSITION

Rather than saying, "You must not do that," parents state, "This is what I expect, and here's why it matters to me," and back it up with consistent action.

The most common question parents ask me when presenting is, "How do I deal with my child's disobedience and still be the kind of parent I want to be?" Today's parenting advice often discards the view of children as "disobedient," encouraging parents instead to interpret pushback as a response to big emotions and to respond with gentle guidance.[1] Yet, in the daily grind of asking kids to cooperate, parents see how hard it can be for their children to accept direction—and how easily a child can oppose even the most reasonable request. While I understand that children are a *work in progress* when it comes to managing those big emotions, and the environment is always at play, I think it's also realistic to acknowledge that children often want to be in charge and do things their own way. Children naturally don't like not getting their own way. Adults react similarly to not getting what they want—but a mature adult has learned to see their own selfishness and curb these reactions. Parents need to help their kids mature in this way. All parents seek a way to set effective boundaries that nurture their child's ability to be cooperative.

Misbehavior—from Within the Child and What's Happening Around the Child

As I see it from a family systems perspective, a child's misbehavior is not just an individual issue—it's also a reflection of the relationships around them. In systems thinking, personal responsibility and relational context are held together. Children (and we adults) are accountable for their actions, but the emotional tone and patterns within the family also shape their behavior. In this view, misbehavior is both something that comes from within the child and something that expresses what's happening in the family and wider system. We need to hold both in view—helping children take responsibility for their behavior while observing how our reactions and the overall family dynamic may reinforce the pattern.

Parents Learning to Define Themselves

In this chapter, I introduce you to one of the most groundbreaking aspects of a Bowen family systems approach to parenting—the "I" position. Rather than relying on strategies to change the child, the "I" position helps the parent change themselves in relation to their child— without reverting to harsh discipline or using threats and punishments. Instead, they learn to take a clear stand on what they can control and what they are willing or not willing to do. It also avoids the impasse that often arises when applying popular parenting techniques, such as giving a child words for their feelings, hoping this will lead to cooperation. What matters most is not the method, but the steady, calm presence of the parent. Developing a solid "I" position helps parents move from reacting to leading, from rescuing to respecting, and from confusion to clarity.

So, let's revisit our three families and see how each applies the shift from trying to change, rescue, or coerce their child to holding firm limits aligned with their parenting goals. You'll see how they began to recognize that much of their previous communication centered around

"You" messages and what it looked like when they shifted to more of an "I" position.

The "You" Position

I wonder if you can recall the descriptions of each of our example parents interacting with their children? As I analyze the examples, remember—this isn't about always getting it right, which is too high a bar for us. It's about shifting focus away from trying to direct the child, which lies outside a parent's control. Please don't read the following scenarios as a negative critique of these parents' best efforts. I aim to highlight the value of recognizing the "You" posture and gradually replacing it with more of what the parent can take a stand on that reflects their parenting goals. This shift isn't something a parent can be expected to make all at once.

For Jason and Amy, thirteen-year-old Sophie seems to be their easiest child, so very little of their energy is invested in trying to change her. In contrast, their worries about the two boys, Henry and Charlie, shape their parenting into a cycle of monitoring and fixing. This fuels a "You" position that focuses on how the parent wants the child to change. It's also important to note that parenting a compliant child, like thirteen-year-old Sophie, presents challenges, as this can involve a subtler form of reactivity that may hinder a child's growth. We return to that later in the chapter. For now, let's look more closely at how Amy and Jason often unknowingly approach their boys from a "You" focus. Their response to Henry's refusal to stop gaming offers a clear example for examining different versions of the "You" position in action.

You'll recall that Amy asks Henry to finish his game and prepare for dinner. Henry ignored her. She walked over and said calmly but firmly, "Henry, you must not ignore me. I know finishing the game you enjoy is hard, but it's time to wrap it up now." Amy is bringing some of herself and her parenting principles to the interaction through a calm voice and an expression of empathy. Still, her focus is on Henry's behavior—his ignoring—rather than on her own limit to which she's agreeable. Can you notice how this remains mostly a corrective "You" message?

Henry replied with irritation: "Leave me alone!" Hearing this from the next room, Jason stepped in sharply, with lots of "You" instructions. His responses easily convey a control-based "You" message. Jason reacts to Henry's tone with a punishment threat, which tries to enforce authority rather than clearly expressing where he stands. The situation escalates with Jason increasing his "You" position. On the other hand, Amy's "You" stance leans toward rescuing, soothing, and avoiding conflict with Henry and between father and son. Both styles bypass the parent's "I" position—where the adult acts from self-definition (i.e., "Here's what's important to me, so this is what I will do"), not reactivity.

In the example with Brianna, Carter, and sixteen-year-old Jada, the "You" position comes through, even though the tone is gentle and caring. A "You" position isn't always loud or reactive—it includes any posture where a parent focuses on managing, rescuing, or fixing the child, rather than acting from clarity about their own values, limits, or responsibilities. Essentially, the "You" position attempts to change another, whereas the "I" position involves changing ourselves.

In her interactions, Brianna walks on eggshells around her daughter Jada. Again, I want to emphasize that this is understandable for any parent whose child struggles to cope. This worry shapes her parenting intent into getting Jada to engage or feel better—a subtle "You" focus (getting her to do something). Reminding Jada of the psychologist's advice about exercise or eating disguises a correction behind another's advice. It's a version of what Bowen called triangling, where we use a third party to communicate our anxious message. Bowen writes, "A two-person emotional system is unstable in that it forms itself into a three-person system or triangle under stress."[2] As we all do so easily when worried about another, we outsource authority ("the psychologist says"), but we're still directing another toward action. When Brianna says to her daughter, "I will take a day off work to take you to therapy, and we can go to your favorite café afterward." It can sound like a generous response. However, it is a "You"-focused rescue at its heart.

As stepdad and husband, Carter reacts to his wife's stress, saying, "You tell me what you want me to do, and I'll help out." Carter is also in a "You" stance where Brianna's anxiety directs his energy. He hands over responsibility for direction, rather than expressing his viewpoint. Carter suppresses his view to preserve emotional harmony, instead of speaking for himself—more on this dilemma in Chapter 13 on marriage and the parenting partnership.

Let's turn to Natalia, Carter, and four-year-old Elena to see how much of their parenting has a "You" direction. In the face of a young child's tantrum, it sure is difficult not to focus on just avoiding the next meltdown. As you read on, consider how the "You" stance shows up—whether through reward, persuasion, rescue, or collapse. Elena mastered her art of delay tactics at bedtime. Natalia has created a list of bedtime tasks for Elena, promising star stickers as she follows the sequence. This behavior-focused "You" approach relies on external motivation to get the child to comply, rather than grounding expectations in the parent's own conviction. Instead of Natalia expressing what she will do, the conversation remains centered on what Elena will or won't receive. It becomes a transaction, not a boundary. Adrian steps in and asks what has made his princess so sad. He promises more incentives, including a new toy the next day.

When the parents give in, things finally calm down—and sure, there's relief. But it's the kind that comes from ending a standoff, not from holding firm. This back-and-forth is part of that exhausting, "You"-driven loop. Adrien has a rescuing "You" stance, focusing on Elena's emotional state, and moves in to comfort, rather than holding a line. So, what does it actually look like to step out of that and lead from an "I" position instead?

The "I" Position—Not to Be Confused with Assertiveness Communication

I hope you're starting to get a sense of what each of our example parents can choose to do differently in how they respond to their child. Shifting their energy from the "You" of the child to the "I" of the parent allows a parent to take charge effectively. It reflects who the parent is and how they see their role in raising a child. It's at the heart of *differentiation-based parenting*, where a parent relates to their child from a strong sense of self—of who they want to be as a parent. We unpack a parent's job description more in Chapter 11, but for now, pause and reflect on your goals as a parent. Are they "You"-focused goals to make your child happy, successful, or compliant? Or are they self-focused goals, such as being present with your child in ways that help them experience self-regulation, responsibility, appreciation, and compassion? Can you hear the shift from who you want your child to be to who you want to be with your child?

Here's how Dr. Bowen explains the "I" position:

> The differentiating force . . . has been called the "I position," which defines principle and the taking of action in terms such as, "This is what I think or feel or stand for" and "This is what I will do or not do."[3]

This concept differs from what you might have heard about an "I" message that is part of assertiveness training approaches.[4] It's less about the words a parent uses and more about a mindset of representing a parent's self. Additionally, it isn't about asserting your voice in a relationship but defining how you think and what you will do to back that up. The popular idea of an "I" message conveys what you want from the other and how the other affects you. This still has a lot of "You" energy. Consider this subtle difference in how it is conveyed in *Parent Effectiveness Training*: "An 'I-message' tells how you feel, what you want, or how the other person's behavior affects you."[5] This self-expression message differs from people drawing a line around what they will and won't do based on their values.

Parents Drawing Their Line in the Sand

Let's look at how an "I" position can be applied in each of our parent examples. I'll share how each parent might shift from a "You" position to expressing themselves more clearly as a parent. These aren't scripts to copy, but examples showing what becomes possible when a parent is clearer about their principles and acts on them. We start with the shift that Amy and Jason make with Henry—a shift that will also influence how they parent their other children.

Amy looked at the clock, then walked to the living room, where Henry was gaming. "Henry, it's 6:00 and I'm serving dinner now," she said. "I'll leave your plate out for fifteen minutes. It's important to me that we all eat together as a family."

Amy isn't scolding or correcting Henry—she's calmly stating what she will do. She's setting a clear limit for herself around dinner time while also expressing an expectation rooted in her role as a parent and her value of shared family connection.

Henry kept playing and didn't respond. Amy paused and repeated her "I" stance: "I'm not going to ask again. I'll be at the table." She walked away and began serving. From the other room, Henry shouted, "I don't want to come now!"

Jason heard the tone and refrained from stepping in angrily. As he walked by, he said, "Hi buddy, I'm looking forward to dinner, and I'm supporting your mom by getting there on time. I hope to see you very soon." By shifting attention away from Henry's behavior and to himself as a dad, Jason kept himself calm and ensured he didn't escalate things.

Henry repeats, "I'm not ready to come to the table. I need to finish this game." Amy calmly replies from the entrance to the living room, "I get that you want more time. I'm not going to argue. I've said all I need to about dinner being ready soon." Ten minutes passed. Amy returned briefly and said, "Five minutes left before I put your dinner away. If you want to eat with us tonight, that's all the time left." Henry grumbled and came to the table. The family kept chatting about the day's activities while Henry sat in a bad mood at the table. Amy and Jason refrained from trying to change his mood. Amy's not trying to force compliance— she's just starting to break her part in a pattern. Jason is ensuring he stops his part in escalating the pattern. After dinner, while Jason and Charlie were cleaning up, Amy sat beside Henry as he finished eating. She says, "I appreciate you stopping your game and coming to dinner. I get it's hard to stop something you're really into. I hope you know how important family dinner times are to me."

Amy's not rescuing or backing off—she's showing emotional steadiness. Jason makes a meaningful contribution by stepping back to let Amy handle it, showing he's committed to family dinner, and doing his part in cleaning up. Both parents create a calmer, more respectful dynamic by shifting from managing Henry's behavior to managing their own responses. Henry still has his habitual defiant reactions, but they're not adding fuel to the escalation. They're not reacting to his emotional pushbacks. Instead, they're expressing clarity and respectful leadership. If this pattern hadn't become so entrenched, the parents' "I" position would look different, confidently conveying expectations to a child. However, when aiming to break out of a conflict cycle, the "I" position is expressed chiefly with just a few words and an effort not to reactivate the futile pattern. Table 9.1 shows what Amy and Jason demonstrate.

Now let's look at a new version of the scene in which Brianna and Carter take clear "I" positions—statements rooted in self-definition rather than reacting to or managing Jada's behavior or emotions. The tone stays warm and supportive, but the focus shifts from fixing to leading with more of the parent's self. Brianna knocked on Jada's bedroom door, saying, "Good morning, Jada. I'm heading out for a walk in a little while, and I'll grab a coffee. I'd enjoy your company, if you're up for it." This is an "I" position in which Brianna shares what she's doing and what she'd like, but doesn't try to coax Jada.

Table 9.1 A Summary of the "I" Positions—Example 1

"I am not willing to . . ."	"I am willing to . . ."
I am not willing to argue about dinner	I am willing to serve dinner at 6:00
I am not willing to ask again	I am willing to leave your plate out for fifteen minutes
I am not willing to escalate this	I am willing to be at the table on time
I am not willing to force you or manage your mood	I am willing to hold dinner as a shared family time
I am not willing to repeat myself	I am willing to state what matters to me calmly
I am not willing to rescue you from discomfort	I am willing to acknowledge how hard transitions are
I am not willing to chase or demand compliance	I am willing to express what's important to me
I am not willing to continue old reactive patterns	I am willing to change my part in this dynamic

Jada didn't respond. Brianna paused for a moment, then said in a relaxed tone, "I'll be back in about thirty minutes. If you change your mind, you can text me and I'll let you know where I am." Later that day, Jada muttered over lunch, "Nothing's helping. I don't want to go back to counseling." Brianna felt her chest tighten, but took a breath. "I hear you. It's hard when things feel stuck. For me I'm committed to supporting your path back to health, and I think counseling may be part of that. I'll keep the appointments for now, but I respect it's your call if you choose to make further appointments. I'll get some coaching for myself so I can be the best support I can be for you."

Rather than bargaining or pleading, Brianna states what she'll support and leaves space for Jada to step into responsibility and own her decisions. Brianna realizes that getting her own support is something in her control that can help her make a difference in the family. On the first day of working on a new pattern, Brianna didn't see much response from her daughter. However, she noticed that Jada engaged a little more than usual with the family members and spent less time in her room.

Later that evening, Brianna shared her new parenting efforts with Carter. She was calm but tired. Brianna expressed her effort not to push, saying, "It's hard, but I feel more solid doing it this way." Carter listened. "I've had doubts, too—maybe all the focus on treatment adds pressure. But I've kept quiet because I didn't want to stress you more." Brianna looked at him. "I appreciate that. But I'd rather we both speak honestly, even if we don't always agree." Carter nodded. "Okay. I'll support what seems right to me, and we'll keep checking in." Now, Carter is stepping out of silence and into honesty, owning his stance rather than suppressing it for harmony's sake. He knows not to criticize in front of the children but to give his perspective when it's just the two of them.

Brianna is working to have an "I" position that is committed to staying connected and supporting her daughter without pushing. She manages her urges to try to fix and rescue, and doesn't give in to panic. Jada is given space to feel and choose without being emotionally managed. Can you see how this scene models leadership through self-definition, not reaction? Table 9.2 summarizes what Brianna and Carter demonstrate.

Turning now to Adrian and Natalia. What does their shift from their anxious "You" position to a clearer "I" position look like? Approaching

Table 9.2 A Summary of the "I" Positions—Example 2

"I am not willing to . . ."	"I am willing to . . ."
I am not willing to coax you into participating	I am willing to share what I'm doing and invite you
I am not willing to panic when things feel stuck	I am willing to stay steady and supportive
I am not willing to manage your emotions or make decisions for you	I am willing to keep structure, like appointments, in place for now
I am not willing to overfunction or try to fix everything	I am willing to get my own coaching to support you better
I am not willing to pressure you into counseling	I am willing to respect your choices while supporting your growth
I am not willing to silence my concerns to avoid stress	I am willing to speak honestly with my partner, even in disagreement
I am not willing to withhold my viewpoint for harmony	I am willing to support what feels right to me and check in regularly

Elena's bedtime, Natalia decided to try something different that was all within her control. Before dinner, she showed Elena the bedtime list and said, "I'll follow this routine tonight. I'll let you select a favorite storybook when you're in bed on time." Natalia sets a clear, non-controlling expectation. Later, when Natalia notices Elena taking out more toys, she walks over and says calmly, "It's time for bed prep. I won't be playing now. I'm going to the bathroom to help with teeth brushing for the next five minutes." Natalia avoids bargaining or distraction. She states what she's doing, not what Elena must do.

Elena eventually follows, dragging her feet. In the bathroom, she asks, "Can I get a rainbow star now?" Natalia replies warmly but clearly: "Remember, I said this is the last week I'm doing our star chart. I'm okay with giving rainbow stars tonight once you're in bed on time and our little bedtime list is complete."

Elena gets distracted and calls her dad, asking him to play with her. Adrian hears her and enters calmly, saying, "I'm not doing any more play tonight because I won't change the bedtime plan. I'd love to play tomorrow when you're all ready for daycare." Adrian offers a connection without collapsing the limit. He doesn't fix or escalate the reward. Elena

Table 9.3 A Summary of the "I" Positions — Example 3

"I am not willing to . . ."	"I am willing to . . ."
I am not willing to play when it's time for bed prep.	I am willing to help with teeth brushing for the next five minutes.
I am not willing to bargain or distract to gain cooperation.	I am willing to follow our bedtime routine calmly and consistently.
I am not willing to change the bedtime plan for more play.	I am willing to play tomorrow when you're ready for daycare.
I am not willing to continue the star chart beyond this week.	I am willing to give stars this week when the bedtime routine is followed.
I am not willing to add extra stories tonight.	I am willing to enjoy our regular story together on another night.
I am not willing to stay up beyond what's reasonable for me.	I am willing to rest so I can be present again tomorrow.
I am not willing to offer rewards when you protest.	I am willing to stay steady and warm while holding boundaries.

sniffles but finishes brushing her teeth. In bed, she asks her mom to do extra stories. Natalia smiles and says, "I'm looking forward to my story with you another night. I'm not adding extra stories tonight." Elena protests: "Please, just one more?" Natalia replies: "I know you want more, but I need time to rest, too. We'll read again tomorrow." She gives Elena her sticker, knowing these rewards won't serve her in the long run. She wants to parent in a way that facilitates Elena's cooperation, not demands. Elena settles in, and bedtime finishes only ten minutes later than usual — a big improvement.

Table 9.3 shows what Natalia and Adrian demonstrate.

Patience Is the Companion of Progress

Not every effort to hold a line based on what you're willing and not willing to do will lead to instant change. But take heart — over time, you're giving your child the steady experience of a parent who's truly on their side. Kids pick up on this and tend to respond with more respect and cooperation over time. They feel loved—not because you always give in, but because you stay connected without losing yourself. The longer a pattern has been in place with a child, the slower the change will be. Parents need to be prepared for this and not get derailed when their child invites them back into the old "You" approach through their expressions of defiance or helplessness. The "I" position gives parents a way forward that doesn't disconnect from the child. Perhaps the most courageous part of this for parents is persevering until the child's "change-back" invitations have ceased. Tolerating a child's upset while staying with your "I" stance is essential to the parenting journey. This is backed up by highly regarded parenting research, such as the work of Dr. Eli Lebowitz, the developer of the SPACE (Supportive Parenting for Anxious Childhood Emotions) program at Yale University. He writes in his book, *Breaking Free of Child Anxiety and OCD*:

> Of course, most parents would prefer that their child be comfortable, but is that really the most important job of a parent? Preparing your child for life in the world can also mean helping them to be strong enough to cope with the less comfortable aspects of life.[6]

Remember, as a parent, it's essential to appreciate that enduring outcomes often result from steady, long-term efforts rather than quick fixes.

Beware the "We" Position—Avoid Making a Project Out of Getting the Other Parent on Board

In each of our examples, both parents change themselves to support their child's growth in resilience and character. This is an ideal, but commonly, just one parent takes the lead in differentiating between changing their child and working on defining themselves. Many parents I've worked alongside in their journey to being the best resource they can be for their children often start to instruct their parenting partner on how to parent. They begin to use a "We" position, with one parent telling the child that "We" both want you to change this way. One parent decides what they want from the other parent, acts to change them, and speaks on their behalf. This is rarely productive in the same way that trying to change a child is unproductive. It leads to defensiveness or pretend compliance from the other parent. Remember the good news that one parent who begins to change their pattern to a more mature "I" position is a trailblazer for the whole family's well-being.

What About the Compliant Child?

It's easy to apply the parent "I" position to challenging behaviors, but holding a clear parent job description is just as vital in parenting a compliant child, such as thirteen-year-old Sophie, the older sister of Henry and Charlie. Compliant children reap the benefits of not being anxiously focused on by their parents, as they get a bit more breathing space. However, they can also become highly sensitive to their parents' distress about their sibling. They grow up reacting to others' stress, working to relieve any additional worry by being the good child—rather than developing their capacity to have a balanced relationship with others. As a result, they can grow into people pleasers who go above and beyond to care for others, which can be at the expense of developing their separate interests and personal projects.

The parents of a child who works to please, such as Amy and Jason, might take an "I" position with Sophie, conveying, "I recognize that I've been letting my worry about your brother spill over to you. I know this isn't helpful to either Henry or you, and I'm committed to finding ways to stop adding to you always being my good child. I'm going to spend more time with you doing things that you really enjoy. Just one-on-one. I want to get to know my daughter afresh."

Principles for Self—Not a Parenting Technique

This chapter has shared examples from various families, but each parent must ultimately consider what resonates and fits their situation.

While many examples focused on setting limits, the deeper goal is to support a child's development in character, responsibility, and resilience through principled leadership. Limit setting isn't about control—it's a way of expressing to a child, "I'm for you." It communicates, "I want to be the best parent I can be, to give you the best chance at a strong and flourishing future." Parents are encouraged to move away from reactive, fear-based parenting—especially the fear of a child's disapproval or distress. Instead, they're invited to take an "I" position—calmly defining what they will and won't do, based on what they can genuinely control. Rather than saying, "You must not do that," they state, "This is what I expect, and here's why it matters to me," and back it up with consistent action. Words alone won't cut through. Children may tune out anxious lectures but pay attention to calm conviction. A thoughtful, firm "I will not" often lands more deeply than a reactive "You will not." As I've frequently said, grown-up parents raise grown-up children[7]—not by trying to control them, but by being a steady, thoughtful presence they can trust and learn from. That's the paradox at the heart of this approach—the more a parent grows in maturity and self-leadership, the better equipped their child is to grow up well.

For Reflection

The Key Principles for Establishing the Parent "I" Position

1. The parent manages themself, not the child.

2. Parents don't try to control what's beyond their own choice to activate.

3. Parents don't expect words to achieve much and are willing to take action on what they say.

4. Parents represent their values about responsible behavior in the way they act, which validates the expectations they convey to their children.

What's in My Control?

Take a few minutes to reflect on your recent parenting efforts. Use the following prompts to clarify where your energy has gone—and where it might be better directed.

What Am I Trying to Change That's Not in My Control?

1. Where have I been trying to control someone else's feelings, behavior, or reactions?
2. Have I focused more on getting agreement, obedience, or cooperation?
3. What have I wanted to *fix* that isn't actually mine to fix?

What Am I Trying to Change That's in My Control?

1. What are the boundaries, principles, or responses I *can* choose for myself?
2. How am I showing up in ways that reflect the parent I want to be?
3. What actions or decisions are truly mine to take?

Looking Back at This Week

1. What did I try to control that led to frustration or tension?
2. What moments showed self-leadership or clarity?
3. What would I like to carry forward into next week?

Note: The "I" position is not self-interested.

Dr Bowen distinguishes between the "responsible I" and the "irresponsible I." He writes:

> The "responsible I" avoids the "irresponsible I" which makes demands on others with, "I want, or I deserve, or this is my right, or my privilege." A reasonably differentiated person is capable of genuine concern for others without expecting something in return.[8]

PARENT LEADERSHIP IN THE DIGITAL WORLD

We set boundaries that don't instigate futile power struggles and open up age-appropriate conversations to help our children develop their own values for the online world.

Probably no aspect of modern parenting is more challenging than navigating the rapidly evolving digital landscape that now defines so much of childhood and adolescence. The digital landscape is changing so quickly with the expansion of artificial intelligence (AI) that it feels impossible to keep up. At the time I'm writing, everyone is talking about Jonathan Haidt's important, groundbreaking book, *The Anxious Generation*,[1] which lays out the profound difficulties parents face in managing their children's digital lives, particularly amid growing concerns about mental health and social development. As new voices raise concerns about the digital world's impact on children, it's clear that technology brings both beneficial advances and profound risks of manipulation, exploitation, and abuse. While parents are vigilant in the physical world, many are unprepared for the online landscape. Haidt argues that children are often underparented online. Society as a whole has been caught off guard by the rapid rise of smartphones and digital platforms, leaving families, schools, and communities scrambling to adapt. Most parents are trying their best but lack guidance in raising kids surrounded by screens.

A major concern for parents today is managing phones and social media. Many kids get smartphones and join social platforms before age thirteen, often because *everyone else has one.* Despite parental hesitation, saying no is hard. But avoiding the issue isn't an option—it needs thoughtful attention. Haidt emphasizes that early digital exposure is reshaping childhood. Instead of playing outside or socializing face to face, kids are glued to screens—moving less, sleeping poorly, and missing chances to develop critical life skills. Mental health issues, especially among teenage girls, have surged in the past decade, linked to the pressures of apps like Instagram and TikTok.

One of the most concerning impacts of the online world on our children is access to porn. With smartphones and little online filtering, children may encounter it as young as nine or ten. This harmfully shapes their views on sex and relationships—and the effects go beyond knowledge—they touch kids' emotional and mental well-being. There are links between frequent porn use and rising levels of anxiety, depression, and social withdrawal, especially in teen and college-age boys.[2] Additionally, porn is designed to be addictive. It can hijack the brain's reward system, making it hard for some teens to stop even when they want to. For parents, trying to deal with this can feel overwhelming. Children are increasingly adept at using technology and often know how to bypass parental controls or conceal their online activities. Even when parents are doing their best, it's tough to work out how to provide leadership in a tech world so different from the one they grew up in.

The normalizing of sharing explicit photos, called sexting, has added to this disturbing online world for our kids. And to add to the concerns about our children's access to their devices, there has been a surge in cases where AI-generated explicit images (deepfakes) of teenagers are created and distributed without consent, leading to emotional distress, reputational harm, and shocking psychological impacts for young people. Various forms of cyberbullying can proliferate in the anonymity of the internet.

Getting Past Helplessness and Fear

As parents and community members, we must face the detrimental impacts of the online world head-on. Yes, the rise of smartphones has brought many benefits to us all, including easier access to information and staying in touch. However, we will continue to underprotect the younger generation if we don't take the statistics on damages seriously. The data on impacts needs to wake us up to action, but not overwhelm us with fear. To truly support parents in navigating this anxious digital landscape, we need more than a flood of alarming statistics. Fear won't build confidence or clarity.

There's an alternative narrative to Haidt's argument, presented by Professor Peter Gray, a research professor at Boston College, who proposes that the loss of free play may have more to do with the decline in mental health than social media. He also provides a helpful reminder that history has had its share of moral panic episodes regarding new media's potential to harm children.[3] Whenever a new technology comes along that creates a revolutionary new means of communication, there is a public voice warning of its hazards to the young, followed by what Gray describes as "a persistent and often gradually growing worry or fear about damage to the young done by the new media."[4] A great deal of fear was generated in the 1850s with the widespread availability of short stories for youth, earning them the label of "Penny Dreadfuls." Then came the motion picture and the post–Second World War comic book panic. In the 1990s, concerns arose about the damage caused by video games. This is a salutary reminder that parents are never helped by any public catastrophizing that generates fear. While I consider Haidt's book timely and invaluable, we must ensure that, as with any warning, our response is measured, not driven by panic.

I've heard many parents report that reading books such as *The Anxious Generation* left them feeling shocked and helpless. One mother wrote, "I can't argue with all the issues kids need protection from, but I've no idea how to start doing this when my kids are already addicted to their phones." Parents need practical, manageable steps to help them show up as calm, loving leaders in their children's digital lives. This begins with a reminder of the parenting paradox—to shift our focus from trying to change or control our children to working on ourselves. This approach is far less overwhelming than chasing outcomes beyond our direct control, such as changing our children's attitudes to improve their sleep or spend more time outdoors. Of course, we want those things—but we won't achieve them through lectures, threats, or constant *you need to* messages. That only creates disconnection and conflict. Shaping an environment that nurtures our children's maturity works better than pushing their mindset in a particular direction. Parents need to take the risks and impacts of the ever-changing digital landscape seriously, but not panic. Our efforts focus on clarifying our job description and values and representing this to our children and teens. We set boundaries that don't instigate futile power struggles and open up age-appropriate conversations to help our children develop their own values for the online world.

Start Where Your Family Is At

There's no one-size-fits-all approach to parenting in the digital age. Every family's situation differs, so parents must clarify a few key realities: How old are my children? What have they already encountered online? How much time are they currently spending on devices? What kind of access to data or Wi-Fi does our family have? Have we had open conversations about both the benefits and the risks of the digital world? What patterns do I tend to fall into when trying to set limits with each child? And perhaps most importantly—how wrapped up am I in my own devices? Honest answers to these questions form the foundation for stepping up as a parent in ways that actually make sense for your family. The answers to these questions from our example families help to see where to start becoming positive influencers in children's digital lives.

Consider How to Share the Positives

Before revisiting how our example families might address the parenting dilemmas specific to their stage of life, it's helpful to recognize that the digital revolution has not been wholly detrimental. It has brought with it incredible innovations and everyday efficiencies that benefit us all. While this chapter focuses primarily on how parents can navigate the many challenges of screen time, it's also the case that the digital world offers real value. When used thoughtfully, screens can be powerful tools for creativity, connection, and learning. Take a moment to reflect on the positives you see in your online life and consider how to share them with your children. Maybe it's how you use video calls to stay in touch with faraway family, join online groups to share photos with loved ones, follow your favorite cultural pages or sports teams, or turn to YouTube for quick how-to videos. Sharing these moments with your child can turn screen time into a shared experience, rather than something done in isolation. By intentionally highlighting the good and modeling time limits for switching off and moving on to something else, you're helping your family build a healthy, balanced relationship with technology.

When Children Are Still Young

Adrian and Natalia have an advantage starting with a four-year-old child. Elena has only been exposed to movies and TV shows on her parents' iPad. Yes, she defies their efforts to restrict the amount she watches, but they can work out how to consistently hold limits. They can set a daily time limit for using the iPad and watching TV. As parents, considering the recommended guidelines and deciding what fits best for their family may be a helpful place to start. For example, the World Health Organization (WHO) recommends healthy screen time access by age group for children under five years old.[5] There should be no screen time for babies under one year old. That means avoiding phones, tablets, TVs—anything with a screen. They need face-to-face interaction, tummy time, and lots of physical and sensory play at this age. The guidance is similar for toddlers between one and two years old. Ideally, one year olds shouldn't have any screen time. By the time they reach two years old, a little bit of screen use can be okay, but it should be limited to no more than one hour a day or less. For preschoolers such as Elena, aged three to four years, screen time should still be kept to a maximum of one hour.

Natalia and Adrian have the advantage of not having to implement restrictions on a child who has already become accustomed to spending more time on screen. Elena remains equally interested in her toys and games, and can be redirected from watching a YouTube show to engaging in real-world, interactive play. To make it easier once she starts school, they can have in place practices such as keeping tablets out of bedrooms and times when the home goes offline. They can practice using their "I" position in managing their daughter's pushbacks, such as "When screen time is finished, I turn it off—even if you're still having fun. I know that can feel hard, but it's my job to help us stick to our plan."

"I know you really want to watch more cartoons, but I've decided that there will only be one show a day. I'm here to help you find something else to do, and I won't change my mind when you get upset."

"I care about your eyes and your brain, so I don't let you have too much screen time. There are lots of other fun things to choose from."

"I use the timer so we both know when it's time to stop. That way it doesn't feel like a surprise."

Probably the most important thing that parents of young children can do is set a good example by modeling the responsible use of their own phones and devices. Additionally, they can ensure that they get some rest and respite from the pressures of work and parenting without relying on screens as babysitters.

Rethinking Parent Respite and Devices

I suspect that underparenting around device use is largely driven by the overwhelming stress that today's parents face, and the relief that screens provide when young children are occupied. I recall this as a parent when portable DVD players became available — it enabled us to have a restaurant dinner with the kids and have some time for adult conversations. This diversion can easily continue into the teenage years, as parents appreciate the peace in the household when the novelties on screens quietly occupy children. Parents also find that scrolling through their phones is a mindless stress-relieving zone. Have you paused to consider how this might happen in your life and parenting, and the actions you can take to create alternative forms of respite and stress management.

Doing a Family Digital Inventory — an Example with Tweens and Teens

Amy and Jason, with preteen and early teenage children, have a different context in which to improve their leadership of Sophie, Henry, and Charlie in the digital world. The stress of their lives, dealing with strong-willed boys, busy work demands, and broader relationship responsibilities, has meant that neither parent has stopped to reflect on a family digital use review. Upon reviewing the family's online activities, they realized that both spent a significant amount of their evenings on screens, which was interfering with face-to-face interactions. They also discovered that thirteen-year-old Sophie, whom they hadn't been worried about, was, as it turns out, spending long hours in her room on the phone she got for her last birthday. She was primarily involved with school friends on Instagram and TikTok. This had been happening unnoticed by her parents, and they had never discussed with her the pros and cons of social media or any time restrictions that might be helpful. Both boys played their favorite games each afternoon, which was part of the daily battle to get Henry to focus on his responsibilities and attend family dinner time. While they had some parental controls in place for their TV streaming content, they had not explored any parameters for Sophie's internet exposure or the possibility of strangers contacting their children through multiplayer games or in-game chats. As Amy and Jason considered their digital inventory, they knew a panicked response would not be well received.

Leading Your Family's Digital Life with Intention

After doing their family digital review, Amy and Jason felt a mix of regret and motivation. There wasn't a panic—just the dawning realization that they had drifted into patterns they hadn't consciously chosen. And with that awareness came the chance to lead differently. "I realized I was spending most of my evening with a screen in my hand," Amy admitted. "I thought I was unwinding, but in fact I was checking out from the people in the room. That's not who I want to be as a mom." Jason had a similar moment. "I'd catch myself telling the boys to get off their games while I was scrolling emails. I wasn't modeling anything helpful. I want to show up better."

The first step they took was with their own habits. They decided to carve out screen-free time in the evening, starting with dinner and the following hour. Not because they read it in a book, but because they realized its impact on their family relationships. They let the kids know what they were trying, not as a rule to follow, but as an invitation to reconnect.

In response to Sophie's social media use, Amy and Jason each decide to adopt a more thoughtful and relational approach. Instead of jumping in with new rules, they determine to begin by gently opening conversations about her phone use, showing interest in what she enjoys, and asking about her experiences on social media. Both parents recognize that they've been largely unaware of how much time she's been spending on Instagram and TikTok, and they take responsibility for not engaging with her sooner. Their priority isn't control but connection, aiming to understand what's working for her online and where she might need more guidance or support. This marks the beginning of a more intentional, ongoing dialogue about her digital life and a greater intention to connect broadly with their quieter daughter.

Amy and Jason begin to rethink how gaming fits into family life— not by blaming the boys, but by reflecting on their own patterns. Amy acknowledges, "I won't just jump in to remove something they enjoy hastily, but I will create clearer boundaries so it doesn't crowd out everything else. I must express my commitment to making family rhythms, like dinner, feel less like a daily battle." Jason sees that his own inconsistencies have contributed to the tension. "I haven't been clear or calm in how I respond, and that's on me. I'll set expectations that are fair and stick to them without turning it into a power struggle." Rather than directing energy to changing their children's behavior, they start with their own—shifting from frustration to structure, and from reacting to leading with intention.

Reviewing Digital Safety Gaps and Being Transparent

They also recognize the overlooked digital safety gaps and take responsibility for closing them. "I won't assume basic controls are enough," Jason reflects. "I'll take the lead in learning how to protect our kids online, especially in games and social media." Instead of making quiet changes behind the scenes, they choose openness. Amy commits to involving Sophie in reviewing privacy settings together. "I'll talk about online safety with her, not to control her, but to support her." These aren't quick fixes. They agree to have regular check-ins, not monitor, but stay connected. "I won't treat this as a one-off fix," Jason says. "I'll keep adjusting how I lead, because this isn't just about screens—it's about becoming the kind of parent I aim to be."

Amy and Jason adopt a long-term, intentional approach to digital life by first changing their own habits, opening ongoing conversations with their children, and leading with clarity and consistency. They didn't get it right all the time and had ongoing messy moments trying to handle themselves calmly, but each had set a new direction for their parenting.

Parenting Past Screens—Reconnect with Each Child

Most importantly, Amy and Jason discovered that they had not been connecting one-on-one with their daughter, just assuming that, as a good child, all was well. Making an effort to communicate with Sophie as a whole person would be much more valuable than focusing conversations solely on social media. It was time for phones to be turned off and for them to organize more shopping trips, sports, and hang out with Sophie's friends' families. Similarly, alternative outings without devices can become a regular part of each weekend for the boys.

How to Intervene When Your Teens Are Already Deep In—Avoiding Futile Power Struggles

For Brianna and Carter, raising seventeen-year-old Jada and fifteen-year-old Xavier, stepping into digital parenting now feels like trying to catch up to a runaway train, with their teens already miles ahead. They've been in the dark about what their teens are exposed to online.

The statistics reveal the realities for their children's age group. A US-based study reported that 93 percent of boys and 63 percent of girls had been exposed to internet pornography before the age of eighteen, with the average age of first exposure being twelve years old.[6] Where do they start to support and protect their almost-adult children?

The message for parents like Brianna and stepdad Carter is that while it's easy to feel late to the game, unsure of how to establish boundaries without causing pushback or damaging trust, it's never too late to start. The goal isn't to control or undo what's already happened—it's to step into leadership with honesty, curiosity, and calm authority. Parenting teens in this space begins with humility—I may not know everything about their platforms, but I can still be a supportive presence. This means opening conversations, setting new expectations respectfully, and—most importantly—modeling the digital behavior you hope to see. The best place to start is to ask genuine questions from curiosity not fear:

Brianna might ask: "What's something you've seen online recently that made you stop and think about ways young women can be shamed online?" "What recent things online feel confusing or stressful to figure out?" "Who do your friends go to when something online feels off?" "Have you ever felt pressure to act a certain way online?" "How do you deal with that?" "What things online help you the most?"

Carter might ask: "What kinds of things do you see your friends dealing with online that you think we adults should be aware of?" "What are the hardest parts of being online for teens right now?" "How do you decide what's okay to post or share?" "What do you think about how young women and their bodies are treated online?" "What are the most positive things for you online?"

I've seen so many parents panic and find themselves in futile power struggles trying to restrict teens' screen use. This is never productive, just as ignoring is unhelpful. Brianna and Carter begin by responding out of their measured concern, which is grounded in care and a willingness to learn.

Brianna says, "I realize I haven't asked much about what you're doing online—not because I don't care, but because I didn't know how to start. I want to understand more now." Brianna might say, "I'm learning that just reacting when something goes wrong isn't enough.

I want to be someone you can talk to before things get confusing or overwhelming."

Carter reflects, "I haven't always been clear about what I expect or why it matters. I want to do better, and that means having these conversations with you."

Can you see how these "I" positions shift the dynamic from confrontation to connection, reducing defensiveness and inviting openness? The good news is that even teens who roll their eyes are watching how their parents respond. Parents who are just starting to lead in the digital space still have significant influence, even when the window of childhood feels like it's closing fast.

Opening up Connection in Awkward Spaces — Conversations About Porn

I remember that, as a teenager, my mom banned certain TV shows, but she never explained the values behind those rules. We heard the restrictions, but there were no real conversations — no sharing of her concerns or asking what I thought. One consequence of those bans, without any connection or dialogue, was that the first thing I did when babysitting at neighbors' houses — unsupervised — was watch the very shows my mom had forbidden. They didn't impress me much in the end, but looking back, the predictability of my reaction was almost funny. I do understand, though, how uncomfortable those conversations must have felt for my parents — and how much more daunting the task is today, in an unfiltered digital world. So, how can parents use their own "I" position to open honest, grounded conversations about tough topics like online porn and sexual exploitation? Below are some parent-led discussion scenarios to consider. They represent an ideal that is never easy to implement in the heat of the moment, but I hope they give a sense of how a parent can best express themselves in this tricky space.

One evening, after basketball practice, Carter and his son Xavier sat quietly in the car. It was one of those low-pressure moments, with just enough space to bring up something that had been on Carter's mind. He glanced over and said, "I've been thinking a lot lately about how different things are now from when I was your age, especially with phones and the internet. There's so much out there that's not a great influence and can be damaging. I just wanted to check in with you about that." Xavier shrugged. "Like what?"

"Honestly," Carter said, "things like porn. I know it's out there, and I know most guys your age have seen it, even if they weren't looking for it. I'm not here to judge—I just realized I've never actually asked what this scene is like and how you think about it."

Xavier hesitated. "I mean . . . yeah, I've seen stuff. It's not a big deal."

"I get that," Carter replied. "And I get why you'd say that. When I was younger, no one really talked about it, but it still had an impact. I didn't realize until later how it shaped the way I thought about women, about sex, even about myself." A brief pause occurred before Xavier said, "I guess it's just . . . everywhere. Like, it's normal."

"Yeah," Carter nodded. "I realize I haven't been brave enough to raise this with you and share my experiences. I want you to feel like you can talk about it without worrying that I'll lose my composure. I want to be someone you can come to, not someone you hide this stuff from." Xavier gave a slight nod. "Okay. I mean . . . it's weird to talk about, but okay." "I know," Carter said. "It was weird for me to bring it up, too. But I care about who you're becoming, not just what you watch. I hope you'll reach out to me if you have any questions or if something makes you uncomfortable. And I won't be wimping out of these discussions from now on. I want to learn from you and walk through it with you. I want to share with you all the positives in the value I have about sex in a committed relationship like my marriage to your mom."

This kind of dialogue models emotional honesty, curiosity, and non-judgmental presence—essential ingredients for building trust with teens. Carter is laying the groundwork for sharing his own experiences and values about sex and relationships.

Here's an example of Brianna as a mother gently starting a tricky conversation about sexual content online. It was a quiet evening at home with Carter and Xavier out at basketball training. Brianna and Jada were in the living room. Brianna hesitated for a second, then glanced over at her daughter. "Hey, Jada . . . I want to bring up something kind of awkward for me, but important?" Jada looked up, curious. "Um . . . okay?" Brianna continued, "I don't expect you to answer anything you don't want to, I just realized I've never talked with you about what you might be seeing online. Especially things like sexual content . . . or porn. I think I've let you down as a mother by avoiding this." Jada blinked, surprised, but didn't shut down. "Oh, I don't think you're a bad mother. I like it when you give me privacy. But yeah, there's a lot of weird stuff online," she said after a moment. "Some of it's gross, some of it's just . . . there. It's not like I go looking for it, but yeah—I've seen things." Brianna replied, her tone calm. "Thanks for being honest, I really appreciate that. I get that this is the harsh reality of the world you're growing up in. I wonder how you work it all out? Especially the stuff out there that gives some pretty distorted messages. About bodies, about sex, about relationships." "Yeah," Jada nodded. "I've noticed that too. So much of it feels fake . . . or kind of extreme." Brianna said. "I remember feeling uncomfortable about things when I was younger and thinking it was just me being weird. But now I see—those feelings were often worth listening to. I wish I could have talked to my mom about it, but we didn't know how." Jada laughed, saying, "Yeah, I can't imagine Grandma managing to talk about sex. I wonder how you worked it all out back then?" Brianna said, "I've come to respect the values my parents had around sex in the safety of a loving marriage, and I'd have loved them to share more of what shaped their beliefs with me."

Brianna took the opportunity to share more of her journey at Jada's age. This was a new type of conversation for them. Brianna was also curious about how Jada figured out what was fake or disturbing, conveying that she wanted to learn from her daughter's experience. The conversation lasted for a little while, with Jada becoming more interested in things from her mom's family growing up. Brianna finished saying, "I want to make sure you feel like you can talk about anything that seems off or confusing. Even if I don't have all the answers, I'm here to figure it out with you." Jada was quiet for a second, then said softly, "That's . . . kind of nice to hear."

Not every attempt at openness led to a deep conversation. Sometimes, things shut down quickly. Brianna used those moments to reflect—not just on Jada's reactions, but on herself. She noticed how often she brought unnecessary intensity to the conversation, especially when she was zeroing in on making a point rather than being genuinely curious. Whenever her anxiety took the lead, the connection stalled. She learned that real dialogue isn't about delivering a message—it's about staying present in the back-and-forth. There are no shortcuts, only slow, steady steps.

Using Streaming Dramas and Documentaries for Side-by-Side Conversations

Recently, I've heard parents speak about the value of watching documentaries and series that have been useful for opening up meaningful conversations about relationships, identity, and online culture. Watching media together can be a natural and non-threatening way to start conversations. Choose content that aligns with your values or raises valuable questions, and use it as a springboard to talk, reflect, and connect. News publications have reported on how the Netflix series *Adolescence*[7] has struck a nerve across the globe because it draws viewers into challenging questions about masculinity, online influence, and parenting in a digital world.[8] Sitting side by side watching dramas like *Adolescence* together can build an emotional connection. Such shows help parents and teens sit together—literally and emotionally—creating natural openings for meaningful conversations without the pressure of a face-to-face talk. It offers a safe springboard for reflection, giving parents natural ways to ask questions like, "How would you feel?" or "Have you seen this online?"

Young Children's Online Sexual Safety

A brief word about what parents of younger children can do to help protect them from harmful online sexual content. Just like we've learned to talk to kids about things like strangers asking to see their private parts or what to do if someone touches them in a way that feels wrong,[9] we can use the same calm, straightforward approach when it comes to online safety.

In addition to our clear boundaries for screen use, parents use clear language that children can understand, such as: "Your private parts are private. If you ever see a video or picture that makes you feel weird or uncomfortable, it's good to tell me." You can help your child understand the importance of trusting their feelings by discussing the "uh-oh" or "yucky" sense they might get if something online doesn't feel right. And as with adolescents, share your values using age-appropriate language. For example, discuss your values regarding body privacy and what you consider special in your grown-up relationship. This can include explaining that when people, especially children, are forced to do private things on camera, it's very wrong and harmful. Let children know it's actually against the law for adults to take pictures of kids in those ways. These conversations don't need to be heavy or frightening—but honest and age appropriate. The goal is to build trust in your leadership, not fear.

Building a Community of Like-Minded Parents

Navigating the complexities of parenting in the digital age can feel overwhelming, but parents don't have to do it alone. Connecting with like-minded parents who share your values can make a big difference. When families agree on boundaries—like holding off on phones until high school—it becomes easier to stick to those decisions and reduces the pressure kids feel when "everyone else" seems to have more freedom. Support from the community and schools can go a long way in assisting parents with the challenges of promoting their children's online healthy habits and setting limits. In a later chapter, we explore further the value of community support for parents. It's so helpful to parents that governments and schools are setting more precise limits on phones and social media, and groups are being established to support smartphone-free childhoods.[10]

From Anxious Fixing to Curious Connecting

The most common pitfall I see parents fall into is getting too caught up in the content about online dangers and moving quickly into trying to fix and impose rules rather than building a relationship. I recall a parent who described becoming immediately vigilant about taking her son's devices away after attending a parenting presentation at her son's school about the negative impacts of today's online world. This resulted in awful conflicts that left them both feeling worse about themselves. When this well-meaning mom saw the effect of her sudden attempt to impose rules, she realized it wasn't working. While her desire to help her son reduce his late-night screen time and improve his sleep was valid, how she approached it was damaging her ability to positively influence him in the future. Her energy needed to shift first to herself as the parent, not controlling the child, but choosing a wiser, more grounded response. This was an opportunity to open conversations rather than impose rules. To ask good questions, listen well, and admit she's learning too.

Using the "I" Position and Protecting the Relationship

Finally, as parents navigate the challenges of this rapidly evolving digital age, it's so helpful to remember to focus on what's within our control—attitudes and actions that make a meaningful difference. Children benefit most from caregivers who are honest about their own struggles, lead with humility, and stay committed to ongoing conversation. I hope you don't hear me proposing a permissive, accommodating approach, but a value-based approach that doesn't add problematic intensity to the parent–child relationship. I've heard from many parents about how they have implemented limits using what's within their control and conveying to their children their loving commitment to their child's well-being. Parents who turn off the family Wi-Fi at set times or use the account to restrict their child's phone connection times. Letting the child know that they will regularly update online safety apps and stay informed about any detections that attempt to violate these. With any of these actions, they don't send an expectation of control, but instead convey care and commitment to being the best parent they can be.

Using the "I" position helps protect the relationship by keeping the parent emotionally steady, avoiding power struggles, and modeling grounded leadership. Instead of saying, "You have to because I said so," the message becomes, "Here's what I believe, and here's how I'm parenting based on that." We won't get it right every time—and that's okay. What matters is making space for age-appropriate conversations, keeping our tone curious and non-judgmental so our children can come to us with questions and concerns. This isn't about reacting out of fear or trying to fix everything—it's about showing up with steady, loving leadership that gives them the balanced support they need to develop their own wisdom to navigate their world.

For Reflection

Parent Leadership in the Digital World

Use these "I" statement prompts to explore what works best for you and your child. These conversations won't always be easy or smooth—but small, consistent efforts matter. The goal is to open honest discussions about online content without shaming or shutting things down.

Conversation-Opening "I" Statements

1. "I realize I haven't asked much about what you see online, and I want to change that."

2. "I know this might feel awkward, but I'd rather talk about it than leave you to figure it all out alone."

3. "I'm not here to judge—I just want to understand what it's like for you."

Expressing Concern Without Panic

1. "A lot of what's online shapes how we see sex, people, and ourselves. That concerns me—because I care."

2. "Some content can affect how people view relationships and boundaries. I'm curious what you think about it."

3. "I'm not here to freak out—I just want to know how this stuff affects you and how we can talk about it."

Modeling Openness and Accountability

1. "I wish I'd started these conversations earlier—I see now how important they are."

2. "I didn't grow up with this kind of access, so I'm learning as I go—alongside you."

3. "I've made mistakes, but I'm committed to being more present and supportive."

Setting Wise Limits

1. "I'll provide some boundaries while you learn to create your own."

2. "I'm putting filters in place—not to control, but to protect you from harmful content and unsafe people."

3. "I'll regularly review apps, share what I'm learning, and welcome your thoughts."

4. "I've decided not to allow an iPhone right now. When you're ten, I'll look into simpler options with ways to stay connected."

Inviting Trust and Connection

1. "I want to be someone you can talk to—even about the uncomfortable stuff."

2. "I'm not trying to control you. I want to share my values and give you space to find your own way."

3. "If anything online ever feels off, I hope you'll know you can come to me."

Sharing Values, Listening with Respect

1. "I believe that sexual content online can be really damaging—I value relationships that are built on trust, commitment, and genuine care, and that's the kind of message I want to share with you. I know you'll be figuring things out for yourself, and I want to be here to talk with you as you do."

11

THE PARENT JOB DESCRIPTION

LOVING LEADERSHIP THAT ENABLES EACH SIBLING TO GROW

Our job description is essentially to be mature leaders who prepare children for adulthood.

Can you imagine starting a new job with an organization and discovering that you have no job description? You're given a title—one of great importance—but no clear goals, no outlined responsibilities, no measurable tasks. No orientation or training, either. This is essentially what parents face when they commence their first day in their new and vital role—holding a tiny, helpless infant in their arms. It's striking to me that almost all parenting courses for expectant parents focus solely on baby care, rather than the broader role of guiding parents through their child's growing years. Courses for expectant parents—often called antenatal classes or prenatal education—prioritize preparing parents for childbirth, early parenting, and the fundamentals involved in the physical care of a baby in the first few months. I recall that my husband and I attended such a course at the hospital where our first child was to be born. We even had a plastic baby to practice diaper changing, swaddling, and other similar practical tasks. We hung on every word of the midwife and prepared ourselves diligently for the arrival of baby number one. So much focused on birth prep and so little on what the heck to do with the dramatic changes to our sleep cycles, routines, and relationships. To this day, parent preparations typically cover the signs and stages of labor, pain relief options, the role of the birth partner, creating a birth plan, and what to expect at the hospital or birth center. It's hard enough to navigate all the unpredictable challenges of the first few months. Where does a parent start figuring out their job description for the next eighteen years?

For some light-hearted fun, I searched online for a comprehensive parent job description and found this perfect script for a job description for parents that I've summarized.

Who Would Apply for This Role?

Chief Operating Parent (Unpaid, Non-Optional)

This long-term, unpaid role requires high energy, no training, and the ability to function on broken sleep and cold tea. Candidates should expect chaotic conditions, twenty-four-hour shifts, and bathroom breaks with small companions asking repeated "why" questions. Responsibilities include emotional diplomacy, toy surgery, rapid-response cleaning, logistics coordination, and maintaining social calendars for humans under four feet tall. Travel is required (rainy playgrounds and endless sports tournaments) without reimbursement. No experience necessary—just resilience, humor, and the capacity to love irrationally. Compensation? None—unless you count endless laundry, spontaneous hugs, and the strange joy of being both indispensable and deeply embarrassing. Bonus skills: stealth, Lego avoidance, and Disney trivia expertise. Advancement opportunities include superhuman patience and the lifelong title of "my parent."[1]

This makes me smile, as it humorously touches on some core realities of any parent's long-term, monumental job. It speaks to the role of parents of younger children. Imagine one for the teen years?

Teen Relations Manager

Looking for someone to take on a role where you're expected to hold the line, offer endless lifts, interpret eye-rolls as communication, and stay calm while being blamed for everything from bad Wi-Fi to the unbearable tragedy of running out of snacks. All this, while quietly hoping that one day they'll look back and say, "You weren't entirely wrong."

Let's explore what makes an effective parent job description—one that supports a parent through every stage of a child's development and accommodates different temperaments. But first, it's worth considering the consequences of not having a clear position description.

The Cost of Having No Clear Job Description

As we've come to know our three sets of example parents, it's become clear that each began by letting their child's shifting moods and behaviors define their role as a parent. Like many who lack a clear job description, they found their responsibilities shaped day by day in reaction to whatever their children brought to them. For Natalia, her role has become doing anything to stop four-year-old Elena's distress. For Adrian, who is trying to do a better job of parenting the second time around, he's being directed by his anxiety that Elena must like her dad and not reject him.

Amy is so conscientious that she is outsourcing her parenting to the latest fad and technique to prevent any issues from developing in her three kids. This has her particularly applying techniques to the child she worries about the most, feisty middle child Henry. Her worry about Henry and her reliance on "expert" online parenting advice had been shaping her as a parent. It resulted in her parenting her children very differently, as if each needed her to have a different job description. As the compliant child, Sophie received less attention, while Henry and Charlie got more intensity from her fixing and soothing efforts. Jason had been shaped by his reaction to Henry's disrespect, which triggered his angry, controlling responses. He didn't want to be that kind of dad, but his emotions were running the show rather than any clear parenting goals.

Brianna's parenting was being formed firstly by her huge investment in daughter Jada's success as a dancer and subsequently by her fear about her declining mental health. Carter was trying to maintain peace with his wife and within their relationship.

These are all examples of parenting without a clear job description. The ups and downs of each child shape the parent, as well as each parent's sensitivity to past relationship experiences and their parenting partner. Parenting led by emotional responses to each child can leave a parent floundering without a clear direction, and risk leaving children without mature leadership. Over the past chapters, we've seen how each parent has begun to redirect their energy into managing themselves and representing their values to their children. This involves clarifying their purpose and value-based job description.

Clarifying the Goal of Parenting — Restoring Character over Happiness

In this era of intensive parenting, with an excessive focus on children, many parents are left with the unrealistic goal of raising happy and successful children. I wonder what first comes to mind for you as you reflect on your purpose as a parent and your goal for your children? Are they realistic goals? Do they factor in life realities, and how do we prepare our children to manage these? Do our goals include children's growth of internal good character?

I have followed the work of family therapist and researcher Phillip Klever for many years. He's conducted fascinating research examining what helps families function well over time. He followed fifty couples over twenty years and has teased out the impact of parent goal setting.[2] The parents who did best had clear, balanced goals — not just for their children, but for themselves as well. These weren't parents chasing perfection or control. Instead, they were guiding their families with intention. And the effect? Their families showed fewer signs of stress and emotional struggle. Drawing from this work, we can contrast higher-order and lower-functioning parenting goals. These goals help define a parent's job description.

Higher-order goals stem from emotional maturity, clear values, and a focus on long-term growth. Such parents prioritize responsibility, self-regulation, and problem-solving, aiming to build character and internal resources over external success. They take a long-term view, accepting short-term discomfort (like letting a child struggle) for lasting development.

In contrast, many modern parenting goals are reactive and image driven, shaped by stress and fear. These focus on external validation—grades, trophies, good behavior—rather than character. They seek short-term ease and control, not long-term resilience. When these goals fail, parents may become emotionally over-involved or withdraw, unsure how to respond to setbacks.

The essence of high-functioning parenting is fostering character and maturity. Differentiation-based parenting emphasizes helping children manage anxiety rather than removing stress, promoting independence and critical thinking over obedience or image. And I think it allows for prioritizing the lost concept of building character and integrity. Crucially, these parents understand that their own emotional functioning shapes the family, so they work on themselves to support their children's growth. As my husband says from his business experience, "leaders cast a broad shadow." As parents, we are the first and most consistent leaders in our children's lives, which means our shadow is long and constant. The key, then, is being intentional about the shape and impact of that shadow. So, what can help us determine the effect of our shadow as parents?

Consider Table 11.1, contrasting an anxious child-focused job description with a parent self-development job description.

How Parents Shift from External to Internal Goals

Can you see how our parental examples have gradually shifted from external to internal parenting goals? Natalia is committing to tolerate Elena's distress and opposition, not to give in, and to remind herself of the essential life lessons that her daughter will learn in the process. Adrian stops using bribes to gain Elena's cooperation and affection. He thinks about the big picture of his daughter learning cooperative teamwork with peers and teachers. The goal of promoting humility to make space for others and the ability to delay gratification starts to shape his parenting responsibilities. He puts energy into steadying himself internally when Elena is mad at him.

Table 11.1 Parent Job Description—Two Ways of Leading

Anxiously Focused on the Child	Calmly Focused on the Parent Job Description
To resolve my child's distress	To tolerate my child's upset sufficiently for them to learn to manage emotions
To solve my child's problems	To invite my child's problem-solving
To direct my child's thinking	To be engaged with my child's thinking and share my own calmly
To push my child to do what I want	To act on what I can control and stay aligned with my values
To pull my child away from risk	To set boundaries and allow space for mistakes and learning
To make my child confident, happy, successful, and popular	To be a consistent, caring, principled, respectful, and loving presence
To make my child my project	To live a principled life that serves as a steady example

Amy shifts her goal from fixing Henry's possible attention problems to cultivating each of her children's independence. This means less rescuing and intervening with Henry and Charlie, and more curious connecting with Sophie. The goal is the same, but it's applied differently to each child. Jason realizes that his angry reactions must be addressed so his sons can develop anger management skills.

Brianna is toning down her investment in both of her teenage children's successes. This is helping her not to catastrophize on behalf of Jada, thinking that she can't be happy in life without being a gifted dancer. This is similar to her co-achieving investment in Xavier's sporting success. Carter is refining his job description and goals as a stepdad. He's setting a goal to be a non-judgmental yet honest resource for his wife, not staying silent when he has a perspective to share, but sharing in a way that isn't imposing his view on Brianna.

Each of these parenting goals aims to support their child's long-term maturity and ability to manage life and relationships—unlike short-term aims like keeping a child happy, maintaining temporary peace, or seeking worldly success.

A Job Description That Enables Each Sibling to Mature

Have you noticed how siblings in the same family often turn out to be very different in their coping capacities? Of course, there are various contributors to this, including differences in genetic temperaments, but one factor that is rarely appreciated is the impact of how parents vary in their worry about and intensity in relating to each child. When parents are more reactive in either protective or controlling ways with one child compared to another, that child is likely to grow up more entrenched in reactivity and dependency, hindering their development of resilience and responsibility. We've touched on this in previous chapters, but it's worth considering how higher-order parenting goals that start with parent awareness can mitigate this disparity in parenting intensity. Child-focused parenting goals lead to reactive parenting. Even if the goals seem good, such as having a well-behaved or a secure child, they are projects beyond a parent's control that easily lead to overparenting.

I mentioned earlier the example of Amy shifting her attention to her big-picture parenting goals, which help her avoid overinvesting in Henry and underconnecting with Sophie. Amy is shifting her goal from fixing Henry's possible attention problems to cultivating each of her children's independence. This shift allows Henry to gradually develop responsibility without relying on his mother to soothe him or align with him when his dad is angry. As attention on Henry lessens, Sophie gains freedom to express her own personality, rather than feeling responsible for reducing her mother's stress. Although she's already more independent than Henry, Sophie benefits from no longer being shaped by the tension surrounding her brother.

The Impact of Uneven Parental Attention on Siblings

I trust I've ignited your curiosity about this perspective on how worry-driven parenting, without a clear value-based map, can lead to differences between siblings. I often remind people that all siblings grow up in both the same and quite different families. They're all born into different circumstances, and each is parented with varying intensity levels. This perspective has been most clearly articulated by Dr. Michael Kerr, who succeeded Dr. Murray Bowen in the leadership role of family systems scholarship in Washington, DC, following Bowen's death in 1990. Dr. Kerr has written about and presented case examples showing that it's not uncommon in families for one child to attract more parental attention—often the one perceived to be struggling in some way, whether academically, behaviorally, or with health issues.[3] When anxiety about a child's functioning rises, parents may naturally respond by becoming more involved, more vigilant, and more directive. While well intentioned, this pattern can lead to overfunctioning on the parent's part and underfunctioning on the child's part. The child becomes increasingly dependent on external help, and opportunities to build their own problem-solving abilities may diminish.

Meanwhile, other siblings, who receive less intense investment, can find more space to work things out for themselves. They're given more room to develop resilience and a sense of agency—not because they are *better off* necessarily, but because the parental focus isn't doing the emotional work for them. These differences in experience can shape siblings in markedly different ways over time. Personally, I find this helpful in reflecting on the family I grew up with, which included my four siblings. At one stage of family life, I was the recipient of my parents' worried focus and struggled to lift out of a "sickness role." The "worry focus" later shifted to another sibling, which has affected their ability to cope with stress in adult life.

How a Goal of Helping Children Can Backfire

We see a growing pattern of over-helping in families and schools. When a child struggles, the instinct is to respond with more involvement—more oversight, organizing, and motivating attempts. This stems from a good-hearted desire to help, but on its own, a goal to help a struggling child isn't a helpful job description. Our higher-order goal is to relate to children supportively and give them space to grow inner character. The challenge isn't doing nothing—it's stepping back enough for the child to face natural consequences and develop the inner resources they'll need as adults. How's this for a parent's job title: *Helping each child grow the resources they need for life*?

Meeting Our Children's Needs, Not Their Wants—Finding the Right Level of Support

A clear part of a parent's job description is giving the appropriate level of support. Parents want to support their child's development of resourcefulness and responsible independence, and to support their child being comfortable in their own skin rather than being a people pleaser or a rebel. Reactive parenting constantly responds to a child's *wants*, whereas more mature parenting responds to their *needs*. I acknowledge that one of the most challenging aspects for parents to determine is their child's specific needs at each stage of their development. Dr. Bowen acknowledged this challenge for every parent whose "overprotective energy is directed more by their anxiety than the reality needs of the child."[4] How do I choose the right amount of support each child needs from me, and when it is too much or too little? Let's look at our parent examples working out their children's *reality needs* at pivotal moments.

Starting with parenting a young child, how do Natalia and Adrian figure out when Elena expresses a *want* versus a genuine *need*? When Elena wants more story time at night, is it a delay tactic and a *want* to have her way? Or is it an age-appropriate *need* for more time to connect and snuggle up with her busy working parents? If Natalia and Adrian can consider their job descriptions, it can help them find a way to give loving support that doesn't promote entitlement. They're clear that their four year old needs regular fun and affectionate interaction with each of them. Additionally, they recognize that they want to encourage Elena's ability to cope with their limits without escalating the situation. In preparation for bedtime, they work out what they'll adjust in responding to Elena's predicted episodes of wanting more play and her habitual tantrums. Each sets aside more regular time in their diary to spend fun time with their daughter, not as a one-off but as part of the weekly routine. They review all of the out-of-home activities they've anxiously enrolled her in and figure out which one they can stop. Putting in the extra and needed parent–child time enables them to say at bedtime confidently:

> I love our storytime and the quiet cuddles with you, too. However, I know good sleep is important, so my answer is no. I know that we have our special playtime tomorrow afternoon.

As parents, they can be committed to special connection time each week, in addition to the caring interactions each morning, night, and weekend. And they can stay equally committed to saying no to more stories to enable sleep time. When Elena protests, they can walk away knowing they've fulfilled the age-appropriate nighttime affectionate rituals and calmly say: **"**I know this is new, but I've decided to be a better parent—one who shows love by saying no when it's best for you. Goodnight, sweet girl. See you in the morning."

In the early stages of this new clarity, they practice ignoring the tears and shouts for five minutes before a gentle restatement of, "No, Elena, I know you can use your imagination to get to sleep happily. I'll leave you to it." No bribes or threats, and both parents have agreed not to cave in to the predictable upset as they set their new course. They quietly lead her back to bed if she comes out of the bedroom in the early stages of testing them out. If it escalates further, they get themselves ready for bed and don't engage with Elena's protests. If it goes on further, one of them says calmly:

> I'm going to sleep now. I know you can choose to return to your cozy bed and rest. While you're getting used to Mommy's no (or Daddy's), you're welcome to sleep on the blanket with your pillow and bunny.

This won't be an easy transition, but both Natalia and Adrian are confident that they're responding to their daughter's needs, adjusting their schedule to do so, and ensuring that they no longer give in to her wants.

Amy and Jason take some separate time to reflect on their job descriptions and then come together as a couple to discuss them. Amy wrestled with Henry's reluctance to do his schoolwork. She carefully considered whether he truly needed her tutoring or would benefit more from being allowed to make his own choices. Her parenting goal was to promote independent problem-solving. With this in mind, she prepared for a gradual shift, recognizing that Henry often completed his work at school. Although energetic and easily distracted, he was capable. Amy focused on creating an environment where he could learn to manage his restlessness and follow through on tasks.

Meanwhile, Jason committed to being a better role model by learning to control his temper. When he slipped, he made a point to apologize. He realized that part of his role as a father was to call out unacceptable behavior without yelling. This decision was his own—not prompted by Amy—though he heard her express how hard it was not to step in when he shouted at the boys. He saw that another part of his parenting job was not making it harder for her. Jason also reflected on what preteens need—role models they admire. He didn't want their only examples to be violent video game characters. He became more intentional about spending active time with his kids—playing catch or going on outings— and made sure not to neglect Sophie. He began learning guitar with her, bonding over music and building a connection beyond just his sons.

Brianna and Carter were dealing with older adolescents who seemed to want to push them away. Determining what constitutes appropriate parent–child time for adolescents on the brink of adulthood was tricky. They often heard that this was the stage for granting considerable independence and allowing peers to become central, but did this truly align with their parenting values? They invested a substantial amount of time in carefully considering this. Brianna knew she felt pulled to do everything for her vulnerable daughter to help her get back on track as an aspiring professional dancer. She also felt pushed away by Jada and wondered if this was because of her age and need to be treated as a grown-up. What are their teenagers' reality needs regarding parental involvement in their lives? Carter was always uncertain about how involved he should be as a stepdad. As he recalled just how long he'd been the central father figure for his two stepchildren, he chose to strengthen his connection with both Jada and Xavier.

Popular views about children's needs often don't align with credible research. For Brianna and Carter, it's valuable for them to know that while peers are more important than at earlier stages, and opportunities to experience more adult independence are also appropriate, adolescents continue to benefit from balanced, warm relationships with parents. Here's an example of a study involving over 15,000 teenagers.[5] It found that when parents are warm, communicate effectively, spend quality time with their kids, and have a strong relationship with them, those teens tend to grow up healthier and happier. As young adults, they are more likely to feel good about themselves, have less stress and depression, avoid drugs and alcohol, and feel more hopeful about the future. We explore this further in Chapter 12, examining the balance of connection in mature parenting.

A Job Description for a Parent Who's Working on Their Own Maturity

How would you write your "parent job description" in light of what you've been reading? By cultivating our own steadiness and differentiation of self, we better support each child's growth into a resilient, values-driven young person—equipped to navigate life's challenges and contribute positively to their relationships. In my previous writing, I said, "grown-up parents help grow-up children."[6] Children benefit enormously from our efforts to steady ourselves, to hold our value-based boundaries, and stay connected in supportive and not stifling ways. Our job description is essentially to be mature leaders who prepare children for adulthood. Whatever the age of our children, we aim to cultivate their progress to increase their capacity for their next stage of life. This is summarized well in this reminder from Dr. Kerr, emphasizing that the "appropriate structure of families is that parents are in charge. This involves reality-driven functioning for the child until the child matures sufficiently not to require it."[7] Put simply, we parents lead by supporting our children to the point where they no longer need our assistance. Yes, they need our love and interest throughout life, but our role is to let them go gradually. I acknowledge that this is no small task. It does call for real self-sacrifice—not in dramatic moments, but in the quiet, consistent effort to stay grounded, to lead with principle, and to love in a way that helps our children stand on their own.

For Reflection

Our Parent Job Description

See what you think of this job description. Is it one you're willing to sign up for? Remember that it's always slow and steady work in progress, and every small step brings growth for the whole family. None of us ever fully meets these ideals, but they give us something for which to aim.

Job Title: Parent (Lead Developer of Maturity and Resilience in the Next Generation)

Key responsibilities:

1. **Provide Leadership, Not Control:** Maintain a clear presence, leading with what is within your control to change. Stay grounded in your values and beliefs, even under pressure, without becoming reactive or authoritarian.

2. **Differentiate Self from the Child's Emotions:** Remain emotionally connected without becoming emotionally fused. Support your child's growth without rescuing, fixing, or taking over their responsibilities.

3. **Respond to Needs, Not Wants:** Make thoughtful decisions based on what fosters long-term maturity and resilience, not on momentary comfort or avoidance of distress—yours or your child's.

4. **Foster Responsibility and Independence:** Resist overfunctioning. Encourage age-appropriate responsibility by allowing natural consequences, supporting problem-solving, and stepping back when needed.

5. **Manage Self, Not Others:** Prioritize your own emotional regulation and growth. Stay curious about your own patterns and triggers, and take responsibility for leading yourself well.

6. **Create a Home Base of Security and Clarity:** Offer consistent structure, love without intensity, and a predictable environment where children can thrive without being overprotected or micromanaged.

7. **Avoid Triangle Detours:** Watch out for the urge to intervene and interfere with your partner's process of figuring out how to relate to your child. And take care not to avoid issues in your marriage by jointly overfocusing on the children.

Core competencies:

- Emotional steadiness under pressure.
- Self-reflection and personal growth.
- Ability to tolerate discomfort without overreacting.
- Respect for the child's individuality and pace of development.
- Healthy boundaries and relational clarity.
- Long-term vision for the child's development.

Reports to:

- Personal values, thoughtful principles, and a commitment to emotional maturity—not social pressure, comparison, or the child's short-term approval.
  - Those with faith positions will also recognize being accountable to a higher power and their faith values.

Success indicators:

- A child growing in self-regulation, problem-solving, and responsibility.
- A parent who is less reactive and more self-directed.
- A family culture marked by calm connection rather than emotional intensity.
- Less energy spent managing behavior and more invested in leading by example.

12

CONNECTION AND LOVE WITHOUT THE PRESSURE

Strong connections are built by not always being involved with our kids—what feels counterintuitive often turns out to be precisely what a child needs.

You may remember Rachel—the mother of Jessica, a teen who had been quietly battling depressive symptoms and engaging in self-harm. Rachel found herself grappling with a painful, persistent question: "How can my daughter be so depressed when we've invested so much love in her?" It's a painful paradox for many modern parents, raised to believe that unconditional love ensures emotional well-being. But when love is driven by worry and a child feels like a project to fix, it can unintentionally hinder their resilience. The instinct to offer more love in the face of distress is natural, yet if it becomes anxious or overbearing, it may do more harm than good. Still, pulling back or becoming emotionally distant is no better. True balance lies in steady, supportive love that encourages independence and growth. Balanced love—not worried love—helps children take risks, learn from mistakes, and develop inner strength. As explored through the parents in Part Two, the key is learning to love without pressure. To explore this, let's return to the three parents we've been following. Each of them is learning what it means to love their child with balance.

Balanced Love Is Connecting Without Worry

In our example families, the parent is working to manage their worry triggers—to notice the urge to fix, control, or rescue—instead staying present in a steady, non-smothering way. They're learning to turn down the dial on their anxiety, so they can genuinely connect with their child. With less intensity directed toward particular children, not only does that child get more space to grow, but all family members benefit from a less tense environment. There is now more space for every relationship to be nurtured and developed. It means reminding themselves of their parenting goals and grounding their actions in those intentions rather than in worry or urgency.

Let's start with Amy and Jason as they work to bring more balance to their parenting. Jason is beginning to loosen his grip on the fear that his sons will grow up disrespectful. Instead of defaulting to correction, he's learning to connect first—and the tone in the home is softening.

Amy still notices when Henry struggles to stay focused, but she's becoming more mindful not to fuel his fidgeting by hovering or over-monitoring. With less energy consumed by managing Henry's every move, she's finding more space to enjoy her other children, reconnect with Jason, and return to parts of herself that had been on hold.

As the emotional temperature in the household cools, Henry begins to sense the shift. He begins to take more ownership of calming himself, responding to his parents with greater steadiness and less reactivity. Sophie and Charlie, in turn, are benefiting from more balanced attention. The family is beginning to breathe together again.

Balanced Love Is Not Always Being Available

A significant shift for Amy is not always dropping everything to intervene if Henry is whining and saying he can't do or doesn't want to do something. She wants all her children to get used to having parents who are not always on duty to serve their needs. This will help Henry learn to tolerate not always being assisted. Consider how useful this will be for him at school, allowing him to manage himself without relying on teachers to direct him all the time. It's another parenting paradox that strong connections are built by not always being involved with our kids. Amy learned to say: "I hear you, Henry, but I can't come until I've finished sending this email to Grandma." Or "I'm looking at Sophie's artwork now, so I'm unavailable." Or "Dad and I are catching up on our days, which is important. So helping you out will have to wait."

This same principle was important for Natalia and Adrian as they supported their daughter, Elena. After prioritizing connecting with Elena when they get home from work and after the daycare pickup, each can say their version of "I'm only available for one game because I have other chores to do." Adrian could say, "That was fun to play pretend kitchen, Elena, you baked the best chocolate chip play-dough cookies! I need to go and help Mom in the kitchen now and hear all about her day."

Like the other parents, Brianna found herself needing to recalibrate her energy direction. She realized she had overinvested in her daughter at the expense of her marriage. She began to let both her teens see that she and Carter regularly prioritized time together, including a regular movie date night. This shift removed a significant amount of reactivity from the mother–daughter relationship, laying the groundwork for a more relaxed mother–daughter bond. It didn't mean that Jada lost connection with her mother, which would have triggered resentment toward her stepdad. Instead, it meant that all family relationships got more balanced, non-intense attention. There was increased space for each family member to be a separate self without feeling that they had to always be for the other. This is part of transitioning from a fused relationship to a differentiated one.

Balanced Love Means Connecting with Each Child Individually, Not Just as a Group

In the busyness of daily life, it's easy to skip making time for each chlid and replace it with group family time—trips to the park, weekend outings, and family vacations. These shared experiences are valuable for building connections and creating lasting memories. But when it comes to deepening the bond with each child, nothing is more powerful than intentional one-on-one time.

Growing up in a family of five siblings and having a grandparent living with us meant my family had plenty of extensive group interactions.

My parents prioritized great family holidays, picnics, trips to the beach, and attending sporting events. Often, our home was full of visiting neighborhood kids enjoying all the activities we had been gifted, such as table tennis, a pool table, and the pinnacle of fun, our swimming pool. This was a significant strength of my family culture—however, what was missing was time to connect with our parents one-on-one. I think that was partly behind my relishing my sick role at age eleven because of the unique time it gave me with my mother. We always stopped at a café and chose a favorite sweet treat before or after each medical appointment. While I cherish the vibrant, social nature of my upbringing, those quiet moments of closeness with my mother remain especially meaningful—a reminder that even in a crowd, personal connection matters deeply. I think each of my siblings would have benefited from more one-on-one time with both our parents.

I've heard of many families who set up family meetings to improve family connection and communication. I do think these can have a place in building family connection, especially in an era when family meal times have been replaced with eating separately in front of screens. I wonder if they often have a "change the children" agenda behind them. They can be used as strategies for enforcing rules and gaining compliance that are particularly targeted at one child. The anxious "child focus" can be hidden behind the group meeting, but the targeted child will undoubtedly pick up the negative focus and react to it. Any disciplinary issues are better addressed honestly in one-on-one conversations.

One-on-One Time and Sibling Rivalry

I know how challenging it can be for parents to allocate this one-on-one time. I also recognize the significant benefits for each child's flourishing. I recall a period of parenting young children when sibling rivalry was at its peak, with regular arguments creating a conflictual family atmosphere on most days. While it was helpful in practice not to over-adjudicate sibling fights about fairness and conveying that I knew each of the kids could find a way to cooperate, this was not what made a breakthrough. The positive change occurred when my husband and I decided to ensure that we each had one-on-one time with each child on the weekend.

Our activities were simple and not indulgent outings; they included things like a trip to the garden center or hardware store, followed by planting our purchases or working on a home project together. This individual connection time resulted in settled sibling interactions. It also built the foundations of a lasting friendship with each child that has carried all the way into their adult lives. We enjoy the times we get to hang out together. Prioritizing simple one-on-one time with each child transformed sibling dynamics in our home, fostering both harmony and enduring parent–child relationships.

Balanced Love Is Connecting to the Whole Child

Each of our example parents recognized that most of their connection with the child they were most anxious about was focused on the child's difficulties rather than their unique, developing character. A "worry focus" connects with a child around what the parent perceives as problems, or by narrowly focusing on their potential for success. What a difference it made when each parent shifted to becoming curious about their children. For example, dad Jason began noticing how his three kids liked to play—how their imaginations worked, what activities they loved to repeat, and which stories captured their interest. From these observations, he expanded his repertoire as a father, connecting with each child through a genuine interest in their unique personalities.

Jason could discuss different types of dinosaurs with Charlie and learn how to draw them effectively. Henry loved discussing soldiers and defenses and drew detailed diagrams for building forts. Jason asked about Henry's designs and his thoughts on how battles unfolded. At one time, Jason might have worried that Henry's fascination with war games meant he was becoming violent—but he came to understand that the opposite was true. Henry had a creative outlet for his interests and could pursue them with the support of a curious parent. This was deeply settling for Henry as he refined his knowledge and skills in defense strategies and construction. It wasn't his only interest, and as each year passed, he expanded into other topics, but what a difference it made to have his parents engage with him as a truly fascinating young human.

The same was true for Sophie, who benefited from her parents noticing her diverse interests and talents, not just approving of her good behavior. It's essential that Jason, Amy, and all of us as parents avoid turning our children's gifts into projects. Becoming overly invested in their success creates a pressure-cooker environment that ultimately hinders their development. Our interest stems from our job description to be a supportive presence for our kids rather than a driver of their achievements.

Balanced Love Is Relating to the Child's Capacities

Here's a challenging idea to consider. When we consistently engage with the immature side of someone, we unintentionally reinforce and cultivate that immaturity. So, what does it look like to relate to the emerging maturity in our kids in ways that help them to grow their capacities? One of the mottos I have taken from Bowen's brilliant theory is to "not do for another what they can learn to do for themselves."[1] Notice that it says what they can learn to do, not just what they can already do. When we relate to our child's learning edge, we can tolerate letting them struggle and make mistakes, and connect with them around how they solved their challenge and mastered something new.

Here are some examples of how parents can have connecting conversations that convey that they believe the child is always learning and growing new life skills. Natalia asks Elena, "How are you figuring out the best way to end your game? What are your best ideas for how to start up the game again tomorrow?" Adrian doesn't jump in to put on Elena's socks, but he comments that he sees she's practicing and admires that she is trying to do it on her own.

Carter notices that Xavier hasn't done a complete job of packing the dishwasher and wiping down the bench. Rather than criticize him, he asks, "What kind of score do you give yourself for the kitchen clean up tonight?" Does he think he's delivered his best effort? After Xavier's dismissive remarks, Carter says, "I know you are capable of a good job, and I really appreciate it when you bring your best to helping out."

Brianna is struggling to decide on an outfit for an upcoming family wedding. She is aware of Jada's growing interest in fabrics and design as a school subject area and as a potential after-school course. She says to Jada, "I respect what a great eye you have for fashion and color, and I could use your help to decide between these dresses I've found online." She asks Jada for her opinion about color matching and accessories. Brianna isn't speaking out of anxiety or trying to boost Jada's self-esteem—conversations like that tend to fall flat. Instead, she genuinely respects her daughter's capacity to think, advise, and contribute, and invites her help in a meaningful way.

Amy sees Henry delaying his homework and simply comments in a cheerful tone, "I wonder what special power you will be able to find today to deliver the work your teacher is expecting." Jason sees Sophie doing more than her share of helping out at dinner clean up and says, "Sophie, I wonder how you work out when you've done your share. I reckon you know when it's enough and you're free to do some relaxing." Amy notices Charlie getting frustrated as he tries to fit everything into his school bag. She doesn't rush in to do it for him but comments, "It looks like packing that bag is just like a tricky puzzle that you're so good at, working out where all the bits fit. I'll be interested to see how you figure it out." When Charlie gets even more frustrated and says he doesn't want to go to school today because he doesn't like the sport they're doing, Amy says, "That's a challenge you've managed before my love, how did you manage to find your strength to push through frustration last week when it was so hard?" And before going to another room to get ready for her day she remarks, "I'll be interested to see how you work it out today."

These examples aren't quick fixes for better outcomes—they reflect a mindset that sees children as developing life skills and strengths, and relates to them accordingly. This helps parents stay attuned to their child's growing maturity without interfering. A powerful way to connect with this maturing self is through curiosity—holding back our own thoughts and asking how they think, showing faith in their ability to reason things out.

Balanced Love Is Sharing Life Both Ways

When we stop overmanaging and start being genuinely interested, we can share ourselves more authentically. Children benefit from knowing their parents as a person, not just as a fixer or authority. Parents show interest by remembering what matters to their child—like a spelling test or school play—and also by sharing something from their day, whether it's a knitting project, a tough moment at work, or hope inspired by world events.

Loving relationships are built on mutual knowing, not one-way attention. Daily life offers chances to share ourselves in age-appropriate ways and stay curious about each child. Sharing family stories and history helps children feel part of something larger, showing them that their parents' lives aren't centered solely around them but part of a broader, meaningful family narrative. We explore this more in the next section.

Balanced Love Is Connecting and Having Realistic Limits

When most parenting advice focuses on helping children feel heard and attuned, it's especially easy to skew parental love toward showing nurture and diminish the need for limits. Hence, I think it is worth revisiting the unarguable evidence-based truth that children need both warm connection and clear limits to flourish, and they need them in equal measure.

I've mentioned previously the work of Laurence Steinberg, a prominent developmental psychologist, who has extensively researched the balance of warmth and limit setting in parenting.[2] He emphasizes that authoritative parenting—characterized by equal measures of high responsiveness and high demands—is most effective in promoting positive child development. "Authoritative parents are warm but firm. They encourage independence while maintaining limits and controls. This style is associated with the most positive outcomes across a wide range of measures."[3] Recent studies continue to support this approach, showing that authoritative parenting fosters emotional well-being, academic achievement, and social skills by providing a nurturing environment with clear expectations.[4]

Let's be clear—this approach isn't the same as authoritarian parenting, which emphasizes strict rules and high expectations, but with little warmth or emotional connection. An authoritarian parent might say things like, "Because I said so," without explaining the value basis of their request.

On the other end of the spectrum, permissive, or what some call over-connecting, parenting is very warm and affectionate, but lacks clear boundaries. These parents might avoid saying "no," want to be their child's best friend, or struggle to set consistent limits. This quote from Dr. Steinberg captures the balance of an authoritative stance:

> Authoritative parents combine warmth, sensitivity, and the setting of limits. In contrast, authoritarian parents are restrictive and punitive, and permissive parents are warm but lack control. The authoritative style strikes the best balance, fostering autonomy and self-regulation in children.[5]

I hope this helps you recover confidence in the value of parenting that isn't fearful of setting limits alongside a loving connection. The most effective path to achieving this balance is remembering the impact of the "I" stance versus a "You" posture. Acting on what we are willing to say yes to and no to, out of love for our child, provides a pathway to balanced love. When parenting from our values, we speak our "connecting no," not an "opposing no." We say our "No" is because we want our children to be best prepared to manage life and relationships.

Recovering the Word "No" in Our "I" Stance

Bowen's idea of working on ourselves and having an "I" position helps parents navigate how to achieve limit setting that doesn't break the spirit of a child or leave the parent feeling helpless and ineffective. Limit setting is expressed with love. Amy says to Charlie when he doesn't want to go to school, "I'm willing to give you a bit of extra time to get on track, even if we're a bit late, but I'm not willing to go along with skipping school today, and I won't write a false sick note for your teacher. I love you and want to be the best parent I can be. I want to give you every support to get all the good things out of school."

Adrian tells Elena, "I'm not going to promise treats anymore to get you to behave. That's not being a good parent and loving you well. I won't give you any extra playtime or toys tonight. I'll wait for you to get your jammies on, then we'll have one story, and then I'm going to help Mom clean up."

Brianna responds to Jada, who refuses to make another appointment with her psychologist. "I respect this is your decision, so I won't force you to go back. I realize I've been pressuring you too much about your treatment and that I'm not helping you make your journey of recovery your own. I'm willing to support your ideas about ways you see you can lift out of any unsafe, restricted eating."

Brianna defines herself to Jada with her truthful, loving commitment, "I'll keep working on my part to be the kind of parent who is honest with you, but not putting you under pressure. When I see any dangerous food restrictions, I'll call it out and ask how you're taking steps to a healthy path. And most importantly, I will keep working on being more of a friend to you, where our relationship is so much more than these mental health challenges."

Combining warmth with appropriate limit setting nurtures a child's emotional well-being and equips them with the skills necessary for success in various aspects of life. Do you see this picture of connection and love, free from pressure, starting with parents defining the kind of parent they aim to be?

Does Differentiation Downplay the Role of Feelings?

Let's revisit differentiation-based parenting and clarify some common misconceptions. Differentiation isn't about rugged individualism or self-interest. It balances individuality with empathy and mutual understanding. Through their connection with their parents, children learn to relate with warmth and respect. This approach means that parents stay true to their values—clear about what they'll say yes or no to—while showing genuine interest in knowing their child. The goal isn't to shape the child into the parent's ideal, but for the parent to offer their best self and build a meaningful relationship.

It's sometimes assumed that Bowen's idea of "differentiation" means staying emotionally distant or shutting down feelings. Mainly, critics[6] think it doesn't leave enough room for emotion. But I think that's a misunderstanding. True differentiation, where we elevate our relationship from fusion into one of growth, doesn't suppress emotional expression. Instead, it creates the internal and external space for more authentic, joyful, and affectionate interactions. By helping parents and children stay connected without becoming emotionally stuck or reactive, differentiation enhances the capacity for positive feelings, playful engagement, and meaningful closeness. Bowen sums this up by saying that "the concept of differentiation of self makes it possible to be connected to others without being consumed by them."[7]

Can you see that emotional maturity isn't about emotional detachment but maintaining one's sense of self while staying meaningfully connected? An accessible, practical resource on this topic is *True to You* by Dr. Kathleen Smith,[8] who writes:

> A person who is working on differentiation of self is giving their relationships a chance to be something different. The less focused we are on keeping others happy, the more we can be truly present in the lives of those we love.[9]

Differentiation is the ability to stay connected to others while maintaining self-direction and responsibility for our own thoughts, feelings, and actions. Strengthening this allows us to remain present and engaged— even in emotional moments—without reacting, withdrawing, or trying to fix others.

What Growth Looks Like When Parents Lead the Change

As we close Part Two on *differentiation-based parenting*, one clear theme emerges—meaningful family growth begins not by changing the child, but by the parent taking responsibility for what is within their control. Jason and Amy, Brianna and Carter, Natalia and Adrian all realized that their intense focus on helping or fixing their child left them depleted, uncertain, and reactive. Their love was never in question, but their direction needed realignment. Rather than continuing to try to manage their child's moods, behavior, or outcomes, each parent began doing the more lasting work—clarifying who they want to be as a parent. They took thoughtful "I" positions that defined their guiding values, and began leading with calm conviction rather than anxious reaction. They stopped overfunctioning and started relating to their child from a more anchored, less emotionally fused position. This internal shift created space for their children to take greater responsibility for themselves. As the parents grow clearer in their role, as steady guides rather than emotional rescuers or constant fixers, each child is growing more capable of regulating their emotions, managing challenges, and developing a grounded sense of self. Jason, Amy, Brianna, and Carter balanced their connections with their other children, ensuring they had one-on-one time with each of them.

This effort from each parent changed the tone in their homes, and it began to change their children. Once locked in power struggles, Henry is slowly learning to regulate himself, handle frustration, and re-engage with school without constant parental intervention. Jada is developing a stronger sense of self—more open emotionally, more grounded in her choices, and more resilient when things don't go as planned. Once prone to meltdowns at every limit, Elena now shows signs of delaying gratification, accepting her parents' "no," managing transitions, and solving small problems with growing confidence.

These changes didn't come overnight, nor are they complete. Each child still has moments of struggle, just as all developing humans do. But they are increasingly standing on their own emotional feet, not because their parents made everything easier, but because their parents stepped back from over-responsibility and began leading with steadiness and self-awareness. This is what differentiation-based parenting makes possible—the parent stops trying to change the child and starts becoming the calm, boundaried, connected presence their child can rely on. In that shift, the entire family system grows, less driven by anxiety, more shaped by purpose. And the children, sensing a new kind of safety and clarity, begin to grow too. That is the gift of the paradox—what feels counterintuitive often turns out to be precisely what a child needs.

For Reflection

Balanced Love Is Connecting Without Worry

1. When you connect with your child, do you notice moments where your love is blended with urgency, worry, or the desire to fix and change them? What do you see as the effect—for you and your child?

2. What helps you stay grounded in your role as a steady guide rather than becoming a rescuer or emotional manager? How might returning to your parenting values help you stay connected without pressure?

3. How might you begin to shift from a connection rooted in concern to one grounded in confidence in your child's growing capacities? What could that sound like in your daily conversations?

Balanced Love Is Not Always Being Available

1. Are there times when your emotional availability turns into over-availability? How might always being *on call* unintentionally communicate pressure or limit your child's coping capacity?

2. How comfortable are you allowing your child to feel disappointed or frustrated in your relationship—such as when you're unavailable or say no? How do you respond internally in those moments?

Balanced Love Is Connecting to the Individual Rather Than Group Time

1. Are your one-on-one moments with each child mostly about managing tasks or correcting behavior—or are there regular opportunities for lightness, curiosity, and shared enjoyment, free from expectation?

2. Are there ways you could shift from group-based connection to more intentional individual moments with each child? What small opportunities already exist in your week?

Balanced Love Is Connecting to the Whole Child

1. Do you tend to focus more on your child's problems or achievements, rather than showing interest in who they are becoming? How might this shape the kind of connection they experience with you?

2. What small observations or questions could help you tune into your child's unique personality, interests and character beyond their challenges or accomplishments?

Balanced Love Is Relating to the Child's Capacities

1. When your child struggles, is your first instinct to step in or to stay steady and allow them space to wrestle with the challenge? What would it look like to connect with them after they've had a chance to try on their own?

2. What does it mean to you to relate to your child's "learning edge"? How might that change the tone of your encouragement or support?

Balanced Love Is Sharing Life Both Ways

1. What messages are you giving your child about who you are— not just as their parent, but as a person? What do they know about your daily life, interests, or challenges?

2. How might sharing parts of your own story or day-to-day experiences help build connection without turning the focus solely on the child?

Balanced Love Is Connecting and Having Limits

1. Are there times you withhold limits or structure out of concern that it might damage your connection? How might a well-defined "I" position actually strengthen your relationship?

2. How clear are you about what you are and aren't willing to do as a parent? How do you express your limits with warmth and consistency?

PART THREE

PARENTING IS A BROADER FAMILY AND COMMUNITY AFFAIR

13

STRENGTHENING MARRIAGE AND PARENTING PARTNERSHIPS

The essence of keeping a marriage strong is continuing to get to know each other. This person-to-person journey never stops, as we and our spouse are continually experiencing different stages of our lives, including parenting children of various ages.

This final part emphasizes that parent–child relationships don't exist in a vacuum. Instead, they are interwoven with family dynamics, especially parenting partnerships and extended family. It also truly takes a village to raise a child, and regaining community connections is vital for sustaining parent–child support. Until now, we've focused primarily on the parent–child relationship. In some ways, this gives a misleading impression that we can work on this relationship in isolation, as if it stands alone. However, this is a relationship situated within a web of other significant relationships—within a marriage, an extended family, all the generations that came before, and within a community. It's a network of relationship systems, each influencing the other profoundly. In Part Three, we draw from a range of new family examples (all de-identified) to bring to life the issues of the broader context of the parent–child relationship.

Earlier, we explored how societal views have shaped the parent–child relationship; now we turn to more personal influences, starting with the parental relationship. While families take many forms, marriage—or the core parental bond—remains a key influence on children. Cultural differences shape caregiving—in many Asian, South Asian, and Latin

American families, care is shared across generations,[1] while Western cultures often isolate parents under greater pressure. For single parents, reflecting on the relationship from which your children came and how it was navigated can be helpful. Regardless of family structure, it's valuable to consider how the parental relationship impacts children, how children affect that relationship, and how our own parents' relationship shaped us.

The Arrival of Children and Marriage

It's easy to neglect working on a marriage when children arrive and demand so much of their parents' energy. Harvey and Brittany enjoyed the freedoms of the first three years of their marriage. They both had established careers and while feeling the pressure of their new mortgage, they could find enough surplus to travel and enjoy their shared love of the outdoors. Their work gave them time apart to experience their individuality, and their joint projects, such as setting up home and planning vacations, gave them a happy sense of partnership. Their love life was easy to sustain without much effort. While they experienced some tension about their occasional differences in desire and some niggles regarding how much contact to have with extended family, on the whole, life was pretty easy. That was until their first child, Camille, was born.

During pregnancy, both Harvey and Brittany shared a bond of anticipation as they welcomed a child into their family. They both imagined they'd be pretty good parents, determined to adjust aspects of how their parents had raised them. Then their daughter, Camille, entered their predictable life, and they found that many aspects of their life had turned upside down. Sleep was dramatically disrupted by frequent night waking and challenges to settle Camille after feeding. While both had parental leave for the first weeks of Camille's life, Brittany continued as a stay-at-home mother over the first year. She felt the loss of adult freedom and envied the escape to the adult world that Harvey maintained.

The marriage relationship no longer seemed fair and balanced. Harvey wasn't prepared for how much of his wife's energy needed to be invested in caring for an infant, and he began to be irritated at Brittany's lack of attention to him. Harvey found himself pursuing Brittany for sex in ways he hadn't previously done—anything to settle his sense of being ignored. Brittany resented the extra pursuit for intimacy and felt that Harvey didn't understand her exhaustion. Both tried not to show their emerging resentments toward each other, as they wanted this time in their family life to be filled with only the positive pictures of the happy family they had imagined. They believed their relationship was robust and that this early strain would soon pass.

Harvey and Brittany were fortunate to have a well-established support network of friends to meet up with, which helped reduce some of the intensity they were experiencing. They also had Brittany's parents and a sister living nearby, and could call on them for help. Yet, even with friends and family close by, they struggled to organize their lives to socialize or go out as a couple. Previously, they hadn't needed to have difficult conversations, and now that tensions were emerging in their relationship, they didn't have any template for raising them with each other. Like many couples going through this huge life transition, they didn't discuss their feelings and thoughts about what they were experiencing. Instead, they acted out their struggles, unaware of patterns of critical tone, pursuing and avoiding. Having a gorgeous baby girl to dote on did help provide some glue to their relationship, but vulnerabilities lay just below the surface of their marriage.

Divorce Rates and the Child-Rearing Years

The strain of raising children within a marriage is well documented. The US Census Bureau's report on the timing of marriages and divorces reveals that the median duration of marriages that ended in divorce was around eight years.[2] Consistently, reports from a range of countries describe the reality of a seven-year itch in marriage, with many marriages experiencing heightened risk of divorce around the seventh to eighth year.[3] Think about what these timings highlight. Not surprisingly, it relates to a period in family life when couples often navigate the arrival of children and the intense demands of early child-rearing. These early to mid-marriage years can frequently be among the most vulnerable, revealing how the pressures of building a family can test the strength of the marital bond.

So, how can a marriage be protected from such strain? The answer begins with awareness—recognizing that this phase is predictably challenging and that strain does not equal failure. Consider the benefits for couples who anticipate these pressures, openly communicate, and intentionally protect time for their relationship. This awareness helps to be better positioned to weather the turbulence. Yet, it's all too easy to neglect the signs of strain and let the children fill the breach that has quietly grown. What does it take to nurture the partnership amid the chaos of the early parenting years?

Not Letting Children Fill a Breach in a Marriage—Seeing Patterns of Avoidance and Triangles

When tension arises in a marriage, it's unconsciously common for couples to shift their focus to the children. Parenting can become a safe and consuming distraction from relational distance and unaddressed tension. Over time, the child or children may come to occupy the emotional space between partners, filling the gap where intimacy, communication, or connection once lived. Can you recognize the seeds of this in Harvey and Brittany's relationship? Both were experiencing challenges in the inevitable upset to the balance of their marriage after the arrival of their first child, Camille. The arrival of a child disrupted their former freedoms and created an uneven dynamic—Brittany stayed home and experienced a loss of adult identity. At the same time, Harvey continued his work routine, feeling increasingly excluded from his wife's involvement with their infant daughter. Brittany grew exhausted and emotionally depleted, while Harvey, feeling neglected, sought more physical intimacy, which only added to her sense of overwhelm. Both began to harbor unspoken resentments but avoided raising concerns, hoping their relationship was strong enough to weather this early turbulence.

Their second baby was born two years later—a beautiful boy named Ezra. While Harvey and Brittany were overjoyed to welcome him, the added demands of parenting two young children quickly intensified the existing cracks in their relationship. Sleep deprivation deepened, personal space vanished, and the small pockets of time they once managed to carve out for each other disappeared almost entirely. With Brittany now caring for two children under four, her exhaustion reached new levels.

Harvey tried to be more helpful at home but often felt clumsy and unacknowledged, adding to his frustration and emotional distance. He found himself investing more in his work, where the structure and affirmation from colleagues offered a sense of competence and value he no longer felt at home. Brittany found solace in feeling needed by two dependent little ones, which gave her a sense of purpose amid the fatigue. She also drew validation from her mother and sister, who reinforced the narrative that motherhood is relentless and that men are often unreliable when it comes to understanding its demands.

Both Harvey and Brittany were seeking external allies to steady them, but neither felt equipped to discuss the growing weight of their changing worlds directly with each other. Relationship triangles were predictably emerging to help steady the marriage. Finding allies can settle us without directly addressing our issues. In the same way, investing in children provides an easy triangle by detouring spouses away from their one-on-one connection to a focus on the easy third party of children.

When they did spend time together, Harvey and Brittany's conversations rarely touched on the emotional strain that each was carrying. Instead, they filled the space between them with the logistics of parenting—sleep routines, feeding schedules, nap transitions, Ezra's latest milestone, Camille's new favorite game, childcare drop-offs, preschool options, what to pack for lunch, what not to forget at the supermarket, whether Ezra's rash needed checking, how to handle Camille's tantrums, or whether screen time rules were being too relaxed. These topics provided a safe and seemingly collaborative layer to their communication—one that felt productive and loving, but also allowed them to avoid the more complex conversations about what it was like for each of them to feel lonely, changed, or misunderstood within their marriage. The children became the glue that kept their interactions constant and the barrier that kept them from reaching one another. Beneath their teamwork as co-parents, the emotional distance continued to widen.

Every couple experiences some version of this in the early years of parenting. If this dynamic continues unaddressed, the intimacy gap can quietly grow, putting the marriage at real risk. I have previously written about this, drawing from Bowen family systems theory.

> When we adults stop being direct with each other about our own concerns and insecurities, one of our children can unknowingly step into the connection gaps that have been left open for them. Children so easily fill a breach in their parents' marriage. The solution lies in one or both parents shifting their focus from their child to their own issues and responsibilities.[4]

The answer is to recognize the avoidance and detouring and start to make time to share what life is like for each spouse. Even small, consistent acts of sharing what life feels like for each of them can begin to repair the thread of intimacy that holds a marriage together.

Recovering Connection Through the "I" Position and Seeing the Family of Origin Pattern

Neither Brittany nor Harvey had great examples of their parents having open person-to-person conversations. In their families growing up, their fathers distanced themselves through work, and their mothers were invested in the children. Awkward disagreements were avoided. In Harvey's family, tensions spilled over into yelling and then avoidance, while Brittany's parents avoided all conflict and did whatever it took to keep the peace. They could see that, despite their goals to the contrary for their family life, they were replicating many of the patterns from their own family.

To recover their connection, they need to practice expressing themselves without blame or criticism. Rather than discussing the children, they could share what they find challenging and joyous about being a parent to each child. They could be curious about each other's experiences, get into each other's shoes, and ask what fatherhood and motherhood are like.

They are practicing their "I" positions. This is the foundation for building intimacy, helping each other truly know the other. Here are examples of how each spouse could express themselves, but please don't see this as a simple script to follow. Just start by thinking about what I miss the most in this transition. What is most challenging for me in adjusting to the changes in our lives? And start taking a risk to describe your own experience. It doesn't matter if the words get muddled—it just matters that you are not putting the other down but are committed to rebuilding the connection.

Brittany might say: "I'm feeling completely worn down lately, and sometimes I don't even know who I am outside of being a mom. I miss feeling like we're in this together."

"Sometimes when you reach out physically, I wish I could respond with more energy. I want us to be close, but right now I feel touched out and emotionally empty."

Instead of "You never have time for me anymore," Harvey might say: "I've been feeling more on the outside of your world lately, and I miss how connected we used to be. I'd love to find a way back to feeling close again."

"I'm trying to be more present and helpful, but I often feel unsure and like I'm doing it wrong. I really want to support you better, and it helps me when I hear what's working."

Brittany and Harvey can begin to bridge the growing distance between them, not by fixing each other but by showing up with honesty and care. It is never too late to recognize what we haven't addressed, how we've detoured and avoided, and how we've contributed to the gap in our relationship. Then, we can truly get to know our spouse again and let them get to know us.

The Problem with the *United Front* in Parenting

When I met Laurel for a parent coaching session, she was clear: the problem in their family wasn't her oppositional fifteen-year-old son Lyle— it was her husband, Malcolm. She expressed frustration that he wasn't backing her up on screen time boundaries and believed nothing would change unless they became a united front. Malcolm was driving Laurel crazy by agreeing to her parenting approach when she pressured him, but then failing to follow through on it. The tension between them was palpable. Laurel blamed Malcolm for not supporting her, while Malcolm avoided conflict by nodding along, all the while quietly disagreeing with her approach to their son. It was tearing their marriage apart. The more Laurel argued for a united front, the more frustrated she became. Her intentions came from a loving place and a belief in this widely accepted parenting mantra. Malcolm was equally adding to the impasse that was breaking them apart. He was quietly pulling away by going along passively and never honestly sharing his differing views.

This call from one spouse to adhere to the "united front" approach is incredibly common. I hear different versions of it from many couples, especially when their child is struggling or pushing limits. If only we could get on the same page, they think, we could finally sort out our child's problem. This kind of pressure can put extra strain on a marriage and will also draw a child into an alliance with the parent who is experienced as less strict. This was indeed the case with Laurel and Malcolm, as Lyle sensed his father's view that his mother was being pushy and unreasonable. Even though Malcolm isn't saying this, his body language gives it away. Laurel's frustration understandably gets increasingly elevated as she feels on the outside of this triangle.

Pushing for a united front is an attempt to change another person, often creating more reactivity and tension within the family. The alternative is to allow each parent to be different. To each find their way as a parent without being critiqued by the other. Children benefit from learning to relate to differences in parenting styles, which will serve them well with various teachers and later with different bosses. Children will be more adaptive when they don't require every adult in their life to be just like mom or dad.

Being Different Parents Without Undermining Each Other

Clearly, the goal is not to have parents undermine each other but to show respect for each other's differences. Both parents come from a value base of wanting to be loving parents who support their children's growth, but they approach things differently. Laurel can express her concern to her son, Lyle, about the impact of his screen time and convey what she will do to set some boundaries around internet access. She can relate to Malcolm that it's important to her to lead in this way and that she's only asking him to accept the shutdown of the family Wi-Fi at 9:00 p.m. each weekday night. Malcolm agrees to support this, but conveys that he will not have many talks with Lyle about screen time (as Laurel has been requesting) because he thinks this is making things worse and damaging the connection. He shares his perspective and doesn't tell Laurel she needs to change. When Lyle comes to his dad to complain about mom's limits, Malcolm doesn't take sides but is honest. He says:

> You know that your Mom feels very strongly about this issue and sees it as an essential part of caring for you. I don't see it as so central, but I won't undermine her. I see other issues as central, such as safety when you're on your bike after dark, and I know your Mom is more relaxed about that. She grew up in the country, where she drove tractors and motorbikes as a teenager, which is quite different from my city childhood.

Can you sense the impact of this approach? Parents respect each other but do not insist that they always think alike. They give each other the space to work out their parenting through trial and error as they go along without critical interference.

Letting the Other Parent Make Mistakes and Grow

Allowing my spouse space to grow as a dad was one of the most valuable lessons I learned from Bowen's theory when our children were still young. I had been the more involved parent when our children were small and had unknowingly started intervening when I watched my husband, David, grapple with his responses to two feisty little ones. It was instinctual for me to take over and smooth things out, drawing on my additional experience with day-to-day parenting. My early training through a family systems lens revealed that I was getting in the way of his learning and growth as a parent. I certainly made plenty of mistakes in the day-to-day interactions when I responded to a child and realized it wasn't constructive. I could adjust accordingly without being watched and corrected by the other parent. Children's reactions teach us what is and isn't helpful, and we don't want to rob the other parent of this learning journey.

I needed to keep working on this at every stage of parenting. I remember hearing my husband getting caught in a conflict cycle with one of our teenagers and holding myself back from stepping in as the peacemaker. If I had, I would have been treating him like another child I was managing, rather than an adult who, like me, was learning through trial and error how to parent adolescents. Later, he was able to reflect that raising his voice wasn't going to get him heard. It would only trigger a counter-response—something teens are exceptionally skilled at delivering.

Couples Being a Resource to Each Other

In the central triangle of parents and the child, there is so much sensitivity to each other that it's hard for parents to become helpful, objective resources. Any comment from one parent about how the other is parenting is typically met with defensiveness. And indeed, if the agenda behind the feedback is to change the other, it is unlikely to be heard as helpful. If we are in a blaming mode toward the other parent, it's best to keep our mouths shut and reflect on how we may be contributing to our partner's responses. Are we sidelining them? Or undermining them? Are we siding with our child about their faults?

However, it's also unhelpful to stay silent out of anxiety about others' negative responses. We can find ourselves going along with our partners' parenting while silently feeling critical. This will definitely find its way into the system. That's where a thoughtful "I" position comes in handy. We say what we've observed and our concern about it in terms of the effect on the child's growth and the impact on our parenting. For example: "I observed our daughter ramp up her defiance when you shouted at her. I know you want to take a stand when she's rude to you, but I observe her taking the moral high ground and looking down at you when she sees you're losing your cool. What do you notice happens?" Or "I'm committed to changing the way I was giving in to our son every time he protests, but when I heard you bribe him yesterday after I walked away, I felt set back in my efforts to be a better parent. What are your thoughts?"

Seasoned systems therapist Margaret Donley has laid out common triangle patterns between parents and their children.[5] She describes a common parenting partnership with a disengaged father who "automatically avoids the discomfort of managing himself with his wife, his child, or the relationship between them." On the other side is a wife who is both critical of her husband's lack of involvement and feels shut out of his life. "She longs for his involvement with the child, yet it is never good enough." Another version is the silently critical parent with an underlying resentment of the other parent's involvement with the child. Each tries to correct the problem they see in the other's parenting by becoming firmer or more lenient. They're acting out their criticisms and not finding a respectful way to discuss them. And a slightly different triangle is like a pretend united front, where it can look like an overly supportive marriage on the surface. Donley describes a parent who consistently supports their spouse's worries about their child and never dares to voice dissent. It can look like a peaceful marriage, but the lack of disagreement conceals differences beneath the surface.

Each of these triangle patterns, in their own way, serves to intensify the focus on the child as a vehicle for avoiding learning how to relate adult to adult. Each triangle pattern shifts the focus away from the adult relationship and onto the child—often to avoid difficult but valuable conversations between partners. The marriage is left vulnerable without fully appreciating the relationship gap and how the child has taken the focus.

My husband has been reading some drafts of this book and reflected to me, "I wish I could have been braver at giving feedback to you and being more open to hearing parenting feedback from you, out of love for our family." Hearing feedback, knowing it isn't imposed on us, and knowing that we have the space to think it through for ourselves is an example of lifting to a higher level of differentiation of self. I smile as I think about writing the book we would have benefited from in our child-rearing years. And yet, the work of differentiation—of growing ourselves up—is never really finished.

Parenting After Separation and the Challenges of Stepparenting

In reality, many marriages don't survive the strain of the parenting years. Divorce is common, particularly as people age. I suggest that if systems thinking were more widely understood, more people could recognize the familiar patterns that predictably lead to resentments and distance, and identify what they can address to prevent the breach from growing. They may be able to repair the relationship before too much damage and blame have been done.

US Census data tells the story of how widespread marital breakdown is. About one in three ever-married adults over the age of twenty has gone through a divorce. The numbers climb even higher with age. Among people in their late 50s and early 60s, close to 43 percent have experienced a divorce.[6] While census data doesn't specify de facto non-registered relationships, plenty of data indicates that cohabiting unions are more likely to dissolve than marriages. Specifically, most cohabiting relationships tend to end within five years.[7] And with second marriages, the stats tell a story of even more challenge, with estimates suggesting that as many as 60–65 percent of second marriages eventually end in divorce.[8] The reasons vary, but the emotional and logistical complexity of blending families, managing co-parenting with ex-partners, and healing from previous breakups all play a part.

These overall statistics underscore the need for a more comprehensive understanding of the stressors and strains on marriages, particularly for parents. They also convey clearly that for those parenting with separate households or blended families, you are not alone but in very good company. A differentiation-based parenting approach continues to apply after a marriage is over and when new blended families are formed. The work for each adult to represent what parenting after separation or in a blended family is like for them is central to navigating the complexities of this process. And it is indeed complex. A marriage has ended, but a continued co-parenting partnership continues.

Each parent needs to be able to work out and express to the other parent what they want to stay committed to, so as not to get their children caught in taking sides in their marital separation. It's not easy at all, but keeping a job description for raising steady and resilient children needs to stay at the forefront of a parent's mind, even when the separation process is painful and confusing. Even if only one parent works to maintain the integrity of their parenting values, this would contribute to a much better outcome for children. There's plenty of evidence that children can adjust to the disruption of their parents' marriage breakdown if their parents keep them out of their conflict. High levels of parental conflict after separation are linked to increased behavioral and emotional problems in children.[9]

I've been inspired by many parents thoughtfully navigating tense post-divorce situations. They've learned to step out of blaming and commit to working on their character as an example for their children. I recall one mother saying to me that she is committed to what she called "Operation Integrity," following a painful breakup where her husband had had an affair. She didn't let her resentment flow into badmouthing her ex to her children. It wasn't easy, but she reflected that her children would do best by staying connected to both parents and that they would gain plenty of lived experience to work out the strengths and flaws of each parent.

The most important principle for stepparenting is not to try to compete with the bond that your new spouse has with their children. To honor the long history behind it without needing to become important in the middle of those relationships. At the same time, the new relationship requires intentional and regular one-on-one time. If the children see that their relationship with their biological parent is given space, they can gradually get comfortable with their stepparent. It takes patience. Each adult needs to convey their experience to one another with honesty, but without hostility.

I recall the story of Carmen and Javier, who navigated marital tension that had become entangled in the dynamics with Carmen's children from a previous marriage. Carmen felt torn between her loyalties, and Javier believed she wasn't firm enough when her daughters excluded him or spoke to him disrespectfully. When they married a year earlier, Javier had entered a family where Carmen's two teenage daughters shared a strong, tightly knit bond with their mom. Eager to be included,

Javier jumped in—offering advice, joining routines, even stepping in to discipline when tensions flared. But the girls pushed back, hard. After a series of honest and difficult conversations, Javier began to shift his approach. He stopped trying to insert himself into every interaction and instead gave Carmen and her daughters the space to stay close to each other. He turned his attention to building quiet, respectful connections with each girl, starting small, with one-on-one moments with no agenda. He would drive to their friends' place and cook dinner together, and gradually, the girls began to include him more naturally, sensing that he wasn't trying to replace or reshape their bond with their mother.

Carmen made a deliberate effort to carve out regular time to talk together. Both opened up to hearing the other share how they were each experiencing the dynamics at home. Each could say how it impacted them and listen well to the other. Carmen told her daughters that she would prioritize time to talk to Javier each day for a short while. In the early months, she had just used the time when the girls visited their dad to get some marital connection time. She realized she needed to demonstrate her marriage commitment to her daughters without reducing her time with them. It wasn't smooth sailing—adolescence came with its whirlwind of emotions—but their ongoing work to manage and represent themselves to one another laid a protective foundation.

Relationship ruptures make it so hard to be our best selves. The marriage bond is full of intensity that starts so positively and can easily flip the other way when things fall apart. Working on bringing our best to each relationship without acting out our resentments is the best way to show love to our children through these challenging transitions.

Protecting the Couple Bond amid Parenting Pressures

Children are well served when their parents work on their relationship. It shows kids that the whole world doesn't revolve around them. It also shows them that they have parents committed to a mature relationship, which helps shape how they will approach relationships as adults. In navigating the pressures children place on any relationship, the work is to grow ourselves and not just be led by our children. The divorce rates for people in midlife are on the rise,[10] and the key reason given is "the empty nest syndrome," where couples reassess their relationship after children leave home. If we neglect working on our marriage and become overly tied to our kids and other distractions, we will discover that when our children leave home, we are left with a spouse who has become a stranger.

The essence of keeping a marriage strong is to continue to get to know each other. This person-to-person journey never stops, as we and our spouse are continually experiencing different stages of our lives, including parenting children of various ages. We want to know what it's like in each other's shoes—how is it being a dad of a two year old? A school-age child? A child who isn't sporty like you? What's it like being a mom to a child who loves to draw and create? How is it being married to a mom or dad of this many kids? What is it like right now, juggling work and kids? How are you managing the sandwiching of caring for your kids and having a father whose health is declining? And on we could go. We don't need to talk about our kids—we can share our experiences of parenting each child and the other adventures and stressors of our lives. This way, we cultivate a marriage that can withstand the many pressure points of parenting because each spouse feels deeply known and accepted by the other.

For Reflection

Navigating Challenges in Marriage and Parenting Partnerships

1. How open am I in my marriage to hearing the other's vantage point and perspective?

2. If I've shut down this communication, what have I replaced it with? Distance? Triangling by talking about others rather than a person-to-person conversation?

3. Are there issues where I hold too much reactive certainty? How does this prevent me from being open to learning about my spouse's different perspectives?

4. Can I revise the idea of a "united front" in parenting—to accept differences but not undermine each other?

5. Has focusing on others (third parties—such as our children, friends, extended family, and work) replaced the effort to get to know my spouse?

6. How can I give my spouse the space and respect needed to grow as a parent through trial and error?

7. If distance has crept in, what are some non-intense ways I can open up curiosity again in this relationship?

And a Quote from Dr. Murray Bowen

In broad terms, a person-to-person relationship is one in which two people can relate personally to each other about each other, without talking about others (triangling), and without talking about impersonal things.[11]

BEYOND THE ISOLATED NEST

PARENTING WITH A WIDER FAMILY LENS

Reminding ourselves that we belong to a broader family network might ease the pressure-cooker isolation of modern parenting and give our children a sense of being part of something greater than their current self-absorbed space.

My maternal grandparents lived around the corner for the first seven years of my life. At the time, I didn't realize what a gift this was for us children and our parents. My grandfather lived with us from when I was eight to twelve years old. He died in his bed at night, allowing me to kiss his forehead and say goodbye. It wasn't until I found myself raising my own kids on the opposite side of the globe, far from any extended family, that I fully understood the difference it makes to have extended family in our lives. Raising children in a single-generation, nuclear family—especially with limited extended support—can be a significant challenge. Fortunately, my grandparents provided a steady and comforting presence throughout my childhood. With five children under eight, my mother had her hands full, and they often helped share the load. I remember walking over to their house, simply spending time there, absorbing the pace and feel of older people's lives.

I gazed on the family heirlooms, imagining the glass-cabinet figurines coming to life and whisking me away on some adventure. A portrait of a girl and her dog—painted by great-aunt Maud and framed in a beautifully carved mahogany border made by a great-uncle—hung over the fireplace, and I'd get lost in its quiet world. When granny and papa returned from overseas cruises, we children lapped up stories of other lands and relished the exotic cultural souvenirs. My granny was a brilliant violinist who had visited a prison to play music for inmates in her earlier years. I aspired to learn to play like her, even though I never developed the self-discipline to put in the necessary practice. I didn't get to meet my paternal grandfather, who died young, and our nana passed away when we were still little. Still, I have snapshots of her home and garden in my memory bank—the emerald green garage door stands out in my mind.

There's a deep richness in being connected to other generations while growing up. Through those relationships, we come to understand aging, death, and mourning not as abstract concepts, but as integral parts of a shared human experience. And yet, so many children grow up without that grounding—whether due to lifestyle mobility or distancing, when generational tensions arise. It's worth pausing to ask, how can we reconnect with the broader stories of our families? Even if the relationships are sometimes challenging? And yes, I will discuss some relational challenges between parents and grandparents in more detail. The big question is, how can we remind ourselves that we belong to something bigger than the here and now? In doing so, we may ease the pressure-cooker isolation of modern parenting and offer our children a sense of connection beyond their self-absorbed world. We might discover that tending to our relationships with our families of origin can help reduce the intensity in our relationship with our children.

The Loss and Recovery of Generational and Kin-Based Child-Rearing

Today's parents are reporting high levels of loneliness. In a recent US Surgeon General report, 65 percent of parents reported feeling lonely.[1] Of course, many factors are at play, such as the impact of remote work and the loss of casual interactions. Still, it raises the question of the loss of extended family and kin networks for many, and how stressful parenting young children can be without such support to share the load. At the same time, data indicates a trend toward multigenerational households and shared childcare as cost-of-living pressures prompt both parents to return to work in the early childhood years. This includes reports from realtors that more buyers are seeking homes that accommodate extended family members.[2] It's fascinating to see the statistics showing how many households are relying on unpaid childcare. A report from the Federal Reserve's Economic Well-Being of US Households, released in 2025, reveals that for adults with children under the age of thirteen, 46 percent relied on unpaid childcare, including that provided by grandparents and other relatives.[3] These trends are based on data from the United States and other Western cultures, and it's important to acknowledge the variations in Asian, South Asian, and Latin American cultures, where caregiving is typically a multigenerational responsibility.[4]

The model of care in small nuclear family households is a unique phenomenon of the industrial world. An article in the *New York Times* by Darby Saxbe, from the University of Southern California, with a standout title "Parents Should Ignore Their Children More Often," caught my attention.[5] She clarifies that throughout most of history, families were large, and kids spent their time in mixed-age groups with relatives and community members, without constant adult supervision. In hunter-gatherer societies, children regularly spent time around their parents, extended family, and tribal kin, joining in daily activities such as foraging. Notice the two standout changes to today's world. Firstly, the communal care of children, and secondly, the lack of intense focus on children who learned to deal with boredom and participate in community economic and relational activities. I had heard Dr. Saxbe present at a conference on her extensive research on parenting, with a particular focus on fathers' experiences.[6] It's refreshing to hear of research that isn't pushing today's popular, intensive, child-focused parenting. It can help us all rethink how we raise the next generation with a less anxious focus and broader engagement with kinship supports.

The Value of Knowing Our Grandparents, Great-Grandparents, and Beyond

Beyond having vital extra support, what benefit is there in raising children who are connected to previous generations? Pause for a moment and think about your interactions with grandparents, uncles, aunts, and great uncles and aunts. How much did you hear stories about your ancestors, and hear about stories of courage, failure, and challenge? I remember my early involvement with my grandparents and my fascination with piecing together my family history. At a very young age, I learned that my grandmother descended from convicts transported for life from England on the First Fleet to Sydney, Australia. Rather than a story of shame, this was a badge of honor for me as I proudly, during "show and tell," told my grade-four class of the ships they arrived on, how they met and married, and their success after being granted free settler status. The seeds of interest in my multigenerational family were planted early.

There's compelling research on the benefits of children knowing about previous generations. Using a set of questions about family history, studies have shown that children who knew more about their family history tended to feel better about themselves, have lower levels of anxiety, and have stronger family relationships.[7] Another study reveals that adolescents' family history knowledge correlates with their emotional well-being and identity development.[8] This suggests that familiarity with family history narratives positively impacts children's emotional health. I've been especially drawn to this research group's study of children's trauma recovery, including the results from children between ten and twelve who lived through the period of the 9/11 attacks on New York City. It's a small study of sixty-five families that commenced with the family history questionnaire just before the traumatic attacks in 2001, and it followed up these children for the next two years. Children in families with more coherent, emotionally expressive storytelling about family history and previous family challenges showed significantly better resilience markers in the aftermath of 9/11.[9] A small research study like this provides more hunches than definitive conclusions, but it certainly gets us thinking.

One question I have about all this research on family history and well-being is about something researchers call directionality—in other words, which way the influence flows. Does knowing our family history actually help improve well-being? Or is it that families with strong, healthy relationships—especially between parents and grandparents—are more likely to share stories and pass down history in the first place? My hunch is that it starts with the latter, having parents who have managed to stay positively connected with previous generations, so the family history stories have become part of the extended family narratives. It turns out that in some such studies, there is a correlation between families who share meals and families who share stories. And hasn't sharing meal times become increasingly challenging when, at the end of the day, parents are desperate to switch off? Perhaps one of the solutions is to find ways to connect more with extended family—to share meals and activities, and to bring out the old hard-copy photo albums (remember them?) and bring to life those who have gone before.

Dr. Bowen had much to say about the value of knowing and connecting with our family histories. He taught that "If you can get a person-to-person relationship with each living person in your extended family, it will help you *grow up* more than anything else you can do in life."[10] This can sound daunting, especially when tensions so easily seep into our broader family relationships.

The Challenges of Cross-Generational Relationships

When I met Ashley, she was juggling raising three young children who all exhibited some symptoms of anxiety. I asked who her key supporters were, and she said that her husband, Ryan, is great at helping out on weekends, but is involved in his own business, which consumes his time and energy during the week. I asked about extended family and learned that Ashley had not been in contact with her mother, Lisa, or her father, William, for over a year. Previously, they had been a regular presence in the family. The story behind this proved to be complicated, involving other family members.

Ashley's younger sister, Stephanie, and her husband, Justin, had had a huge falling out with her parents over a financial matter. Lawyers were involved, and the ruptures had rippled through the family network, drawing people into taking sides. Ashley had always been extremely close to her sister and heard regular phone updates on how badly she believed their parents had treated her. Stephanie conveyed how important it was to her that her sister backed her up and did not continue a relationship with their parents. Ashley had drifted into this agreement, and after a year had gone by, she mentioned to her sister that their mother had asked to visit her kids for the holidays. She reported that Stephanie became hysterical and spoke about how dependent she was on Ashley's support. Stephanie was on antidepressants and seeing a therapist. Ashley truly felt trapped, feeling that she couldn't risk adding to her sister's emotional distress. Meanwhile, she realized that her children had lost connection with their grandparents and had been told an untrue story that their nan and grandad were not very well and were unable to see them. It left her children confused and Ashley without the valuable support she needed.

This isn't an unusual example of how easily discord can spread through families and get stuck. The side-taking creates a pattern of triangles, where insiders stop relating to outsiders. Ashley's parents had her brother on their side, which meant her kids were also disconnected from that family and their cousins. It wasn't a quick resolution, but Ashley did find her clarity and courage to define herself to her sister. She conveyed that she loves her sister and would not stop supporting her, but at the same time, she wanted to give her children their grandparents back. There was strong pushback from Stephanie, who felt betrayed and stopped phoning or taking calls from Ashley for a few weeks. Ashley kept in contact with occasional newsy texts that maintained the same old loving emojis. She was clear with her parents that she wasn't going to talk about the upset that belonged between them and her sister and her husband. She conveyed how much she missed them and that her children did as well. Ashley was also aware of similar ruptures in her generation's past that had gone into an emotional freezer, never to thaw. She didn't want to pass on this pattern to her children's generation.

While Ashley's story may be more severe than typical cross-generational relationship tensions, it's easy to avoid addressing the inevitable upsets that occur. So often, people resort to distance, and visits with grandparents and other relatives become dutiful and not nourishing. The steps to cultivating mutually supportive connections with extended family are similar to all the principles conveyed about parent–child relationships—not to try to change or blame another, but rather to work on not being reactive and getting clear about what's important to us. We develop our "I" positions and convey them calmly—always making space to listen to the other. We can say we think differently, but that doesn't stop the affection felt for the other. And as Ashley did, we stay our course even when pushbacks happen.

For relationships to be repaired, patient, continued, non-intense contact is required. We don't have to relive and try to process every past upset, as that will only fuel the intensity. Staying in contact and avoiding taking sides are the key ingredients to sustainable connections. Consider the impact on the next generation to see their parents relate maturely to their grandparents.

The Pain of Family Cutoffs

Ashley's and her sister Stephanie's break in contact with their parents is an example of estrangement, or what Bowen theory calls a cutoff. Sadly, these generational cutoffs seem to be on the rise, reflecting another symptom of the increasingly anxious times in which we live. More and more, we hear of adult children divorcing their parents. Grandparents are being told that they are no longer wanted around their grandchildren. I have read and listened with interest to Karl Pillemer, professor of human development at Cornell University, speak about his research on family estrangement and reconciliation,[11] which reports that around 27 percent of American adults are currently estranged from at least one family member—parent, child, sibling, or other relative.[12]

While estrangements are less common in more traditional cultures, generational tensions are increasingly reported. In East Asian cultures, the relationship between mothers-in-law and daughters-in-law is often characterized by tension and power struggles.[13] I have valued the work of family systems therapist Peggy Chan in Hong Kong, who has written and presented on Bowen theory applied across cultures. She makes a strong case that, despite cultural differences, the processes by which humans manage relational tension appear to be biologically embedded and universal.[14]

According to the Cornell Family Reconciliation Project, there is a long list of causes of family estrangement, including emotional abuse, toxic family dynamics, value conflicts—such as over religion, politics, or identity— parental divorce, mental illness or substance abuse, and interference from in-laws or extended family. I hear more and more young adults describe one of their parents as *toxic*, which justifies a cutoff. Concerningly, many have been given this label by a professional counselor, leaving them with the view that their parent is to blame, they will never change, and their life will be better without contact. This is an individual, not a family systems lens, and can rob people of the ability to navigate upsets and develop resilience and compassion along the way. Remember that a family systems lens views us all as affecting each other, rather than just one person causing all the problems. Additionally, the cutoff is not really about the content of a disagreement, but rather about our capacity to manage our reactions to each other—something we can all work to improve over time.

I've witnessed many people shifting from *writing off* a parent and grandparent to learning to see them as fellow human beings, *muddling* their way along with the patterns of previous generations shaping their reactions. Terence is a dad of school-age kids who went along with his wife's view that his mother, Latoya, was a toxic influence on their kids. Yes, his mother had overstepped their parenting requests at times, and she did behave in dramatic ways when she felt her son was ignoring her. Terence didn't know how to appease his mother and his wife, and ended up passively allowing a cutoff to ensue.

He started reconnecting with his mother one-on-one, explaining to his wife, Kiara, that he wasn't asking her to be part of this. He put some effort into making more sense of his mom's family upbringing, seeing her anxious relationship with her parents. He saw how much he had contributed to her feeling too important to him, allowing her to be preferential to him above Kiara. For Terence, this had consistently reinforced his sense of specialness. This helped him see how put out Kiara was when he so easily got drawn into his mother's complaints about being ignored. Gradually, he forged a more adult-to-adult relationship with his mom and began to bring the grandchildren on visits. It wouldn't be a quick fix, but Terence ensured it would not become another estrangement statistic.

As Terence did, can we learn to see our parents as human beings, rather than give them fixed negative labels? Bowen spoke of the benefits of this effort, writing:

> More knowledge of one's distant families of origin can help one become aware that there are no angels or devils in a family; they were human beings, each with his own strengths and weaknesses,

each reacting predictably to the emotional issue of the moment, and each doing the best he could with his life course.[15]

At the same time, it is up to each person to weigh the advantages and disadvantages of breaking away from a family member. Indeed, there are instances when a cutoff is a way of taking a mature stand in response to the devastating impact of abuse from a family member. Sometimes, a period of distance is beneficial in providing respite and regrouping time, allowing for better preparation to re-engage. Dr. Michael Kerr speaks to this weighing up of the pros and cons of cutting off, explaining that:

> The principal advantage is that it can provide some peace from difficult and painful interactions with one's family—the principal disadvantage is that it intensifies future relationships and the problems associated with an even more anxiety-driven fusion.[16]

It's worth keeping in mind that any relationship rupture we walk away from stays with us in our sensitivities in future relationships, including how we relate to our spouse and children. Ashley and Terence's efforts in bridging their cutoff have grown their relational wisdom. They have strengthened their emotional muscles to avoid being drawn into blaming and avoiding, and to be less easily thrown off course when a family member disagrees with their stance. Consider how beneficial this will be for their leadership as parents. And consider the impact of cutting off the next generation, expressed well by Bowen theory leader and therapist Dr. Anne McKnight:

> When a child grows up without knowing grandparents, aunts, uncles, or extended family, not only are the relationships not available, but the child observes and internalizes that tension is best handled with distance, superficial contact, or cutoff.[17]

Children Can Grow Through Every Family Tie—Even the Tough Ones

You may be surprised to hear that keeping regular contact with relatives you find challenging can still benefit your children. In particular, it diffuses some of the emotional intensity between you and your kids, as your attention gets spread across other relationships. Paradoxically, navigating stressful extended family dynamics can ease the pressure on your relationship with your children. This gives them a bit more space—and a chance to grow their own resourcefulness. It also offers children a beneficial vantage point for seeing what real-life relationships can be like. Being exposed to these dynamics safely and in a manageable way provides children with invaluable lessons. In watching their parents, they can learn how to set boundaries, extend empathy without losing themselves, and tolerate discomfort without running from it. These are essential life skills—not just for family, but also for friendships, school, work, and eventually their own adult relationships. It's not about exposing children to chaos—it's about letting them witness what it means to stay connected even when it's difficult.

Adopting Kin When Family Isn't Around

In some instances where extended family is just not available or able to be a resource, it shouldn't leave parents trying to go it alone. Children will benefit considerably from an intergenerational community, particularly when paired with select older adults who genuinely want the best for them and have their interests at heart. Firstly, if direct grandparents are not a resource, it's worth looking for more distant relatives who share a family history and can be helpful in the child's life. I recall reading about a small experiment that a family systems psychiatrist did working with a group home of teenage girls who were removed from their parents. The effort to reconnect them through letters and visits resulted in more settled and reduced risky acting-out behaviors. There was one exception. A teen for whom any efforts to connect with a parent resulted in increased disruption. Then, the case workers conducted some ancestry research and found an aunt who was interested in being involved in this young woman's life. What a difference it made to her life functioning![18]

For adopted children, connections to the stories of both their birth and adoptive families can be equally meaningful in shaping a sense of belonging within a rich intergenerational narrative. The adoptive family is the child's primary psychological family, which passes on many generational patterns and sensitivities. Every family situation has its unique nuances that require careful consideration and attention. Still, wherever parents can facilitate their children's involvement and knowledge of history, they can be sure that they are enhancing their sense of belonging in the world. Helping children experience a sense of connection beyond their immediate family—through extended relatives, cultural heritage, and caring older community members—fosters a more profound understanding that they are part of something larger than themselves.

A Word to Today's Grandparents— Valued, but Not at the Helm

I now have the great joy and privilege of being a grandparent. The radiant smiles on my grandchildren's faces when they see me fill my heart with profound delight. I will never forget the wonder I felt when I held my first grandchild in my arms, looking down at him and thinking to myself, "How amazing that my baby I carried in my womb, gave birth to, and raised to adulthood, has had her own baby!" Yet, grandparenting is not all straightforward and has some critical challenges to navigate. Just as parenting requires a shift in focus from the child to managing ourselves, so too does grandparenting.

We need to think through our job description and not just jump in to respond to our grandchildren's every whim or protest. Our role is now about supporting our children and their spouses in raising their children. As a parent, I made "in-the-moment" decisions for my children. What they ate, when they slept, how to respond to defiance, and what TV they could watch. The trap for me as a grandparent is not making the vital adjustment to recognizing that my grown-up children and their spouses are now in the driver's seat. I can jump in without thinking and give a sweet treat just before bedtime without respecting that it's the parents whose nighttime sleep will be disrupted by a child's sugar high. All of my instincts are to respond to the child without pausing and asking the parent how they want to handle the situation. Our relationship with our adult children and their partners must take precedence over our relationship with our grandchildren. We must be careful not to skip over a generation.

A grandparent recently shared concerns about how much time their grandchildren spend on digital devices. They were listening to the public discourse about the harms of children's screen time and felt compelled to intervene for the good of their grandchildren. While they might serve as a resource by sparking curious conversations with parents about their thoughts on screen use, I believe the problem arises when we become so focused on addressing one issue that we overlook the broader picture of the relationship. There is a significant risk to the relationship in overstepping and speaking critically about the next generation's parenting approach. We can add significantly to our grandchildren's development by fostering a loving and respectful relationship with their parents, our adult child, and their spouse. From this foundation of mutual respect and trust, we can engage in open, two-way conversations about our grandchildren's well-being, sharing insights into how parenting and the world around us have changed from one generation to the next. But it's worth remembering that words alone don't provide support and perspective—it's achieved by coming alongside each other.

Yes, Tensions Happen—and That's Part of the Journey

Tensions will inevitably occur between the generations, and this doesn't need to cause panic or a cutoff. The key is how we respond to these tensions rather than trying to avoid them. For grandparents, we need to ask questions rather than give uninvited advice. "I'm keen to hear how you're approaching that with the children and how you'd like me to support you?" Our questions need to be honest. That means we want to put ourselves in the shoes of our adult children on their parenting journey, without judgment. We don't use questions as a guise for giving our opinions. Building trust in the grandparent and parent relationship sets the stage for being a valuable resource, where our children start to seek our input. My motto is not to give advice, even if it's asked for, before asking what advice the person is giving themselves. It helps keep me from slipping into my default mode of over-helping. I'm far from perfect at it, but it's a principle that keeps me grounded.

Many ruptures between generations involve the in-law relationship. If we primarily communicate with our adult children without honoring the authority of their spouse, we are destined to trigger upset. This is a difficult adjustment to make when our children get married and have their own children. However, we can be such a valuable resource if we know how to detriangle and not leave the son or daughter-in-law in an exclusion zone, as we relate to our birth children. It comes down to the simple things, such as what we say on a phone call with our adult child: "We'd love to come and visit on the weekend. Can you chat with X and let us know if that works for both of you?"

Giving Your Parents Feedback

You've probably heard the saying that "big problems start as small problems ignored." I do like the more poetic way this proverb is often expressed—"small leaks sink great ships."[19] However awkward it can feel to raise a sensitive issue with our parents, it's so important to find a way to do it before too much time has lapsed. To convey that you know your parent means well, and raising this issue is uncomfortable, but you don't want small things to mount up and get in the way of a special bond. Remember to communicate from the "I," not at the "You." For example:

> I am working to not give in to our child, and it makes it extra hard for me when you are quick to give him what he wants in the moment. Could you please consider this and support me in this while you're with the grandkids?

Or

> I understand that you did parenting differently in your day, but I find it hard when you jump in to correct me. I'm doing my best to find the best way to manage a two year old with a strong personality. It helps our relationship when I feel you're giving me space to find my way as a parent.

Or

> I know it isn't intentional, but I need to give you feedback on the impact on my husband when you assume you are welcome to visit without making room for his input.

If your parent is reactive to your efforts, see that as predictable and don't give up. Growth in any relationship requires staying on course, representing ourselves calmly, and giving the other person time to adjust.

Remember to work on the back-and-forth of the relationship, not just one-way communication. Take an interest in your parents' experiences of raising children—their challenges, their joys, and what shaped their journey. Also, ask about their hopes for their role as grandparents. Asking curious and thoughtful questions can lead to new awareness on both sides of the conversation, fostering greater self-understanding and strengthening the bond between generations.

Recovering Intergenerational Bonds

I hope you're reflecting on the value of cultivating bonds with the broader family, particularly with parents transitioning to becoming grandparents. It isn't easy to adapt to a new phase between the generations. It requires responding thoughtfully to inevitable tensions. Still, the rewards are great for all three generations if we commit to working on these relationships. It brings much-needed support for parents in sharing childcare demands. It allows marriages to get some attention when grandparents can enable date nights. For our children, we provide a broader web of relationships to enhance their capacities to relate to others. For grandparents, there is a sense of purpose in old age in being a resource to our children and their children. In fact, there is a plethora of research on the health and well-being benefits of interacting regularly for both children and grandchildren, including lower depression rates in both groups.[20]

Parents can cultivate their resilience in many ways by connecting across previous generations and with extended family. As I've previously written, understanding the generational patterns our parents inherited helps us move beyond blame and toward a deeper insight.[21] We don't need to idealize them, but seeing their context fosters our maturity—we stop taking things personally and can begin to see family as a resource, not a burden. By widening our lens beyond the isolated nest, we not only share the load of parenting, but we also rediscover the strength, wisdom, and resilience that flows through the broader family network.

For Reflection

Thinking About Your Own Upbringing

1. What role did extended family play in your own childhood, and how might that still influence how you parent today?

2. What patterns in how your family related—such as managing conflict, closeness, or distance—can you now see repeating in your own generation?

3. What stories about earlier generations have been passed down in your family? What are the gaps in your children's knowledge about past generations?

Looking at Current Extended Family Relationships

1. Are there extended family members with whom you've lost contact? What led to that, and what has been the long-term impact?

2. When tension arises in your extended family, do you find yourself stuck in the middle or taking sides? How do you usually handle this?

3. How do you respond when family members disagree with your parenting or choices? Do you tend to avoid, react, or stay steady?

Taking Small Steps to Stay Connected

1. Is there one extended family relationship you'd like to show up in with more calm and clarity, even if there's been distance or tension?

2. How could you involve extended family in your children's lives in ways that expand their experiences of connection and difference?

3. If relatives aren't available, are there trusted older adults you could include in your child's life as a steady presence?

Reflections for Grandparents

1. Am I supporting my adult children in their parenting, or unintentionally undermining their authority?

2. Do I pause to ask the parents how they want to handle a situation, or act based on my own instincts?

3. How can I build trust and open communication with both my child and their partner?

4. What do I prioritize? Connecting with my grandchildren or nurturing a respectful relationship with their parents?

EMBRACING THE VILLAGE

HOW FAMILIES THRIVE IN COMMUNITY

Both children and parents grow stronger when surrounded by consistent relationships—not just support but a shared sense of belonging.

We all know, deep down, that families aren't meant to go it alone. Children grow best when wrapped in the steady fabric of connection, and parents breathe a little easier when the weight of raising kids is shared. The well-worn proverb "it takes a village to raise a child" captures this truth. Although often quoted today, its roots are deep—originating in African cultures and brought into Western consciousness. While most parents instinctively agree with the sentiment, today's lived reality often looks quite different. Community trust is threadbare. Inner cities, once humming with neighborhood life, have become fragmented. Local schools, clubs, and faith groups that used to be safety nets now struggle to connect with families overwhelmed by time pressures, disconnection, and the mental toll of modern parenting. And trust in institutions has been shaken, particularly after widespread revelations of abuse in places once assumed to be safe. But rebuilding these networks isn't about nostalgia. It's essential—because today's intensity in parenting and children's growing emotional challenges tell us that families were never meant to carry this alone.

As a parent reading this, perhaps you've felt the longing—for familiar faces on your street, for a playgroup where your child lights up in the company of others, or for collective routines that aren't formal services, but natural rhythms of support. These everyday connections may seem small, but they matter. When families are part of a broader care circle, both children and parents benefit from the steady rhythm of shared life. In a world that often feels hurried, isolated, and transactional, the question becomes: How can we begin to rebuild the circles of support our families so deeply need?

The Modern World's Erosion of Community

A 2025 article for *The Atlantic*, by respected journalist and author David Brooks, caught my attention. I value his reflections on society and relationships as exemplified in his book, *How to Know a Person*.[1] In his article, Brooks reflects on how modern society's emphasis on personal autonomy and reason—an inheritance of the Enlightenment—has eroded shared moral frameworks. He argues that individuals increasingly make decisions based on personal preference rather than communal responsibility without a common ethical foundation. This moral fragmentation, Brooks suggests, has profound political consequences, where society supports leaders who act from self-interest and power rather than from a sense of ethical obligation to the public good.

Even cultural groups with a strong collectivist heritage are experiencing increased loneliness in today's urbanized world.[2] Yet, humans are wired for community—we thrive in it and wither without it. To move beyond just getting by, we must rebuild the supportive village that helps everyone flourish. Parenting can be stressful, but it becomes a little more bearable when surrounded by people who have our backs. It's about ensuring our children get the care they need while also looking after our well-being along the way.

Natural Versus Professional Communities

Many parents I meet are deeply committed to enriching their children's lives, and often invest heavily in extracurricular activities to do so. Week by week, kids are dropped off at music lessons, tutoring, swim classes, therapy sessions, and developmental appointments. These experiences can be valuable. They can offer structure, skill building, and—let's be honest—some breathing room for parents. But something is missing. These programmed activities rarely create lasting connections. Parents often don't speak to each other in waiting rooms or at pick-up. Children move from one structured environment to another, without ever experiencing the organic, relational web a natural community provides. These services are paid, time limited, and largely transactional. Unlike structured ones, organic communities grow naturally through shared habits and local traditions. They emerge from collective need and mutual investment, not commercial offerings. They often involve neighborly interactions, co-created events, and parent volunteerism. They also provide essential opportunities for kids to explore independence and for families to build practical and personal connections. Natural communities might look like a local sports club run by volunteers, a weekly playgroup in a nearby hall, or an impromptu bike-riding crew that gathers after school. These experiences don't just fill time—they deepen roots.

When Work Steals from Community Life

Another factor that leads to little engagement in the threads of a natural support village is how much of a parent's energy is invested in work. I'm not saying that working parents neglect their children—on the contrary, most are more conscientious in their involvement with their children than previous generations. The issue is that we all have limited affiliative energy, and increasingly, adults are investing this in work relationships. This depletes what is available for natural extended family and community involvement.

Murray Bowen noticed this pattern—the more we cut ourselves off from family, the more likely we are to overinvest in work relationships. He writes:

Those who use physical distance in "cutting-off" from the parents tend to have the most intense relationships with those outside the family. A wide spectrum of people find work relationships to be more useful than social relationships for fulfilling emotional "needs."[3]

Bowen says that workplaces are better when guided by purposeful, goal-directed tasks rather than seeking emotionally fulfilling relationships in the workplace—a tendency reinforced by organizational cultures and leaders that promote a "happy family" atmosphere, often blurring the lines between professional roles and emotional dependency. Work easily becomes the new emotional home, not just a place to get things done. When this happens, it can quietly drain the emotional energy that working parents might otherwise invest in building natural connections within their neighborhoods, schools, or broader communities. The result is not just individual exhaustion, but a weakening of the informal social networks that once helped families thrive. Perhaps this is part of what is driving parents increasingly to outsource their children's activities—sports, lessons, enrichment programs—to external providers. This replaces engaging in communities that give children positive experiences, including their parents' involvement.

When Community Was Just Part of Growing Up

Can you remember natural communities from your growing-up years? For me, they were the heartbeat of childhood and full of rich, lasting memories. I think of neighborhood scooter races—I still carry a small scar from a crash around a corner I took too fast—candlelight carols at Christmas, baking for the local town show kids' competition, and being part of the local swimming squad. These experiences shaped my siblings and me in ways we didn't fully realize at the time.

A standout memory comes from when we moved to a new neighborhood, and my mother discovered there wasn't a local softball club. Rather than accept it, she took action—forming a committee that established the Castle Hill Softball Club, which still thrives some forty years later. I remember the buzz of trying on uniforms, choosing club colors, and gathering with other families. I trained, competed, and eventually coached the under-10s team in my teenage years. Three of my sisters played, and my brother found the same spirit in soccer and rugby. We weren't just participating as individual kids from one family—we were part of something bigger. That was the magic of community camaraderie.

One example of an established community in Australia that helps raise resilient children is Nippers, a beach-based surf lifesaving program that builds physical confidence, teamwork, and community spirit. The Nippers program in Australia has its roots in the early twentieth century. Surf lifesaving clubs began organizing junior activities for boys and girls in the 1920s and 1930s. The program was officially launched in the 1960s and has become an iconic expression of an active, outdoors family community. I didn't grow up near the beach, so for me, local sporting clubs became my version of that weekly gathering—a place where I regularly stepped out of my physical comfort zone and was shaped by shared effort, encouragement, and challenge. Nippers is an excellent example of what a village support community can provide children and parents.

New York Times journalist Damien Cave wrote about the value of such a community. In his book *Parenting Like an Australian*,[4] he reflects on how enrolling his children in Nippers—a surf lifesaving program—transformed their confidence and resilience. Initially hesitant, his children learned to navigate challenging surf conditions, leading to newfound boldness in and out of the water. Cave observed that this exposure to managed risk, supported by a community of involved parents, fostered physical competence and emotional growth. In an interview, he reflected, "You had all these parents taking care of all these children—not just their own kids—and you had all these kids who were expected to move in these risky situations together."[5] This communal approach to parenting, emphasizing collective responsibility and trust, contrasted sharply with his previous experiences and highlighted the value of community engagement in child development.

Simple Ideas, Big Impact—Ways Communities Are Restoring Connection

While our childhood memories of neighborhood life may feel distant now, they reflect a sense of everyday belonging that many parents still deeply desire. Programs like Nippers and Little League baseball and softball—rooted in decades of tradition—continue to offer that sense of connection. At the same time, new initiatives have emerged to meet the challenges of modern life. Some of these efforts stand out for their creativity and commitment to rebuilding natural community—spaces where kids are free to grow, and families feel part of something greater than themselves. Let me share two of my favorites:

1. **The Let Grow Movement.** This not-for-profit movement emerged to counter the modern decline in children's independence, free play, and community connection, which had eroded due to society's heightened safety fears and a culture of constant supervision. Founded by Lenore Skenazy[6] and advocates such as Jonathan Haidt and Peter Gray, Let Grow promotes the idea that when children are given the freedom to explore and play independently, they develop confidence and resilience and help rebuild natural communities. There are excellent resources to build school and parent partnerships, and a brilliant initiative, the Let Grow Project and Play Club.[7] Play clubs usually take place before or after school and offer a safe space where an adult is nearby, kind of like a lifeguard—there to keep an eye out, but not to step in unless really needed. This gives kids the chance to work out problems on their own, make up games, and interact without constant adult direction. A big part of what makes it work is having kids of different ages together—older ones naturally take on leadership roles, and younger ones learn by watching and joining in.

    As a parent and grandparent, I've experienced firsthand the benefits of loosely structured community play groups. Can you hear the importance of not having an imposed structure so that children are not externally managed but given space to grow in connection with peers and other families?

2. The Walking School Bus[8] began as a simple idea with powerful roots—what if getting to school could be healthy, social, and safe—all without a car? The concept took off in the 1990s, first in my home country, Australia, when parents and community

organizers started organizing small walking groups along regular routes. Each "bus" had adults acting like walking chaperones, picking up kids along the way at designated stops. The idea spread quickly—first across the UK, then into the United States and beyond—as schools and parents realized how many problems it quietly solved. For families, it meant less morning chaos and less guilt about screen-heavy routines. It was a burst of freedom for kids: time outside, friendships formed on the sidewalk, and a growing sense of independence. But at its core, the Walking School Bus did something even bigger—it reconnected neighborhoods. Walking together, kids and adults rebuilt the casual, daily ties that make a community feel like home. It's not fancy. It's not expensive. It's just people walking together—and sometimes, that's enough to change everything.

These examples remind us that rebuilding community doesn't require perfection—just intention, consistency, and a willingness to show up. Both children and parents grow stronger when surrounded by consistent relationships—not just support but a shared sense of belonging. Perhaps they'll inspire you to seek out or spark similar initiatives in your own neighborhood.

Like extended family life, community is rarely neat or tension-free—that's not the reality of human connection. But that's precisely the point. Communities give us and our children the everyday joys of belonging and the essential practice of relating to people who are different from us. In natural, unstructured settings, kids learn to work through conflicts, cooperate, and adapt—not by being constantly managed, but by engaging with others. At the same time, trusted adults stay close enough to guide, not control. These experiences help children follow a cooperative structure and teach them how to navigate real relationships. Ultimately, community—messy, imperfect, and deeply human—is not a luxury. It's foundational to our children's development and our mutual well-being.

As we think about rebuilding the village around our families, it's also worth exploring a deeper layer of connection—faith communities—not as institutions, but as communities where meaning, belonging, and shared purpose can take root across generations.

Reclaiming Sacred Spaces for Our Families

Jonathan Haidt's writing highlights many profound societal insights, including his call to rediscover the sacred in communities. He proposes that this generation's mental health has been devastated not just by the rise of the smartphone and the loss of children's free play but also by the absence of a higher purpose and sense of spirituality. He writes, "The phone-based life produces spiritual degradation, not just in adolescents, but in all of us."[9] Haidt discusses how faith communities' shared experiences and rituals contrast starkly with the isolation and emptiness of what is done on a screen alone in a bedroom. While he doesn't adhere to a particular faith lens and explains much of the yearning for higher-order awe and contemplation through Darwinian natural selection, he does see that "There is an emptiness in all, that we strive to fill."[10]

Dr. Lisa Miller, a clinical psychologist at Columbia University, has done substantial research showing that children are naturally spiritual beings. Her book *The Spiritual Child* explains how supporting that part of a child's inner life can build emotional strength and resilience. Her data shows that this longing for connection and more profound meaning is as much a part of being human as learning to speak or feeling empathy. Educators have seen this too—kids ask big, thoughtful questions about life, purpose, and what comes next.[11] They're reaching for something beyond themselves.

Across the world, people belong to diverse faith communities and spiritual traditions. Personally, I'm grateful for growing up in our local church communities. They provided regular spaces to wonder, reflect, and explore spiritual questions openly. I relished the stories and songs from my Christian faith tradition—they became companions I carried with me, adding joy to moments of awe in nature and offering steadiness during tough times. I've seen my children navigate their personal faith convictions in the various communities of kids' clubs, youth groups, and camps. As a parent of a teenager, it was such a welcome partnership to have young adults leading their youth groups, whom my daughters looked up to as people who cared, knew how to have loads of fun, and demonstrated integrity of character.

In an increasingly secular age, it becomes more difficult for families to access what Haidt refers to as a sense of transcendence, with the messaging we need to hear about being slow to anger, quick to forgive, and to do unto others as we would have them do unto us. Wisdoms that counteract the current climate of self-promotion and judgment, personal branding, and social status. No doubt in our faith organizations, we all need to do a regular hypocrisy check in these areas and not get the beauty of the message confused with polarizing political allegiances. As parents begin to reconnect with their own yearning for purpose, community, and something more profound than the material, they have an opportunity—and a responsibility—not to silence that same longing in their children. Young kids often show a natural openness to wonder, connection, and meaning. Rather than brushing it aside or overscheduling it out of them, we can make space for that spark to grow into something sturdy—something that will help carry them through the joys and struggles life inevitably brings.

The time I most deeply experienced the support of my church community was one of great turmoil and grief. My mother was diagnosed with metastatic breast cancer that returned two years after her initial cancer surgery and treatment. She was in her early fifties, and we children ranged from mid-teens to early twenties. It was harrowing to witness her decline and confront the harsh reality of our mother's impending death. Yet, amid this, many from our church community offered practical and emotional support. As a young adult, I witnessed prayers offered at her bedside that were full of love, lament, and hope. I watched my mother draw peace-filled strength from her faith community and inner beliefs that showed her eternal perspective. The pastoral care of our minister, who was like a friend to our family, helped carry us through the season of grief and confusion. Not every family member shared our mother's faith, but all of us were shown gracious care. That season of loss showed me how deeply families—especially children and young adults—need communities that show up with consistency, care, and presence. At their best, faith communities create a space where parents and children can wrestle with big questions, experience belonging, and find strength during life's most painful times.

Of course, that sense of belonging has been shaken for many families. As much as faith and community spaces can offer care and meaning, they have also, tragically, been places where trust was broken. To move forward, we continue to face those failures honestly and commit to rebuilding with accountability and care.

Restoring Safety and Trust in Faith and Community Organizations

Tragically, faith organizations and other community organizations for children have let us down by not taking seriously the risks of sexual predators hiding in the cloak of trusted spaces for children and families. I am deeply relieved that this has come to light, and checks and standards of behavior for any volunteers or employees of these organizations have been legislated to hold institutions accountable.[12]

Across many countries, institutions are now subject to regular safety audits and must demonstrate compliance with safeguarding protocols. Child safety training is now mandatory for all who work with children in any organization, including sports clubs, schools, and faith communities. It will never be water-tight, but I think it's essential that "safetyism,"[13] a mindset where safety is treated as the highest priority, doesn't take hold for parents. We don't want to over-elevate risk avoidance and rob our children of the beautiful gifts found in community organizations, where belonging, support, and collective purpose can flourish when accountability and safety are taken seriously. Parents, too, can play a role by doing their due diligence on an organization's safety practices, just as we do when navigating our children's growing risks online.

Strengthening School and Parent Partnerships

Just as communities like sports teams, faith groups, local clubs, and neighborhood gatherings can offer families a sense of connection and shared experience, schools provide another vital layer of support in family life. While the focus differs, both can become part of the wider village circle that helps raise and shape our children.

Our relationship with schools, like any partnership, can sometimes be complex. There are moments of encouragement, joyful collaboration, and sometimes of misunderstanding. What if we saw schools not just as institutions, but as partners—places filled with people who care about our children's learning and growth? Let's take a closer look at how we can show up in those relationships and build trust. If we're open to it, schools can become more than just drop-off zones—they can be part of our village support network.

Think about it—school is where our kids spend the bulk of their time during childhood. From ages five to eighteen, at least a quarter of their waking hours is spent in classrooms, playgrounds, and hallways. That's a massive chunk of their development—and a key place for partnership. So, how do we show up in that relationship? When our kids struggle, it's natural to feel protective—and just as natural to look for something or someone to blame. Schools often become the target, whether it's a teaching style that we think doesn't suit our child, a rough patch with peers, or a perceived lack of support. There are growing reports of tension between schools and parents, with principals saying that relationships are becoming more strained.[14] This reflects a broader trend where school leaders report being increasingly burdened by heightened parental expectations and confrontations, often exacerbated by social media platforms.[15] The shift from direct communication to online interactions has made it more challenging for educators to address concerns constructively, contributing to stress and burnout among school staff. We envision schools as a vital part of the child-raising village, but the growing societal stress spilling over onto parents and teachers risks undermining this shared ideal.

I recall meeting parents of teenagers, Anthea and Matt, who had moved their two anxious children five times over the school years. Every time one of their daughters reported hating school or complaining about a teacher or other student, the parents would start searching for an alternative. They were desperate to find an educational environment where their teens would be happy. There was a brief honeymoon period at every move, but it wasn't long before the same pattern of upsets emerged. Can you see how this pattern would impact these young people's development? They had come to expect to be rescued whenever they reported unhappiness. And Anthea and Matt had become disillusioned with the country's education system, blaming it for its lack of attention to their children's "special" needs.

As always, this came from a loving place, and I can report that as parents, they stepped back and became more thoughtful about the part they were playing in their children's disengagement from school. This began a new way of relating to their teens' school. Rather than asking for extra special needs support, they shared their plan to help their kids recover resilience with teachers. They would no longer be swift to rescue, but recognized they needed patience as their teens found their way to regular engagement with the school program. Previously, Anthea had written long emails of complaint to school leadership when things weren't working out for their children. But now they were each committed to meeting in person with teachers to explore how to be partners in their efforts to help their children meet their learning and social needs.

Creating a positive, trusting relationship between parents and schools can significantly improve a child's learning and well-being experience. While most parents sincerely want the best for their children, it's not always clear how to engage with a school constructively. Over the years, I've been involved with parents and educators, who have taught me much about improving this vital partnership. Here are some standout ideas for parents to consider about things that can both help and unintentionally hinder their relationship with their child's school.

What Helps and What Hinders Parent–School Partnerships

What Helps

1. **Build Trust in Teachers.** Recognizing the expertise and dedication of teachers is foundational. Trust that they genuinely care for your child and are committed to their growth. While their teaching style might differ from your preferences, this variety helps children adapt to different personalities, just as they will in life. Yes, many teachers and parents are increasingly stressed, but we want to ensure we don't add to that stress with a critical attitude.

2. **Communicate with Openness, Respect, and Curiosity.**
   Difficult topics—like bullying, learning challenges, or emotional
   concerns—are best addressed through calm, respectful
   dialogue. Choose a time and format (ideally in person or by
   phone) that allows for mutual understanding rather than rushed
   or reactive exchanges. Start conversations with a shared goal:
   "We both want the best for my child." See the school as a
   source of fascinating observations of your child's strengths
   and challenges. Often, children are quite different at school
   than at home, and it's great for teachers and parents to share
   these different perspectives to see how much the environment
   shapes each child.

3. **Stay Engaged and Visible.** Don't wait for a crisis to contact
   the school. Introduce yourself early, share helpful insights
   about your child, and take advantage of opportunities to
   connect with the school. Being visible helps the school see
   you as a collaborative partner, not just a concerned voice
   when something goes wrong. Teachers can help by taking the
   initiative to make contact with parents who seem particularly
   anxious and reactive.

4. **Practice the Art of Stepping Back.** While it's natural to want
   to protect your child, letting them experience challenges and
   solve problems with support is vital, as distinct from jumping in
   to rescue. This builds resilience and independence, preparing
   them for life beyond the classroom.

What Hinders

1. **Over-Involvement or Micromanagement.** Constantly
   stepping in to solve problems or challenge decisions can
   undermine your child's growth and the school's ability to teach.
   It also signals to your child that they may not be capable of
   handling things on their own.

2. **Withdrawing from the School Community.** Some parents
   hold back due to past experiences, fear of being judged, or
   feeling unsure about their role. But disengagement can lead to

disconnection for both you and your child. Schools genuinely want parents to be involved—not to take over teachers' responsibilities but to support them.

3. **Relying on Emails and Group Chats for Complex Issues.** Digital communication has its place, but sensitive or emotional topics are easily misunderstood in writing. Face-to-face conversations (or a phone call) are more effective for resolving issues and preserving respectful relationships. Sharing complaints in group chats or social media can spread misinformation, increase anxiety, and harm relationships. Venting complaints to other parents (a form of triangling) doesn't lead to resolution and may unintentionally involve children, undermining their appropriate, respectful stance toward their teacher.

4. **Expecting Perfection.** Every child will have ups and downs; not every classroom or teacher will be an ideal fit. That's okay. These moments offer valuable opportunities for children to build adaptability and for families to have meaningful conversations about the real world.

In the end, a strong parent–school relationship isn't always about agreeing—it's about shared purpose, respectful communication, and mutual trust. Children thrive when the adults around them model how to work together, even when things get hard.

Rebuilding Shared Life Around Families

Parents were never meant to raise children alone. Yet today, many families find themselves increasingly isolated, leaning heavily on formal services to meet their children's emotional and developmental needs— needs that organic community groups once supported and can still fulfill with far greater depth and connection. Parents' relationship energy often gets consumed in their workplaces, which leaves little left over for growing local bonds in family-centric communities. Children receive far more when families engage through schools, sports teams, neighborhood groups, creative programs, hobby clubs, or faith communities. They gain mentors and experiences that nurture a deep sense of belonging. They learn to problem-solve, relate to people of all ages, and build emotional resilience from facing challenges together. Parents, too, feel the difference—less alone, more supported, and anchored in shared experience.

As Anthea and Matt's story shows, meaningful change rarely comes from new programs or professionals. It begins with a shift in how we choose to show up—in our homes, schools, and communities. Real communities aren't flawless, and that's what makes them formative. In the mix of personalities, perspectives, and shared routines—on the sports field, at youth group, around a school fundraiser, or during a neighborhood chat—children learn how to live with others, not just alongside them. Yes, trust has been broken in some places. But the answer isn't to retreat. It's to rebuild—with wisdom, care, and a renewed commitment to showing up for each other. Everyone grows stronger when families are seen, supported, and surrounded—whether by a neighbor, a coach, a teacher, or a fellow parent. Because thriving doesn't happen in isolation, it happens in belonging.

For Reflection

Growing Your Village in Everyday Life

1. What positive memories do you have of growing up in informal, local communities, such as neighborhood play, sports teams, church groups, or schoolyard friendships? What stands out to you about those experiences?

2. Who were the adults (outside your immediate family) who influenced or supported you as a child? What did they offer that made a difference?

3. Did you experience unstructured or loosely supervised spaces where you learned to problem-solve, collaborate, or enjoy being with others? How did those experiences shape your confidence or social skills?

4. Looking at your current season of parenting or family life—do you feel connected to any natural support networks? What helps and what's missing?

5. Do you rely mainly on paid services (activities, appointments, structured programs) to meet your family's needs? What would it take to rebalance that with more organic, community-based support?

6. What small steps could you take to reconnect with or help build a natural support community—whether that's introducing yourself to a neighbor, joining a local group, or showing up more consistently in a shared space like a park, school, or place of worship?

7. How can you create or reclaim sacred spaces in your family's daily life to nurture connection, meaning, and resilience?

8. How might you support your child's natural curiosity about life's more profound questions, and what role can your spiritual or reflective practices play in guiding that journey?

9. Whether or not you had strong community connections as a child, what kinds of community experiences do you hope for your children? What would you love to see more of in their daily life that supports connection, independence, and a sense of belonging?

16

BALANCED LOVE
THE SUSTAINABLE LONG GAME OF PARENTING

When parents grow their understanding of themselves in each family relationship, the whole system begins to shift—and that's where real, lasting change begins.

I began this book with one parent's resounding question: "How can this happen to our daughter when we've given so much love?" As you've journeyed through these pages, I trust you've begun to see the surprising, but sustainable path to truly loving your children well. The issue isn't that there is too much love, but that love without clarity of self as a parent can become entangled with anxiety. When love becomes overly child focused, we as parents can lose our way. There is, however, a balanced way to love our children at every stage of life. When grounded in self-regulation, clear responsibilities, values, and thoughtful presence, love transforms. Our growth as parents becomes a steady foundation for our children's emotional security and adaptive development.

At the heart of this venture lies a powerful paradox: the more we anxiously focus on our children—trying to protect, perfect, or pre-empt their every challenge—the more we unintentionally undermine their ability to mature. And in doing so, we lose the space we need to grow our parenting awareness. The turning point comes when we stop managing our children as projects and instead focus on how we show up in our relationships with them. Rather than hovering, rescuing, or absorbing our children's distress, we learn to hold ourselves well in the face of their struggles.

Another Paradox—Slow Change Is Lasting Change

Reading parents' comments after completing differentiation-based parenting courses is always fascinating. Parents reflect on their habitual behaviors and how they can shift with comments such as: "It shone a light on my deeply ingrained behavior," "It helped me realize the intensity of my parenting." Notice that this feedback concerns parent self-awareness, not knowledge about their child. A repeated theme for parents is that they see that they can stop looking for a quick fix technique for the present challenge and instead start thinking about their long-term goals. One parent writes: "I see that a parent has to be willing to play the long game. Knowing that it is a process that takes time has given me hope. I wish I had known this five years ago."

How does parenting for the long game provide hopefulness that a short-term technique can't deliver? The issue with any short-term parenting technique to deal with a challenge is that it will stop being effective after some early successes. The child learns to play the technique games and adapts to find a new way to avoid or oppose. This experience becomes discouraging for a parent and can lead to a sense of giving up. While quick-fix techniques can have a place in the moment, they are essentially child focused, and the parent isn't developing their leadership for the whole parenting journey. However, when a parent asks themselves: "Am I representing my goal to provide a context where my child grows to be a responsible and good adult?", they can tolerate the many times when things don't go well and see that they didn't give up or give in.

Hope grows because parents stop judging their success by whether their child complied or improved on any given day. Instead, they measure progress by seeing examples of managing what's within their control—demonstrating a steady commitment to creating a family environment that fosters maturity. In my family systems parenting talks, I convey that rather than evaluating our parenting at the end of the day by asking, "Has my child been behaving? Has their mood been good today?"—we can take a different stance. This child-focused lens sets us on a chaotic rollercoaster, with our sense of success rising and falling based on our child's ever-changing behavior. Instead, we can ask ourselves, "Have I been parenting in line with my values and job description today?" This question offers a steadier path for our own growth over the long term. It helps us recalibrate and get back on track during those inevitable days when we're exhausted and running empty.

Returning to one of my favorite parenting metaphors, playing the long game as a parent can be likened to growing a tree. Other writers have used this metaphor in response to the age of overparenting. For example, Alison Gopnik, professor of psychology at the University of California, describes in her writing the parent as a gardener, not a carpenter—someone who cultivates rather than constructs.[1] When planted, a tree is provided with the essential ingredients for healthy growth—water, good soil, and sunlight. These must be provided consistently, but as the roots deepen, the tree becomes more self-sufficient and requires less intervention. Overwatering or overcrowding can stunt its growth. We cannot speed up the process by pulling on the tree—it grows in its own time. What it needs is patience and the right kind of attention. Over time, it becomes a tall, sturdy, shade-giving tree, able to withstand the changing seasons and storms that come its way. Can you see the parenting parallels? Children need consistent care early on, but gradually develop resilience and independence. Rushing or overmanaging their development backfires. The long-term outcomes are hallmarks of grounded, well-adjusted young adults.

Inspiring Shifts That Parents Make— from Frustration to Hope

When I first met Belinda, she was at her wits' end as a parent of her teen daughter. Belinda expressed the depth of her despair, saying: "My daughter's defiant behaviors were killing me inside." This is a raw, honest statement that many parents feel but rarely admit. It highlights the emotional toll that ongoing futile parenting efforts create. Belinda started taking a different path back to confidence as a mother. Here is a summary of her pathway to awareness and change, drawing from Belinda's actual words.

> "I was inciting her without realizing it. And even when I did realize it, I couldn't stop myself."

She began to see that it wasn't just the words that escalated conflict—it was her feelings of moral indignation, the deep sense of "I will not be spoken to like this!" that poured fuel on the fire. "I knew all I was doing was beating my head against a brick wall, trying to change her. And it wasn't working."

That was the turning point: the realization that control tactics weren't creating change, just exhaustion. Something had to give. Then came the core insight that flipped everything: "I can't control her, but I can control how I react to every situation." Letting go of control didn't feel empowering at first. It felt like surrender.

> "When I stopped reacting, I thought I was being a doormat. But actually, I began to feel stronger."

Belinda discovered that silence in this situation isn't weakness—it's self-control. And in that calm, a new mindset emerged. She found strength in clear phrases that held space without inflaming the situation: "It felt like I was finally holding the reins." She responded differently when old conflictual invitations came her way: "You've been heard. I have nothing more productive to add." She learned to shift from exasperation and blame to conveying who she was as a parent—her "I" position. "It's not: 'you can't talk to me like that.'" "It's: 'I'm upset by how I was spoken to.'"

And Belinda learned to wait—delaying consequences until the heat had passed: "I don't do consequences in the heat of the moment anymore."

The results? Real. Tangible. Hopeful. "We have fewer explosions now. She's happier. We're all happier." "She's including her siblings now. I never thought I'd see that."

Belinda doesn't claim perfection. But she has reclaimed her footing. "Things aren't perfect, but I'm committed. I don't want to return to those ugly days."

For Belinda and many other parents, the shift to loving with the long game in view came in steps:

1. Recognize the unhelpful patterns and emotional triggers.

2. Let go of the need to change or control the child.

3. Redefine strength through calm boundaries and self-regulation.

4. Respond intentionally rather than reacting emotionally.

5. Stay committed to the process and trust gradual change.

Observing Yourself in Relationships— Rather Than Following a Tribe

Belinda could not have progressed without becoming a better observer of her patterns. Many approaches promote individual self-reflection, but few espouse the value of reflecting on how you are triggered and predictably respond with others—and, in turn, how they predictably react to you. Attention is on yourself, the impact on others, and what you can adjust to build a more growth-promoting environment for all family members.

We are learning to observe the emotional process in our family. Emotions aren't just what we feel—they're built into our physiology and help drive how our bodies and relationships function. We can't see this emotional process directly, but we can notice its impact. In that way, it's a lot like observing the wind: you can't see the wind itself, but can see what it moves. The way trees sway, clothes flap on a line, or a flag whips in one direction—all show you where the wind is going and how strong it is. Likewise, emotional currents reveal themselves through patterns in behavior, tension, or reactivity. We practice seeing this relationship system and our part in it.

I've noticed that many parents feel strongly about their chosen parenting style, often defending it passionately, especially if it's linked to a popular influencer or approach. But let's step back from all the labels for a moment. The real question is not whether I'm in the right tribe, but whether my way of responding to each of my children helps them grow in independence over time. If our observation of our back-and-forth patterns confirms the answer is yes, then you're on the right track— there's no need to change just because someone else is doing things differently. What matters most is whether your framework is helping or hindering. We observe our children's responses and ask ourselves: Are they becoming more self-regulated, or are they stuck in cycles of dependence or defiance? Is our way of relating helping to cultivate their character, resilience, and ability to manage the next step in their social and emotional development? Parenting isn't about following a tribe or a charismatic influencer. It's about staying curious, observing, and adjusting ourselves based on what our children need to thrive.

The Strength in Letting Go

Mei Ling is a single mother of a young adult daughter. She has separated from her husband, who returned to the country of their birth. Mei's is an example of a step-by-step journey of change with her depressed daughter, who was struggling to do her college work. This is a massive trigger for Mei Ling, who has sacrificed many things to promote her child's educational success. It was a Sunday morning, and Mei's daughter, Grace, said she couldn't finish her assignment for the next day. Mei's anxiety surged. Her daughter had gone to her room and refused to go to church, and all Mei could think was, "This is a disastrous backward step." Mei shifted into fix-it mode, offering solutions and suggestions to get her daughter back on track. But then came the unexpected response: "I don't want solutions. I just want you to listen." This time, it wasn't as emotionally heightened as it had been in the past—no tears, no yelling—and that gave Mei a chance to pause. She regrouped and returned to her daughter's room, starting over: "I see how hard this is for you—how hard it is to find motivation." Mei showed her daughter—and herself—that she could change. That she could respond differently.

The next day, however, the old pattern reappeared. Mei started offering ideas again—gentle suggestions, ways to break down the assignment—and her daughter pulled the blanket over her head and shut down. Mei Ling now saw clearly—giving advice was her own anxiety management strategy, not what her daughter needed.

It wasn't an instant shift. At work the next day, Mei obsessively checked her phone, waiting for a photo of the finished assignment. Her body was tense, her mind racing. "Is she doing it? Is she still in bed?" But then she asked herself: "Where is my energy going right now?" The answer—toward managing her daughter, something that was not within her control. She realized, "This is my work now. I need to calm down and redirect my energy to where it can actually make a difference—me." She walked around the block, listened to a podcast, and resisted the urge to text or drive home to check. "Managing her is not a strategy available to me anymore." It took her an hour to get herself grounded. And when she got home, she stayed out of rescue mode. Her daughter hadn't finished the assignment. She was in her room. Mei didn't push. She simply said, "Grace, you know what you're capable of right now, and you'll work it out. I'm here if you want to talk." Later, Grace came out of her room and joined her for dinner. They didn't talk about school. They just chatted—about life, food, whatever came up.

"This feels like abseiling," Mei declared. "You lean back and trust the harness will hold you, but it's terrifying. That's what it feels like to let go of my daughter's life. To trust she will find her way." She realized it wouldn't be a tragedy even if her daughter quit the course. It would simply be where she was right now. Mei began to believe: "I'm not a bad parent for letting go. I'm not in charge of controlling outcomes. Grace has skills. I've seen her use them. She will find her way."

With less intensity in the parent–child relationship, Grace began to reach out—not for help or advice but for connection. They joined a community orchestra together. On the drive home, they laughed about the quirks of the other members and sang the melodies they were learning. "We connect for fun now—not for fixing," Mei reflected. She conveyed a new understanding that letting go isn't giving up—it's giving space—space for her daughter to rise, stumble, choose, and return on her own terms. It's not perfect. It's not fast. But it's movement. And that is the long game she's now committed to playing.

Another layer of change came when Mei began to look at herself in all her relationships: "If I'm not the fixer or the peacemaker, then who am I?" She saw that this role had deep roots. It shaped how she functioned in her family of origin, her previous marriage, and even at work. She'd poured so much energy into rescuing her daughter that she hadn't processed the grief of her marriage ending. She hadn't thought about her future as a single woman, or what an empty nest might mean. This wasn't just about parenting. It was about reclaiming her own life.

These two examples of Belinda and Mei show growth in their awareness of self in a relationship and the changes this enabled. Many other parents have also shared their stories of playing the long game of shifting how they love their children. A father tells his son, "I will not have these conversations after dinner when I'm tired. I know I can't be useful when I'm tired, and I do not want to lose my cool and contribute to a negative relationship between us." Another dad reflects, "I want to remember the long picture. Think about the skills my child needs when he walks out of our house at eighteen and into the world. How can I facilitate this?" They are all learning to parent with intention, keeping the bigger picture in mind even in everyday moments.

We heard how Mei described her growth as a parent as learning to abseil—terrifying at first, like stepping off a cliff. But over time, she learned to trust the harness and realized that letting go isn't losing control but finding a new kind of strength. It's a hope-generating shift many parents come to—a turning point where growth is measured not by quick fixes but by the steady, realistic effort to represent love without overreaching.

The Value of a Family Systems Coach

Learning to see the family as a system—and to manage ourselves within it—can feel like swimming against the tide or learning a foreign language. Even when we know our old patterns aren't working, they're familiar and easier to fall back on. This is where outside support can help. But not the kind that simply validates our emotions or tells us what to do. We need support that helps us better understand ourselves in the context of our relationships and clarifies what we can work on to bring our best to the family.

I suggest it's worth finding a family systems–trained clinician or coach who can help us stay on track and continue to learn about ourselves in our relationships. I've lived this out in my own parenting, particularly when one of my children has hit a rough patch. I've acted on my belief that a parent doing their own growth work will have a more lasting impact on a child's well-being than simply outsourcing support to an individual therapist for the child.

A trained family systems coach partners with parents to shift from worry-driven to awareness-driven parenting. The term "coach" is intentional—it reflects a collaborative process, not a fixing one. Together, you explore your unique family dynamic and create a new game plan rooted in self-awareness and differentiation. It's a valuable investment. As we grow in understanding ourselves within each family relationship, the system begins to shift—and that's where meaningful, lasting change begins.

Paradoxes Everywhere

It's time to bring this book together. While I've titled it *The Parenting Paradox*—singular—the reality is that parenting is filled with paradoxes, plural. This perspective is far richer and more layered than any single contradiction could capture. A quote attributed to Dr. Bowen's communications speaks directly to the central paradox outlined in this book: "You can't control a whole damn family, but you can control you, and anytime you can control you, the family is a healthier organism."[2] Our children and whole family gradually improve when we change focus, improve our self-control, and draw on our principles. Parenting, when viewed through the lens of differentiation and emotional maturity, invites us into a world where many things are true in tension. Even within this final chapter, several key paradoxes have emerged. At the center lies the overarching *paradox*—the guiding tension that shapes the entire journey:

1. **Letting Go and Growing Ourselves**

   The more we let go of trying to manage or fix our children, the more we're able to grow ourselves—and in doing so, create the conditions for our children to grow. From this counterintuitive lens flows a range of connected paradoxes.

2. **Love Without Role Clarity Becomes Anxiety**

   When love lacks clarity and boundaries, it easily morphs into anxious overfunctioning rather than offering calm and steady guidance.

3. **Slow Change Is Lasting Change**

   While quick fixes may feel satisfying, they rarely hold. Sustainable change is slow, deliberate, and grounded in long-term vision.

4. **Silence Can Be Strength**

   Withholding a reactive response might feel like passivity, but it's often a form of mature emotional regulation that de-escalates conflict.

5. **From Managing the Child to Managing the Self**

   Our most significant influence doesn't come from controlling behavior but from managing our own emotional reactivity and staying grounded.

6. **From Connection Through Crisis to Connection Through Curiosity**

   Connection doesn't have to be built around fixing or rescuing our children. It thrives on curiosity, allowing for shared joy and humor in everyday life.

7. **Defining Our Limits Creates Secure Connections**

   Although it may seem counterintuitive, steady and respectful limits grounded in what we can control create trust and security, enhancing rather than damaging connection.

8. **Support That Broadens, Not Just Empathizes**

   The help that truly enables change doesn't affirm our opinions or empathize with our feelings—it invites us to see beyond them, understand our part in the system, and grow from there. We might feel good if a helper takes our side and agrees with our viewpoints (a triangle), but this can get in the way of growth-promoting change.

These paradoxes are not contradictions—they're tension points that hold insight. Learning to live with that tension, rather than relieve it, is the deeper work of parenting and differentiating. It's what makes the long game sustainable and rewarding.

The Paradoxes for Professional Helpers

Other paradoxes apply particularly to those of us in helping roles—supporting parents and families. For us helpers, learning to work with the tension of these counterintuitive principles is part of our professional development, and what makes long-term growth possible for families and sustainable for us as helpers.

1. **Prioritize Work with the Parent, Over the Symptomatic Child**

    The instinct is to focus treatment on the struggling child, leading to parents being sidelined. However, more profound, lasting change happens when the parent works to shift their own patterns within the family system.

2. **Helpers Don't Give Directives, They Facilitate Parent Discovery**

    Earlier in this book, I shared my guiding question for anything I offer to parents: "Does this help them think and act for themselves, rather than follow a directive?" When parents come to their own insights, they develop the clarity and ownership needed to move forward. But if they're trying to follow an expert's advice, that change often lacks staying power. It's a parallel paradox to that of the parent to the child. A helper draws on their understanding of typical interaction patterns, explores the parent's exchanges, and asks thoughtful questions about their back-and-forth with their child and partner—questions that spark new awareness and an achievable action plan for the parent. The more we helpers resist the urge to direct, the more we empower parents to grow in their own capacity—and that's where meaningful, sustainable change truly begins.

The Long Game of Love, Leadership, and Letting Go

When parents focus on growing themselves rather than changing their children, they begin to ease their hold and create more space in the relationship. This marks a profound philosophical shift—from seeing children as something to own or control, to hosting their growth toward independent adulthood. A change from seeking satisfaction and purpose through our children. It echoes the Judeo-Christian ethic of having no idols. Indeed, the majority of the world's religions warn against misguided attachments to children. Religious scholars convey that idolatry happens when a good thing becomes the ultimate thing—something we depend on for identity or meaning.[3] Our children are deeply precious, but not meant to occupy a place of ultimate importance. Elevating them too high burdens them and distorts the parent–child relationship. In letting go, we don't abandon our children— we honor their separateness. And in doing so, we find our growth as well. Central to the parenting journey is our gradual letting go. As Dr. Michael Kerr, a leading voice in Bowen theory, puts it:

> It is a gradual process of parents separating appropriately from the child, which fosters the child separating appropriately from them. . . . Parents have the task of toning down anxiety-driven togetherness urges as the child matures.[4]

As you turn the final pages of this book, I hope it continues to bring clarity to your own "balanced parent project"—an ongoing journey that honors your deep love for your child while anchoring that love in your own growth. It allows you to stay close while also learning to let go. This isn't about perfection. It's a steady, trial-and-error journey—shifting from anxious reactivity to calm, confident relating, from child-led overwhelm to parent-led clarity. In the ongoing patient work of making space for growth, we foster an environment where our children can become their best—and where we learn to step back, cultivate mature connection, and take genuine joy in watching them grow.

NOTES

Introduction

1 Jonathan Haidt, *The Anxious Generation: How the Great Rewiring of Childhood Is Causing an Epidemic of Mental Illness* (New York: Penguin Press, 2024).

2 Murray Bowen, in David E. Butler, *The Origins of Family Psychotherapy: The NIMH Family Study Project* (Lanham: Jason Aronson, 2013).

3 Salvador Minuchin, *Families and Family Therapy* (Cambridge, MA: Harvard University Press, 1974).

4 Daniel J. Siegel, *The Developing Mind: How Relationships and the Brain Interact to Shape Who We Are* (New York: Guilford Press, 2020).

5 Jenny Brown, *Growing Yourself Up: How to Bring Your Best to All of Life's Relationships*, 2nd ed. (Wollombi: Exisle Publishing, 2017).

6 Parent Hope Project, *Parent Hope Project*, accessed July 2, 2025, https://parenthopeproject.com.au/.

Chapter 1

1 Vivek H. Murthy, *Advisory on Parental Stress as a Public Health Issue* (Office of the US Surgeon General, 2024).

2 UNICEF UK, *UNICEFUKReport* (2023).

3 Dorothy Briggs, *Your Child's Self-Esteem: Step-by-Step Guidelines for Raising Responsible, Productive, Happy Children* (New York: Harmony, 1988).

4 Peter N. Stearns, *Anxious Parents: A History of Modern Childrearing in America* (New York: New York University Press, 2003), 1.

5 Jennifer Senior, *All Joy and No Fun: The Paradox of Modern Parenthood* (London: Hachette, 2014).

6 Jonathan Haidt and Greg Lukianoff, *The Coddling of the American Mind: How Good Intentions and Bad Ideas Are Setting Up a Generation for Failure* (New York: Penguin Press, 2018).

7 Stearns, *Anxious Parents*, 23.

8 Benjamin Spock, *The Common Sense Book of Baby and Child Care* (New York: Duell, Sloan and Pearce, 1946).

9 Stearns, *Anxious Parents*, 23.

10 Andrew Francis, "Stigma in an Era of Medicalization and Anxious Parenting: How Proximity and Culpability Shape Middle-Class Parents' Experiences of Disgrace," *Sociology of Health & Illness* 34, no. 6 (2012): 927–42.

11 Darby E. Saxbe and Magdalena Martínez-García, "Cortical Volume Reductions in Men Transitioning to First-Time Fatherhood Reflect Both Parenting Engagement and Mental Health Risk," *Cerebral Cortex* 34, no. 4 (2024): 126.

12 Lyn Craig, Abigail Powell, and Ciara Smyth, "Towards Intensive Parenting? Changes in the Composition and Determinants of Mothers' and Fathers' Time with Children 1992–2006," *The British Journal of Sociology* 65, no. 3 (2014): 555–79.

13 Suniya S. Luthar and Shawn J. Latendresse, "Children of the Affluent: Challenges to Well-Being," *Current Directions in Psychological Science* 14, no. 1 (2005): 49–53.

14 Patrick Ishizuka, "Social Class, Gender, and Contemporary Parenting Standards in the United States: Evidence from a National Survey Experiment," *Social Forces* 98, no. 1 (2019): 31–58.

15 Haidt, *The Anxious Generation*.

16 Jennifer E. Lansford, "Cross-Cultural Similarities and Differences in Parenting," *Journal of Child Psychology and Psychiatry* 63, no. 4 (2022): 466–79.

17 National Health Commission of the People's Republic of China, *Guidelines for Healthy Care and Nurturing of Children Under 3 (Trial Implementation)* [《3岁以下婴幼儿健康养育照护指南（试行）》] (Beijing: National Health Commission, 2022), accessed July 23, 2025, https://www.gov.cn/zhengce/zhengceku/2022-11/29/content_5729421.htm.

18 Jia-Yu Li, Jing Li, Jing-Hong Liang, Sheng Qian, Rui-Xia Jia, Ying-Quan Wang, and Yong Xu, "Depressive Symptoms among Children and Adolescents in China: A Systematic Review and Meta-analysis," *Medical Science Monitor: International Medical Journal of Experimental and Clinical Research* 25 (2019): 7459.

Chapter 2

1 Pew Research Center, *Parenting in America Today* (Washington, DC: Pew Research Center, January 24, 2023), https://www.pewresearch.org/social -trends/2023/01/24/parenting-in-america-today.

2 David E. Butler, *The Origins of Family Psychotherapy: The NIMH Family Study Project* (Lanham, MD: Jason Aronson, 2013).

3 Murray Bowen, *Family Therapy in Clinical Practice* (New York: Jason Aronson, 1978).

4 Jennifer L. Hudson and Ronald M. Rapee, eds., *Psychopathology and the Family* (Amsterdam: Elsevier, 2005).

5 Michael Thomasgard and William P. Metz, "The Two-Year Stability of Parental Perceptions of Child Vulnerability and Parental Overprotection," *Journal of Developmental & Behavioral Pediatrics* 17, no. 4 (1996): 222–8.

6 Ronald M. Rapee, "Family Factors in the Development and Management of Anxiety Disorders," *Clinical Child and Family Psychology Review* 15, no. 1 (2012): 69–80.

7 Eli R. Lebowitz, *Addressing Parental Accommodation When Treating Anxiety in Children* (New York: Oxford University Press, 2019).

8 Jenny Brown, "We Don't Need Your Help, but Will You Please Fix Our Children?" *Australian and New Zealand Journal of Family Therapy* 29, no. 2 (2008): 61–9.

9 Jonathan Haidt, *The Anxious Generation: How the Great Rewiring of Childhood Is Causing an Epidemic of Mental Illness*. (New York: Penguin Press, 2024), 68.

Chapter 3

1 Julie Lythcott-Haims, *How to Raise an Adult: Break Free of the Overparenting Trap and Prepare Your Kid for Success* (New York: Henry Holt and Co., 2015).

2 "Parent Hope Project," *Parent Hope Project*.

3 Queensland University of Technology, "Helicopter Parents Take Extreme Approach to Homework," *ScienceDaily*, February 2, 2016, https://www .sciencedaily.com/releases/2016/02/160202110726.htm.

4 Bowen, *Family Therapy in Clinical Practice*.

5 "Oxytocin," *AP Psychology Key Terms*. Fiveable, accessed 2025, https:// library.fiveable.me/key-terms/ap-psych/social-bonding.

6 Minuchin, *Families and Family Therapy*, enmeshment discussed in chapter 4.

Chapter 4

1 Matt Richtel, "'It's Life or Death': The Mental Health Crisis Among U.S. Teens," *The New York Times*, April 23, 2022.

2 Kaiser Family Foundation, "Recent Trends in Mental Health and Substance Use Concerns Among Adolescents," KFF, August 24, 2023, https://www .kff.org/mental-health/issue-brief/recent-trends-in-mental-health-and -substance-use-concerns-among-adolescents/.

3 "NHS Referrals for Anxiety in Children More Than Double Pre-Covid Levels," *The Guardian*, August 27, 2024, https://www.theguardian.com/ society/article/2024/aug/27/nhs-referrals-for-anxiety-in-children-more-than -double-pre-covid-levels-england.

4 "The Courier Mail," *Experts Say 8 to 12 Are Years Kids Hit with Mental Health Decline,* February 2024, https://www.couriermail.com.au/news/ queensland/experts-say-8-to-12-are-years-kids-hit-with-mental-health -decline/news-story/ef04a7e16420d2ec1fc4aeac715ab47e.

5 Jenny Brown, "Parents' Experiences of Their Adolescent's Mental Health Treatment: Helplessness or Agency-Based Hope," *Clinical Child Psychology and Psychiatry* 23, no. 4 (2018): 644–62. Jenny Brown, *Facilitating Parents' Agency in Child and Adolescent Mental Health: Helplessness to Hope* (Newcastle upon Tyne: Cambridge Scholars Publishing, 2023).

6 Peter Churven and Bronwyn Cinto, "An Application of Strategic Family Therapy to a Residential Child and Family Psychiatry Service: Redbank House," *Australian and New Zealand Journal of Family Therapy* 4, no. 2 (1983): 77–83.

7 Committee on Bioethics, *Informed Consent in Decision-Making in Pediatric Practice*, *Pediatrics*, 2018, accessed March 5, 2025, https://pmc.ncbi.nlm .nih.gov/articles/PMC6279730/.

8 Australian Institute of Family Studies, *Family-Inclusive Approaches When Working with Young People Accessing Mental Health Support*, accessed March 5, 2025, https://aifs.gov.au/resources/short-articles/family-inclusive -approaches-when-working-young-people-accessing-mental.

9 Aine Schlagel, Nora Walsh, et al., "Parent Participation Engagement in Child and Family Mental Health Treatment: A Review of the Literature," *Clinical Child and Family Psychology Review* 18, no. 2 (2015): 133–50.

10 Golda S. Ginsburg, et al., "Results From the Child/Adolescent Anxiety Multimodal Extended Long-Term Study (CAMELS): Primary Anxiety Outcomes," *Journal of the American Academy of Child & Adolescent Psychiatry* 57, no. 7 (2018): 471–80.

11 Benjamin Zablotsky and Amanda E. Ng, "Mental Health Treatment Among Children Aged 5–17 Years: United States, 2021," in *NCHS Data Brief, no. 472* (Hyattsville: National Center for Health Statistics, June 2023), https://www.cdc.gov/nchs/products/databriefs/db472.htm.

12 Sonya Kurzweil, "Involving Parents in Child Mental Health Treatments: Survey of Clinician Practices and Variables in Decision Making," *American Journal of Psychotherapy* 73, no. 3 (2023): 107–14.

13 Jenny Brown, "The Reciprocity Between Parents and Their Child's Mental Health Treatment Systems," *Family Systems* 14, no. 2 (2020): 124.

14 American Psychiatric Association, *Diagnostic and Statistical Manual of Mental Disorders*, 3rd ed. (Washington, DC: American Psychiatric Association, 1980).

15 Greg Lukianoff and Jonathan Haidt, *The Coddling of the American Mind: How Good Intentions and Bad Ideas Are Setting Up a Generation for Failure* (New York: Penguin Press, 2019).

16 John Bowlby, *Attachment and Loss*. Vol. 1, *Attachment* (New York: Basic Books, 1969).

17 Elizabeth Meins, "Sensitive Attunement to Infants Internal States: Operationalizing the Construct of Mind-Mindedness," *Attachment & Human Development* 15, no. 5–6 (2013): 524–44.

18 Robert J. Noone and Daniel V. Papero, eds., *The Family Emotional System: An Integrative Concept for Theory, Science, and Practice* (Lanham, MD: Lexington Books, 2015).

19 Daniel V. Papero, "The Family Emotional System: Seedbed of Symptoms or Garden of Recovery" (presentation, Family Systems Institute Annual Conference, Sydney, Australia, August 21–22, 2024).

20 Jenny Brown and Daniel V. Papero, "How Bowen Family Systems Builds Hope for Worried Parents," *The Parent Hope Podcast*, hosted by Jenny Brown, Season 2, Episode 7, September 10, 2024, audio podcast, 40:02, https://podcasts.apple.com/us/podcast/season-2-ep-7-how-bowen-family-systems-builds-hope/id1653517551?i=1000669085470.

Chapter 5

1 Barnardo's, *The Missing Link: Social Prescribing for Children and Young People*, October 10, 2023, https://www.barnardos.org.uk/research/missing-link-social-prescribing-children-young-people.

2 Darby Saxbe, "This Is Not the Way to Help Depressed Teenagers," *The New York Times*, February 23, 2025.

3 *Let Grow: Helping Kids Do More on Their Own*, accessed March 6, 2025, https://letgrow.org.

4 Olivia Sappenfield, Cinthya Alberto, Jessica Minnaert, Julie Donney, Lydie Lebrun-Harris, and Reem Ghandour, *National Survey of Children's Health: Adolescent Mental and Behavioral Health, 2023 Data Brief* (October 2024), US Health Resources and Services Administration. https://mchb.hrsa.gov/data-research/national-survey-childrens-health.

5 American Psychiatric Association, *Diagnostic and Statistical Manual of Mental Disorders*, 5th ed., *Text Revision (DSM-5-TR)* (Washington, DC: American Psychiatric Publishing, 2022).

6 American Psychiatric Association, *Diagnostic and Statistical Manual of Mental Disorders*, 5th ed.

7 Michael E. Kerr, *Bowen Theory's Secrets: Revealing the Hidden Life of Families* (New York: W. W. Norton & Company, 2019).

Chapter 6

1 Jenny Brown, "Differentiation-Based Parenting: Part One," *The Parent Hope Project*, June 11, 2024, https://parenthopeproject.com.au/differentiation-based-parenting-part-one/.

2 Bowen, *Family Therapy in Clinical Practice*, 261.

3 Jenny Brown and Lauren Errington, "Bowen Theory Revisited: Observing Self in the Family System," *Australian and New Zealand Journal of Family Therapy* 45, no. 1 (2024): 12–25.

Chapter 7

1 Sigal G. Barsade, "The Ripple Effect: Emotional Contagion and Its Influence on Group Behavior," *Administrative Science Quarterly* 47, no. 4 (December 2002): 644–75.

2 Elizabeth A. Miller and Camille R. Elder, "Balanced Parenting: Proposing a Differentiation-Based Parenting Approach Informed by Bowen Family Systems Theory," *Family Process* 64, no. 1 (2025): 13092.

3 Nathan A. Fox and Susan D. Calkins, "The Development of Self-Control of Emotion: Intrinsic and Extrinsic Influences," *Motivation and Emotion* 27, no. 1 (2003): 7–26.
   Ruth Feldman, "The Development of Regulatory Functions from Birth to 5 Years: Insights from Premature Infants," *Child Development* 80, no. 2 (2009): 544–61.

Mary K. Rothbart and Beth E. Sheese, "Temperament and Emotion Regulation," in *Handbook of Emotion Regulation*, ed. James J. Gross (New York: Guilford Press, 2007), 331–50.

4 Susana Rodríguez, Rocío González-Suárez, Tania Vieites, Isabel Piñeiro, and Fátima M. Díaz-Freire, "Self-Regulation and Students' Well-Being: A Systematic Review 2010–2020," *Sustainability* 14, no. 4 (2022): 2346.

5 Laurence Steinberg, "We Know Some Things: Parent–Adolescent Relationships in Retrospect and Prospect," *Journal of Research on Adolescence* 11, no. 1 (2001): 1–19.
Angela L. Duckworth and Laurence Steinberg, "Unpacking Self-Control," *Child Development Perspectives* 9, no. 1 (2015): 32–7.

6 Kathleen Smith, *Everything Isn't Terrible: Conquer Your Insecurities, Interrupt Your Anxiety and Finally Calm Down* (New York: Hachette Books, 2019).

7 Smith, *Everything Isn't Terrible*, 21.

Chapter 8

1 Jelena Obradović, Michael J. Sulik, and Anne Shaffer, "Learning to Let Go: Parental Over-Engagement Predicts Poorer Self-Regulation in Kindergartners," *Journal of Family Psychology* 35, no. 5 (2021): 664–74.

2 Laurence Steinberg, "A Social Neuroscience Perspective on Adolescent Risk-Taking," in *Biosocial Theories of Crime* (New York: Routledge, 2017), 435–63.

3 Beate Herpertz-Dahlmann, Johannes Hebebrand, Bodo Müller, Sabine Herpertz, Nicole Heussen, and Helmut Remschmidt, "Prospective 10-year Follow-up in Adolescent Anorexia Nervosa—Course, Outcome, Psychiatric Comorbidity, and Psychosocial Adaptation," *Journal of Child Psychology and Psychiatry* 42, no. 5 (2001): 603–12.

4 Pew Research Center, *Parenting in America: Outlook, Worries, Aspirations Are Strongly Linked to Financial Situation* (Washington, DC: Pew Research Center, December 17, 2015), https://www.pewresearch.org/social-trends/2015/12/17/parenting-in-america/.

5 Pew Research Center, *Parenting in America Today*.

6 David Murphey and Vanessa Sacks, *Parenting Young Children: Supporting Parents' Protective Instincts* (Bethesda: Child Trends, September 2022), https://www.childtrends.org/publications/parenting-young-children-supporting-parents-protective-instincts.

Chapter 9

1 Marc A. Brackett and Susan E. Rivers, "Teaching Emotional Intelligence in Early Childhood," *Young Children* 72, no. 2 (2017): 28–35.

2 Bowen, *Family Therapy in Clinical Practice*, 478.

3 Bowen, *Family Therapy in Clinical Practice*, 218–19.

4 Andrew J. Lange and Patricia Jakubowski, *Responsible Assertive Behavior: Cognitive/Behavioral Procedures for Trainers* (Champaign: Research Press, 1978).

5 Thomas Gordon, *Parent Effectiveness Training: The Proven Program for Raising Responsible Children* (New York: Three Rivers Press, 2000), 84.

6 Eli R. Lebowitz, *Breaking Free of Child Anxiety and OCD: A Scientifically Proven Program for Parents* (New York: Oxford University Press, 2020).

7 Brown, *Growing Yourself Up*. Jenny Brown, *Confident Parenting: Restoring Your Confidence as a Parent by Making Yourself the Project and Not Trying to Change Your Child* (Sydney: Family Systems Practice, 2020).

8 Bowen, *Family Therapy in Clinical Practice*, 495.

Chapter 10

1 Haidt, *The Anxious Generation*.

2 Christina Camilleri, Justin T. Perry, and Stephen Sammut, "Compulsive Internet Pornography Use and Mental Health: A Cross-Sectional Study in a Sample of University Students in the United States," *Frontiers in Psychology* 11 (2021): 613244.

3 Peter Gray, "A Brief History of Moral Panics About Kids and Media," *Psychology Today*, January 20, 2025, https://www.psychologytoday.com /us/blog/freedom-to-learn/202501/a-brief-history-of-moral-panics-about -kids-and-media.

4 Gray, "A Brief History of Moral Panics About Kids and Media," para 2.

5 World Health Organization, *Guidelines on Physical Activity, Sedentary Behaviour and Sleep for Children Under 5 Years of Age* (Geneva: World Health Organization, 2019).

6 Grace Coca and John Wikle, "What Happens When Children Are Exposed to Pornography?" *Institute for Family Studies*, April 30, 2024, https://ifstudies.org/blog/what-happens-when-children-are-exposed-to -pornography.

7 *Adolescence*, directed by Anna Biller, season 1, Netflix, 2025.

8 Sonia Rao, "'Adolescence" Is Inescapable Right Now," *The Washington Post*, March 27, 2025, https://www.washingtonpost.com/entertainment/tv/2025/03/26/adolescence-netflix-tv-show/.

9 Lisa Jay, *Body Safety with Ollie: My Body, My Rules* (Sydney: Ollie Publishing, 2023).

10 Smartphone Free Childhood, Home, accessed 2025, https://smartphonefreechildhood.co.uk/.

Chapter 11

1 GCFL.net., "Parent Job Description," *GCFLearnFree.org*, accessed May 28, 2025, https://www.gcfl.net/archive/index.php?msgid=25842.

2 Phillip Klever, "Goal Direction and Effectiveness, Emotional Maturity, and Nuclear Family Functioning," *Journal of Marital and Family Therapy* 35, no. 3 (2009): 308–24.

3 Michael Kerr, "Why Do Siblings Often Turn Out Very Differently?" in *Human Development in the Twenty-First Century: Visionary Ideas from Systems Scientists*, ed. Alan C. Fogel, Barbara J. King, and Stuart G. Shanker (New York: Cambridge University Press, 2008), 221–44.

4 Bowen, *Family Therapy in Clinical Practice*, 381.

5 Carol A. Ford et al., "Associations Between Mother-Adolescent and Father-Adolescent Relationships and Young Adult Health," *JAMA Network Open* 6, no. 3 (2023): 233944.

6 Brown, *Growing Yourself Up*, 113. Brown, *Confident Parenting*.

7 Kerr, *Bowen Theory's Secrets*, 29–30.

Chapter 12

1 Brown, *Growing Yourself Up*, 253.

2 Steinberg, "We Know Some Things," 1–19.

3 Sidney M. Moon, "Beyond the Classroom: Why School Reform has Failed and What Parents Need To Do," *Gifted and Talented International* 11, no. 2 (1996): 89–90.

4 Sanober Khanum, Rabia Mushtaq, Muhammad Danish Kamal, Zuhaib Nishtar, and Kashif Lodhi, "The Influence of Parenting Styles on Child Development," *Journal of Policy Research* 9, no. 2 (2023): 808–16.

5 Laurence Steinberg, *The Ten Basic Principles of Good Parenting* (New York: Simon & Schuster, 2004), 30.

6 Carmen Knudson-Martin. "The female voice: Applications to Bowen's family systems theory," *Journal of Marital and Family Therapy* 20, no. 1 (1994): 35–46.

7 Bowen, *Family Therapy in Clinical Practice*, 540.

8 Kathleen Smith, *True to You: A Therapist's Guide to Stop Pleasing Others and Start Being Yourself* (New York: Balance, 2024).

9 Smith, *True to You*, 46–7.

Chapter 13

1 Organisation for Economic Co-operation and Development (OECD), *OECD Family Database*, updated 2024, OECD, https://www.oecd.org/en/data/datasets/oecd-family-database.html.

2 US Census Bureau, *Number, Timing, and Duration of Marriages and Divorces: 2016*. Current Population Reports, P70-167 (Washington, DC: US Government Publishing Office, 2021), https://www.census.gov/library/publications/2021/demo/p70-167.html.

3 Australian Bureau of Statistics, *Marriages and Divorces, Australia*, December 2023, https://www.abs.gov.au/statistics/people/people-and-communities/marriages-and-divorces-australia/latest-release. Office for National Statistics, *Divorces in England and Wales: 2022*, November 2023, https://www.ons.gov.uk/peoplepopulationandcommunity/birthsdeathsandmarriages/divorce/bulletins/divorcesinenglandandwales/2022.

4 Brown, *Growing Yourself Up*, 115.

5 Margaret Donley, "Unravelling the Complexity of Child Focus," *Family Systems* 6, no. 2 (2003): 152–3.

6 US Census Bureau (Divorce Statistics by Age Group): US Census Bureau, *Number, Timing and Duration of Marriages and Divorces: 2016*. Current Population Reports, P70-117 (Washington, DC: US Government Publishing Office, 2021), https://www.census.gov/content/dam/Census/library/publications/2021/demo/p70-167.pdf.

7 US Census Bureau, *Cohabitation, Marriage, and Union Dissolution: Findings from the Survey of Income and Program Participation* (Washington, DC: US Census Bureau, 2018), https://www.census.gov/content/dam/Census/library/working-papers/2018/demo/SEHSD%20WP2018-07.pdf.

8 Andrew J. Cherlin, *The Marriage-Go-Round: The State of Marriage and the Family in America Today* (New York: Vintage Books, 2010).

9 Stephanie Hess, "Effects of Inter-Parental Conflict on Children's Social Well-Being and the Mediation Role of Parenting Behavior," *Applied Research in Quality of Life* 17, no. 4 (2022): 2059–85.

10 Lixia Qu, Jennifer Baxter, Catherine Andersson, and Rebecca Jenkinson, *Divorces in Australia: Facts and Figures 2024*. Australian Institute of Family Studies, 2025, https://aifs.gov.au/research/facts-and-figures/divorces-australia-2024.

11 Bowen, *Family Therapy in Clinical Practice*, 340.

Chapter 14

1 U.S. Department of Health and Human Services, *Our Epidemic of Loneliness and Isolation: Supporting the Health of Parents in America* (Washington, DC: Office of the US Surgeon General, August 2024).

2 Frank DeVito, "Multigenerational Living: A Step Back to Healthy Communal Life," *The Public Discourse*, July 22, 2024, https://www.thepublicdiscourse.com/2024/07/90045/.

3 Federal Reserve, *Economic Well-Being of US Households in 2024* (Washington, DC: Board of Governors of the Federal Reserve System, May 2025), 26.

4 Organisation for Economic Co-operation and Development (OECD), *Doing Better for Families* (Paris: OECD Publishing, 2011), https://doi.org/10.1787/9789264098732-en.

5 Darby Saxbe, "Parents Should Ignore Their Children More Often," *The New York Times*, September 15, 2024, https://www.nytimes.com/2024/09/15/opinion/parenting-independence-children.html.

6 Darby Saxbe, *Dad Brain: The New Science of Fatherhood* (New York: Flatiron Books, May 2026).

7 Robyn Fivush, Marshall P. Duke, and Jennifer G. Bohanek, "Do You Know? The Power of Family History in Adolescent Identity and Well-Being," *Journal of Family Life* (2010): 748–69.

8 Rachel S. Breen, Jordan C. Booker, and Robyn Fivush, "Knowing Family History Is Associated with Identity Development in Emerging Adulthood," *Genealogy* 7, no. 1 (2023): 13.

9 Marshall P. Duke, Amber Lazarus, and Robyn Fivush, "Knowledge of Family History as a Clinically Useful Index of Psychological Well-Being and

Prognosis: A Brief Report," *Psychotherapy: Theory, Research, Practice, Training* 45, no. 2 (2008): 268–72.

10 Bowen, *Family Therapy in Clinical Practice*, 540.

11 Karl Pillemer, *Fault Lines: Fractured Families and How to Mend Them* (New York: Avery, 2022).

12 Karl Andrew Pillemer et al., *The Cornell Family Reconciliation Project: Estrangement and Reconciliation Between Parents and Adult Children* (Ithaca: Cornell University, 2020), https://contemporaryfamilies.org/wp -content/uploads/2021/03/Cornell-Family-Reconciliation-Project-Report.pdf.

13 Molly Han, Yan Bing Zhang, Teri Terigele, and Shu-Chin Lien, "Mother/ Daughter-in-Law Conflict: Communication in Family Intergenerational Relationships in Chinese Culture," in *Intergenerational Relations— Contemporary Theories, Studies and Policies*, ed. Isabel C. Duarte and Ricardo Rodrigues (London: IntechOpen, 2023).

14 Peggy G.Y. Chan, "Bowen Theory, Culture and Therapeutic Applications to Asian Families," *Australian and New Zealand Journal of Family Therapy* 45, no. 2 (2024): 132–41.

15 Bowen, *Family Therapy in Clinical Practice*, 492.

16 Michael E. Kerr, *Bowen Theory's Secrets: Revealing the Hidden Life of Families* (New York: W. W. Norton & Company, 2003), 144.

17 Anne S. McKnight, "Two Perspectives on Family Rifts: The Concepts of Estrangement and Cut-Off," *Australian and New Zealand Journal of Family Therapy* 45, no. 2 (2024): 176.

18 Roberta M. Gilbert, "Addressing Cutoff in Residential Care of Disturbed Adolescents," *Family Systems: A Journal of Natural Systems Thinking in Psychiatry and the Sciences* 6, no. 2 (2003): 135–46.

19 Commonly attributed to Benjamin Franklin, though original authorship is unverified.

20 Sara M. Moorman and Jeffrey E. Stokes, "Solidarity in the Grandparent– Adult Grandchild Relationship and Trajectories of Depressive Symptoms," *The Gerontologist* 56, no. 3 (2016): 408–20.

21 Brown, *Growing Yourself Up*, 49.

Chapter 15

1 David Brooks, *How to Know a Person: The Art of Seeing Others Deeply and Being Deeply Seen* (New York: Random House, 2023).

2 "Loneliness Beyond Borders: Cultural Insights and Trends," *Glass & Sand*, January 29, 2025, https://glass-and-sand.com/2025/01/29/loneliness -beyond-borders-cultural-insights-and-trends/.

3 Bowen, *Family Therapy in Clinical Practice*, 462.

4 Damien Cave, *Parenting Like an Australian: One Family's Quest to Fight Fear and Dive into a Better, Braver Life* (Naperville: Sourcebooks, 2023).

5 Damien Cave, "Nippers Training Made His Kids Confident in the Water and Out. He Wondered if He Could Follow Their Lead," *ABC News*, October 7, 2021, https://www.abc.net.au/news/2021-10-08/nippers-training-kids -confidence-what-would-happen-to-him/100519180.

6 Lenore Skenazy, *Free-Range Kids: How Parents and Teachers Can Let Go and Let Grow* (Hoboken: Wiley, 2021).

7 Let Grow, *Let Grow Play Club: Rebuilding Childhood Through Free Play*, accessed June 27, 2025, https://letgrow.org/program/play-club/.

8 Victoria Walks, "Case Study – Walking School Buses," accessed June 27, 2025, https://www.victoriawalks.org.au/walking_school_bus/.

9 Haidt, *The Anxious Generation*, 199.

10 Haidt, *The Anxious Generation*, 216.

11 Jennifer Mata-McMahon, Michael J. Haslip, and Shahin Hossain, "How U.S. Early Childhood Educators Understand Children's Spirituality: A Framework of Essence, Origin, and Action," *Early Childhood Education Journal* 53 (2025): 973–84.

12 Royal Commission into Institutional Responses to Child Sexual Abuse, *Final Report: Volume 16—Religious Institutions, Book 2* (Canberra: Commonwealth of Australia, 2017).

13 Lukianoff and Haidt, *The Coddling of the American Mind*.

14 Kevin Nguyen, "St Andrew's Cathedral School Principal Warns Parents over Aggression," *ABC News*, July 2, 2018, https://www.abc.net.au/ news/2018-07-02/st-andrews-cathedral-school-principal-warns-of-parent -aggression/9929004.

15 Jordan Baker, "Parents' Worsening Behaviour on Social Media Creating Stress and Heavier Workloads, School Principals Say," *Sydney Morning Herald*, May 18, 2022, https://newsflash.one/2022/05/18/parents -worsening-behaviour-on-social-media-creating-stress-and-heavier -workloads-school-principals-say/.

Chapter 16

1 Alison Gopnik, *The Gardener and the Carpenter: What the New Science of Child Development Tells Us About the Relationship Between Parents and Children* (New York: Farrar, Straus and Giroux, 2016).

2 Bowen Center for the Study of the Family, "Learning & Development," *The Bowen Center for the Study of the Family*, accessed July 7, 2025, https://www.thebowencenter.org/learning-development.

3 Timothy Keller, *Counterfeit Gods: The Empty Promises of Money, Sex, and Power, and the Only Hope That Matters* (New York: Penguin, 2011).

4 Michael E. Kerr, *Bowen Theory's Secrets: Revealing the Hidden Life of Families* (New York: W. W. Norton & Company, 2019), 99–100.

BIBLIOGRAPHY

Bowen, Murray. *Family Therapy in Clinical Practice.* New York: Jason Aronson, 1978.

Brown, Jenny. *Confident Parenting: Restoring Your Confidence as a Parent by Making Yourself the Project and Not Trying to Change Your Child.* Sydney: Family Systems Practice, 2020.

Brown, Jenny. *Facilitating Parents' Agency in Child and Adolescent Mental Health: Helplessness to Hope.* Newcastle upon Tyne: Cambridge Scholars Publishing, 2023.

Brown, Jenny. *Growing Yourself Up: How to Bring Your Best to All of Life's Relationships.* 2nd ed. Wollombi: Exisle Publishing, 2017.

Brown, Jenny. *Parent Hope Project: Parent Manual.* Sydney: Parent Hope Project, 2024.

Brown, Jenny. *Parenting with Clarity: A Guide for Parents, Caregivers, and Their Supporters Who Want to Contribute to Children's Flourishing.* Sydney: Parent Hope Project, 2024.

Brown, Jenny. "Parents' Experiences of Their Adolescents' Mental Health Treatment: Helplessness or Agency-Based Hope." *Clinical Child Psychology and Psychiatry* 23, no. 4 (2018): 644–62.

Brown, Jenny. "The Reciprocity Between Parents and Their Child's Mental Health Treatment Systems." *Family Systems* 14, no. 2 (2020): 103–25.

Brown, Jenny, and Lauren Errington. "Bowen Theory Revisited: Observing Self in the Family System." *Australian and New Zealand Journal of Family Therapy* 45, no. 1 (2024): 12–25.

Brown, Jenny, and Daniel V. Papero. "How Bowen Family Systems Builds Hope for Worried Parents." *The Parent Hope Podcast.* Hosted by Jenny Brown. Season 2, Episode 7. September 10, 2024. Audio podcast, 40:02. https://podcasts.apple.com/us/podcast/season-2-ep-7-how-bowen-family -systems-builds-hope/id1653517551?i=1000669085470.

Butler, David E. *The Origins of Family Psychotherapy: The NIMH Family Study Project.* Lanham: Jason Aronson, 2013.

Cave, Damien. *Parenting Like an Australian: One Family's Quest to Fight Fear and Dive into a Better, Braver Life.* Naperville: Sourcebooks, 2023.

Chan, Peggy. "Bowen Theory, Culture and Therapeutic Applications to Asian Families." *Australian and New Zealand Journal of Family Therapy* 45, no. 2 (2024): 244–56.

Donley, Margaret. "Unravelling the Complexity of Child Focus." *Family Systems* 6, no. 2 (2003): 147–60.

Duckworth, Angela L., and Laurence Steinberg. "Unpacking Self-Control." *Child Development Perspectives* 9, no. 1 (2015): 32–7.

Gopnik, Alison. *The Gardener and the Carpenter: What the New Science of Child Development Tells Us About the Relationship Between Parents and Children.* New York: Macmillan, 2016.

Haidt, Jonathan. *The Anxious Generation: How the Great Rewiring of Childhood Is Causing an Epidemic of Mental Illness.* New York: Penguin Press, 2024.

Hudson, Jennifer L., and Ronald M. Rapee, eds. *Psychopathology and the Family.* Boston and Oxford: Elsevier, 2005.

Kerr, Michael E. *Bowen Theory's Secrets: Revealing the Hidden Life of Families.* New York: W. W. Norton & Company, 2019.

Klever, Phillip. "Goal Direction and Effectiveness, Emotional Maturity, and Nuclear Family Functioning." *Journal of Marital and Family Therapy* 35, no. 3 (2009): 308–24.

Lebowitz, Eli R. *Addressing Parental Accommodation When Treating Anxiety in Children.* New York: Oxford University Press, 2019.

Lebowitz, Eli R. *Breaking Free of Child Anxiety and OCD: A Scientifically Proven Program for Parents.* New York: Oxford University Press, 2020.

Lukianoff, Greg, and Jonathan Haidt. *The Coddling of the American Mind: How Good Intentions and Bad Ideas Are Setting Up a Generation for Failure.* New York: Penguin Press, 2019.

Lythcott-Haims, Julie. *How to Raise an Adult: Break Free of the Overparenting Trap and Prepare Your Kid for Success.* New York: Henry Holt and Co., 2015.

McKnight, Anne S. "Two Perspectives on Family Rifts: The Concepts of Estrangement and Cut-Off." *Australian and New Zealand Journal of Family Therapy* 45, no. 2 (2024): 168–79.

Noone, Robert J., and Daniel V. Papero, eds. *The Family Emotional System: An Integrative Concept for Theory, Science, and Practice.* Lanham: Lexington Books, 2015.

Pillemer, Karl. *Fault Lines: Fractured Families and How to Mend Them.* New York: Penguin, 2022.

Saxbe, Darby. *Dad Brain: The New Science of Fatherhood.* New York: Flatiron Books, 2026.

Senior, Jennifer. *All Joy and No Fun: The Paradox of Modern Parenthood.* London: Hachette, 2014.

Skenazy, Lenore. *Free-Range Kids: How Parents and Teachers Can Let Go and Let Grow.* Hoboken: John Wiley & Sons, 2021.

Smith, Kathleen. *Everything Isn't Terrible: Conquer Your Insecurities, Interrupt Your Anxiety and Finally Calm Down.* New York: Hachette Books, 2019.

Smith, Kathleen. *True to You: A Therapist's Guide to Stop Pleasing Others and Start Being Yourself.* New York: Balance, 2024.

Stearns, Peter N. *Anxious Parents: A History of Modern Childrearing in America.* New York: New York University Press, 2003.

Steinberg, Laurence. "We Know Some Things: Parent-Adolescent Relationships in Retrospect and Prospect." *Journal of Research on Adolescence* 11, no. 1 (2001): 1–19.

INDEX

ABOUT THE AUTHOR

Dr. Jenny Brown has been a dedicated leader in child, couple, and family mental health for over four decades, working across Australia, the United States, and the UK. With a career grounded in family therapy and Bowen family systems theory, her long-term focus has been strengthening families, primarily by empowering parents to support their children's emotional and psychological well-being. Through decades of clinical practice and research, Jenny noticed a troubling trend: parents often feel sidelined in their child's mental health care, losing trust in their own instincts. Her PhD research explored this dynamic and led to the creation of the Parent Hope Project—a groundbreaking suite of resources designed to restore parental agency and build lasting confidence in navigating their child's challenges.

Jenny is the author of the widely read *Growing Yourself Up: How to Bring Your Best to All of Life's Relationships*. She has authored several publications, including *Facilitating Parents' Agency in Child and Adolescent Mental Health: Helplessness to Hope*. Jenny is the founder and director emeritus of the Family Systems Institute in Sydney, and her contributions to family therapy have earned her recognition and awards in Australia and the United States.